DAVID C. B̶A̶R̶R̶O̶W̶S̶

Crime in the Public Mind

Crime in the Public Mind

Kathlyn Taylor Gaubatz

Ann Arbor
THE UNIVERSITY OF MICHIGAN PRESS

Copyright © by the University of Michigan 1995
All rights reserved
Published in the United States of America by
The University of Michigan Press
Manufactured in the United States of America
⊛ Printed on acid-free paper

1998   1997   1996   4   3   2

A CIP catalogue record for this book is available from the British Library.

Library of Congress Cataloging-in-Publication Data

Gaubatz, Kathlyn Taylor.
    Crime in the public mind / Kathlyn Taylor Gaubatz.
    p.   cm.
    Includes bibliographical references (p.   ) and index.
    ISBN 0-472-10582-5 (hardcover : acid-free paper)
    1. Criminal justice, Administration of—United States—Public
opinion. 2. Crime—United States—Public opinion. 3. Public
opinion—California—Oakland. I. Title.
HV9950.G38   1995
364.973—dc20   94-25221
                                                        CIP

For Kurt

Contents

Acknowledgments

Many individuals and organizations made contributions that were critical to the completion of this study. I am grateful to the Research Program in Criminal Justice at Princeton University for providing the funding for participant solicitation, interviewing, and tape transcription. I appreciate also the financial support of the Roothbert Fund and the "Taylor Family Fund." The First Baptist Church of Oakland generously provided the use of a conference room in which many of the interviews took place.

Fred Greenstein offered advice during the initial conceptualization of the project and made the very fruitful suggestion that I use a screening questionnaire in order to secure interviewees from different points on the opinion spectrum. Jim Rodgers reviewed and commented on my proposed interview questions. Jameson Doig and John DiIulio provided helpful critiques of early drafts of the manuscript. Jennifer Hochschild gave inspiration and advice at every stage of the journey from nascent idea to final publication.

At those times when the fog seemed impenetrable, my husband, Kurt Taylor Gaubatz, always could be counted upon for light: he has been colleague, counselor, co-parent, and more. Our children, Jayne and Andrew, gracefully endured the preoccupations of their mother.

John Taylor, Doris Atchison, Lester Flint, Steve Reimer, and Karen Willstadter served as pretest subjects: I can thank them by name because their views are not included in these pages. I cannot divulge the names of the twenty-four Americans who dared to let a stranger into their homes or to meet her elsewhere sight unseen. These individuals gave me hours of their time and a large piece of their minds. They made my task not merely educational, but downright pleasant as well. The fact of some small honoraria notwithstanding, I remain in their debt.

CHAPTER 1

Introduction

Barbara Damon is trying to make up her mind about whether the court system is harsh enough on criminals. "Part of me says not harsh enough, because if it was harsh enough ... it wouldn't be happening as much ... I don't think I think at all that it's too harshly ... It seems like maybe now we're going more towards harsher punishment, but I don't think that the courts are too harsh." Why should we be harsh on criminals? Because "they have done something wrong. Nobody said that punishment was supposed to be nice ... If you just threaten them, they're gonna turn around and do it again." And if stiffer sentences were handed out to more criminals? "Maybe it would get better. Maybe somebody would think twice before they did something."

Anne Girard has not heard Barbara speak. Yet she as much as offers a rebuttal. Anne feels that the courts respond "inappropriately" to crime. "What needs to happen is that the people who have broken the law need to be rehabilitated somehow ... Harshness isn't going to do that. Instead, reeducation, giving them work, for instance, to do, that will make them feel good about themselves ... Give them a sense of self-worth and pride, rather than ... treating them like they're bad—with disrespect. It's only going to make them angrier and more lacking in self-esteem, and thus ready to go out and do more lawbreaking. To be harsh is just not going to work. So any harshness would be too much."

Barbara Damon and Anne Girard do not agree about what we should do about crime, but it seems that most Americans do. Across the United States, there is a striking public consensus about how we should respond to crime. In national polls that asked respondents, "In general, do you think the courts in this area deal too harshly or not harshly enough with criminals?" compiled results from ten polls spanning 1982 to 1991 show that an average of 83 percent believed they were "not harsh enough."[1] We have become accustomed to living in this climate of public unity, but if we stand back for a moment to examine it, we will recognize it to be a truly remarkable phenomenon. How can it be that on the subject of crime—an issue of such enormous complexity and intractability—there can exist any kind of a public consensus regarding a solution?

This book is about that consensus. In order to understand the roots of the consensus, I focus on individual Americans and how they form and structure their ideas about crime and criminal justice. Although I draw upon existing survey research, aggregate data have proven inadequate for producing a comprehensive explanation of this phenomenon. In contrast, my work takes an intensive look at a cross section of everyday Americans. In these pages I present a detailed analysis of the varied attitudes people hold about how our society should respond to crime. I explore at length the motivations that lead them to favor particular approaches to crime: what are they trying to achieve with the policies they prefer? I also examine the relationship between their views on criminal justice and their broader political beliefs. Then, based on this foundation, I offer an in-depth theory about who joins and who spurns the consensus—and why that consensus came into being.

As I write, crime is making headlines once again, with state and federal governments rushing to consider rigid "three strikes" sentencing laws, and some commentators calling crime *the* political issue for the 1990s. Extraordinary levels of resources are being expended on police, courts, and the penal system, and still the problem proves unyielding. In the face of all this, almost the entire American public seems to agree on what to do. Yet, as I will demonstrate throughout this book, public opinion about crime is not a seamless web. The public that wants a greater use of incarceration also believes that our prisons are not particularly effective; the public that calls for harsher courts also believes that an attack on socioeconomic problems would do more to reduce crime. In fact, public opinion is stitched from more than one cloth, and each deserves our careful attention. Major policy decisions will continue to turn on figuring out what the public really wants, and why they want it. If we are ever to address the urgent problems we face, the challenge for the future will be to move beyond the apparent contradictions in order to identify responses to crime that are politically feasible, practically effective, and democratically satisfying. I address this book to anyone who is interested in either the politics of crime and justice or the way individual Americans come to grips with "the challenge of crime in a free society."[2]

To begin, we must examine more closely the nature of the consensus— its history, the context in which it came into being, and its full dimensions.

The History and Context of the Consensus

A broad consensus about criminal justice has not always existed. In 1965, Americans were first asked what was to become a standard poll question about crime: "In general, do you think the courts in this area deal too harshly or not harshly enough with criminals?" In that year, only 48 percent of Americans considered the courts "not harsh enough." But in the decade that followed, this figure rose by thirty percentage points, and it has remained at or above this level ever since.[3]

As public opinion has grown harsher, changes in criminal justice policy have followed. Beginning in the 1970s, prison populations rose steeply: by 1989, roughly three times as many prisoners were being held in state and federal institutions as when the huge growth began.[4] By year's end 1992, over 880,000 individuals were incarcerated at the state and federal level; when the roughly 450,000 prisoners held in local jails are added to this total, we can see that there are now well over one million persons behind bars in the United States.[5]

This growth has squeezed our country's prison capacity to the bursting point. Despite a nationwide increase in prison space of over two hundred thousand beds in the decade following 1978, in 1988 state prisons were estimated to be operating at 115 percent of capacity, and the federal system at 153 percent of capacity.[6] By 1990, state prisons were estimated to be operating at 121 percent of capacity, and the federal system at 151 percent of capacity.[7]

In a review of the get-tough changes of the Reagan era, Susan Caringella-MacDonald writes that during the late 1970s and the 1980s "virtually all states have altered sentencing codes in some form or fashion. Indeterminate sentences have been replaced or augmented with mandatory, flat, determinate, and presumptive sentencing stipulations. Additionally, probation has been disallowed for certain crimes and criminals, and parole has been abolished in more than a dozen states."[8] At the national level, the Federal Crime Control Act of 1984 capped a decade of Congressional debate by bringing determinate sentencing to the federal justice system, as well as abolishing parole and eliminating youthful offender legislation.[9] The late 1970s also brought the reinstitution of the death penalty, which by 1991 was legal in thirty-six states and the federal system.[10]

In 1988, James Austin and Aaron McVey wrote that "the principal factor fueling prison population growth over the next five years for most states is an increasing length of stay resulting from numerous laws adopted by states to 'get tough' with criminals."[11] In addition, data from the U.S. Bureau of Justice Statistics indicate that "there is some evidence that during the period 1980–89 changes in criminal justice policies have increased a criminal's probability of being incarcerated from levels existing in prior years." Between 1960 and 1970 the ratio of prison commitments to adult arrests for a number of serious crimes decreased from 299 to 170 per 1,000. After a relatively stable period during the 1970s, it increased from 196 to 332 commitments per 1,000 adult arrests during the years 1980 to 1989.[12]

In the state of California, where the prison system is the largest in the nation, 113,000 persons are now incarcerated—a nearly sixfold increase from the 1977 population of 19,000. This overcrowded system now runs at 180 percent of maximum capacity. From the kickoff in 1976 with passage of the Determinate Sentencing Law, over one thousand laws that either established new offenses, or lengthened sentences for existing ones, were passed in California. Costs for these changes have been astronomical. According to the San Francisco–based Center on Juvenile and Criminal Justice, "in 1980 state funding for the prison system was $300 million; by 1994 it is expected to reach $3 billion." They estimate that *each* of the one thousand–plus prisoners serving sentences of life-without-parole will cost the state more than a million dollars over a lifetime.[13]

In short, our political leaders have set in motion a nationwide "crackdown on crime." But which came first—the public's expressed desire for harsher policies toward criminal offenders, or the words and deeds of politicians who campaigned, legislated, and generally made political hay out of the "crime crisis"? Barry Goldwater led the flock in his 1964 presidential campaign with talk of a "growing menace . . . to personal safety, to life, to limb, and to property," but he went down to defeat.[14] Lyndon Johnson picked up the torch (while moderating the tone of his opponent's message) and in 1965 created a presidential Commission on Law Enforcement and Administration of Justice.[15] Recall that in the same year, when that first national poll asking respondents about the tendencies of the courts was conducted, still only 48 percent of the public said that they were "not harsh enough." By 1968, that proportion had already risen to 63 percent,[16] and candidate Richard Nixon rode into office on words like these: "Our judges have gone too far in weakening the peace forces as against the criminal forces. Our opinion-makers have gone too far in promoting the doctrine that when a law is broken, society—not the criminal—is to blame."[17] Five years later, following Nixon's second inauguration, 73 percent of the public felt that the courts were "not harsh enough"—an increase of twenty-five percentage points in just eight years.[18]

President Ronald Reagan was nothing if not tough on crime. And George Bush gained much of the momentum that propelled him to the White House by casting Michael Dukakis as the kind of soft-on-crime liberal who sponsored work-furlough programs that allowed predatory criminals to destroy the lives of innocent citizens. The presidencies of these two men span most of the era of harsher sentencing and prison expansion detailed above. As Bush wrapped up his presidency, he was still calling the nation to "do something about crime and drugs . . . It is time for a major, renewed investment in fighting violent street crime," he asserted in his final State of the Union address.[19] Few may remember, however, that Ronald Reagan was not always the standard bearer of the get tough-movement. In an account of changes in California's criminal justice system, Caleb Foote writes that "during Ronald Reagan's tenure as governor, his administration first ordered the [Adult] Authority, as an economy measure, to reduce prison population by increasing parole release rates, a policy which enabled the state to close one prison and underpopulate San Quentin and some other prisons. Then the Reagan administration, attacked from the southland for being soft on crime . . . , reversed course and ordered the Authority to tighten ship."[20] We know that the tides of public opinion began their harsh upswing during the years of Reagan's first governorship, and here is the revelation that his actions as a political leader were not always oriented to a crackdown on crime. So we may surmise, as Foote suggests, that Reagan took up the get-tough mantle because it was politically advantageous.

It is difficult to tell whether the broader trend follows this pattern as well. The surge in harsh public opinion was well under way by the time presidential candidates, starting with Richard Nixon, began winning on law-and-order platforms. On the other hand, the intervening presidency of Lyndon Johnson and the work of his famous crime commission obviously did much to highlight the issue in the public eye. Stuart Scheingold, who has made a detailed study of the politicization of crime, points out that

> National politicians . . . have strong incentives to politicize street crime. For them it provides a unifying theme and thus a valence issue. While victimization is experienced differentially according to class, race, gender, and geography, the *threat* it poses to property and person evokes comparable fears throughout the society. National political leaders can, therefore, deploy the fear of crime to unify the public against the criminal.[21]

Of course, whether the egg followed the chicken or the other way around, once the momentum got started, it no doubt fed itself in both directions. Again, we can turn to Scheingold's work:

> The politicization of crime is an interactive process combining elements of responsiveness with elements of manipulation. Politicians do not so much "expropriate our consciousness" as take advantage of punitive predispositions about crime that are rooted in American culture. The public engages and disengages from the politicization process for reasons that have at least as much to do with the place of crime in the culture as with the impact of criminal victimization in our lives . . .

> Law-and-order political candidates, then, simply take advantage of opportunities provided by the public's state of mind to build an

effective election campaign. Nor is it necessarily the case that these politicians are cynical manipulators of the public's anxieties. As members of the public, politicians may be just as outraged about the crime problem as their constituents are, and may be just as inclined to believe that cracking down on criminals will solve or at least alleviate the problem.[22]

In sum, three things happened, perhaps in this order: public opinion on criminal justice became increasingly harsh starting in the late 1960s; politicians, with the help of the media, picked up and escalated the get-tough message; and policymakers instituted a responsive crackdown on crime.

The Dimensions of the Consensus

While politicians and policymakers obviously heard the dominant chords of the growing public consensus, it is not at all clear that they caught the underlying nuances. We too must not jump to overly broad conclusions about the nature of public agreement regarding crime. There is a consensus, but it is a thin one. It resides solely in the general belief that intentionally harsh policies must be pursued. On questions such as why and to what degree they should be pursued, and whether and to what extent milder policies should be pursued alongside them, survey research has shown us that public opinion is often diverse and sometimes appears contradictory. Indeed, a substantial proportion of the American public could reasonably be said to have mixed views on the topic of criminal justice.

We know that the vast majority of Americans call for harsher sentencing of offenders. But more specific poll questions tell us that beneath this general agreement lie a variety of subsidiary views. A Gallup poll that asked respondents what the main aim of imprisonment should be found that 26 percent selected "to re-educate the prisoner," 33 percent chose "to protect other citizens," 29 percent selected "to make those who have done wrong pay for it," and 8 percent chose "to act as a deterrent to others."[23] Gallup also found a variety of views when they asked respondents whether anything could be done to reduce recidivism rates, and then pressed those who answered "yes" for what that might be. Thirty-six percent said "stronger rehabilitation" and 8 percent mentioned "jobs when released"; another 36 percent said "stiffer sentences"; and a total of 31 percent mentioned "no parole," "less leniency in prison," and "enforce capital punishment."[24] Surveys have indicated that 74 percent of Americans favor the use of the death penalty for murder, and 91 percent favor "tougher parole boards."[25] Yet also, 89 percent will agree to the proposition that "increasing employment opportunities for youths could prevent a lot of serious crimes."[26] And

79 percent of a national sample chose the statement that "in most cases society would be better served if non-violent criminals were not jailed but were put to work and made to repay their victims," over the assertion that "non-violent criminals must be kept in jail because allowing them out represents too great a risk to society."[27] To say that there is a public consensus about harshness does not mean that Americans across the board hold *thoroughly* harsh views about criminal justice. Clearly, a majority holds views that contain both harsh and mild elements. We need to know more about how they put these views together.

These important underlying nuances notwithstanding, a striking public consensus about harsher responses to crime unquestionably exists, and few policymakers have bucked its tide. Our nation now spends billions of dollars annually pursuing policies that have produced the highest incarceration rate in the world but are widely recognized as having done next to nothing to reduce crime in our society to an acceptable level.[28] In fact, the vast majority of Americans acknowledge that jails and prisons are not very effective at discouraging crime.[29] Yet they support increasing our use of incarceration.[30] In 1991, still 91 percent of the American public felt either that the courts were not harsh enough (80 percent) or that they were about right (11 percent).[31] What is going on here? Why do Americans stand so firmly behind a policy that they themselves believe is not working? Are they simply misinformed or misguided? Are they so terrified that they grasp at any straw? Does the public have any conception of the price tag on the policies they have called for and received—or the magnitude of the costs they still ask our nation to incur? Or are they simply out for vengeance, at any price?

Why Consensus?

It is time to look at some possible explanations, starting with those above. The public, of course, is ignorant of many of the facts. Certainly the public is fearful. But I will present survey data that indicate that those who support the get-tough consensus are no more fearful than those who oppose it. And new evidence collected for this study suggests that the accuracy of the information possessed by those who favor harsh policies differs little from that of those who prefer alternative methods. Likewise, I will show that the underlying views about forgiveness and vengeance of the two groups are remarkably similar.

So what is happening here? Is the public being manipulated by some powerful hand? Politicians and policymakers, it seems, have as much followed as led the growth in harsh public sentiments, their primary role being one of escalating the growing momentum. Could the media be responsible? Or is there some other force—a striking set of circumstances, a powerful ideological tide—to which the public has uniformly responded? It would be easy to believe, for instance, that attitudes about crime have become more uniformly harsh in recent decades because crime rates have dramatically increased during this time. Certainly, much in the media creates the ongoing impression that we are suffering from crime waves of unprecedented proportions. The hard evidence, however, does not support this conclusion. In the years since 1973, when reliable data on national victimization rates began to be collected annually, rates of violent crime have held remarkably steady, while rates of both household crime and personal theft have dropped significantly.[32] Even if crime had increased, it still would be a mistake to tag the national consensus as a logical response to such a phenomenon, for as I will detail in chapter 5, research has shown that those groups most affected by crime—that is, those who show the highest levels of victimization, fear, or salience—are no more punitive than the rest of the population. In sum, we will need other hypotheses.

Alternately, it would be easier to understand why public attitudes about criminal justice have become so entrenched at one end of the opinion spectrum, if attitudes about other social issues involving questions of tolerance had also moved neatly in that direction. But in fact, we know that while public opinion regarding criminal justice has become more conservative in recent decades, attitudes about certain other social issues—race and gender relations, abortion, civil liberties, and issues surrounding sex—have liberalized.[33] Arthur Stinchcombe and his colleagues, in their 1980 analysis of changing public attitudes about crime and responses to crime, devoted considerable attention to this mystery. The conventional wisdom is that less harsh views on criminal justice are a part of a general complex of liberal social attitudes,[34] and indeed, they found small but consistent correlations between less harsh views regarding penal sanctions and liberal views on these other social issues.[35] But Stinchcombe et al. discovered that the correlation between these attitudes is primarily due to "a very few ideological liberals who view penal philosophy as a part of their liberalism," and they concluded that most Americans see no strong connection between "the treatment of criminals by the courts" and other questions of "Enlightenment liberalism."[36] Left unsettled, however, is the question of why they do not make stronger connections between these issues.[37] All we know is that the surprise of consensus on crime cannot be explained away as a subset of a larger consensus.

We should be skeptical, as well, about arguments that link consensus with success. Some might suggest that this overwhelming agreement formed when members of the public who had previously held less harsh views noticed that our policymakers had begun to institute tougher penal policies—and these citizens then realized that tough policies work. But this cannot explain why another 30 percent of the American public jumped onto the get-tough bandwagon, because the movement in public opinion largely preceded the changes in policy. Not to mention that these policies have *not* worked. In fact, little credit for steady or falling crime rates should be claimed by the proponents of harsher policies: population research has shown that this phenomenon is largely due to demographic changes that have reduced the percentage of our citizenry who are in the crime-prone age bracket.[38] And even the biggest advocates of get-tough actions would not argue that we have arrived at such a nirvana of public safety that all who disagreed with them must now be convinced that they were right all along.

What about the media? The public's exposure to crime, most of the time, is not through direct victimization, but through the stories they hear and read. Likewise, politicians may play on the issue of crime incessantly, but by and large, the public hears their proclamations not through face-to-face contact, but through the intercession of the media: newspapers and news magazines, television and radio. In his history of crime and punishment in America, Lawrence Friedman writes that

> Throughout the country, newspapers, movies, and TV spread the word about crime and violence—a misleading word, perhaps, but a powerful one. Even people who live in quiet suburban enclaves, or rural backwaters, are aware of what they consider the crime problem. They, too, may feel fearful and besieged: safe where they are perhaps, but conscious of a dangerous world beyond their doorsteps.[39]

Certainly there is evidence that media output on crime—real and fictional—tends to concentrate on the most frightening offenses, and reinforces the myth that most violent crimes are committed by predators unknown to the victims.[40] Furthermore, fictional programs generally play into harsh views by depicting a world in which the bad guys are invariably caught and punished, rendering the studio "streets" safe enough at least for the next week's show to go on—and encouraging the viewer to feel that justice has been done. The effect of the media on the public's perceptions of crime and criminal justice has been a subject of considerable research and speculation—but with varied results. Many researchers have found no direct relationship,[41] while others have found limited connections hinged to the type of content, and the degree to which individuals find that content to be realistic or relevant.[42] Most likely, as with the relationship of politicians and the public, there is a reciprocal effect: people who are already more concerned about crime than others consume more media output about crime—real and fictional.[43] But experts disagree about whether this output reinforces or alters their views about crime and justice.[44] A role for the media in shaping harsh public attitudes certainly cannot be dismissed completely, but there is insufficient evidence to consider it a major cause of public consensus.

Of course, the study of public opinion about crime is well-traveled territory.[45] The reader may ask why these questions about consensus cannot be answered easily from a review of the existing research. Indeed, many analysts have sought to discover some correlation between citizens' opinions about appropriate responses to crime and other of their attitudes or attributes—something that might explain differences in the degrees to which citizens want harsh responses to crime.[46] But while the body of available information about public opinion on crime and criminal justice is large, it is not sufficient. From the existing data, no analyst has been able to piece together a complete answer to the questions I have put forth about consensus. There still remain important gaps in our knowledge. Plainly stated, the most important missing element in crime-related opinion research has been depth. Almost without exception, survey research has been the only game in town.[47] Such quantitative research, when well designed, has the obvious advantages of being straightforward to analyze, and reliably generalizable. The nature of the enterprise is such, however, that the resources have seldom been available to ask a substantial number of crime-related questions of a large sample. And even then, there have been limits, generally, on scope or detail, and always on the latitude that is given respondents for the expression of their thoughts. Thus, a thorough study of the existing literature, while providing a useful background, cannot provide a comprehensive answer to the mystery of consensus.

In truth, there does not seem to be an easy explanation for this overwhelming public consensus about how government should respond to crime. One by one, the obvious answers fail, leaving the glaring question: why consensus? Most people cannot agree on vanilla versus chocolate, let alone genuine political issues like free trade or Bosnian intervention: how is it possible that almost all of us have the same outlook on crime?[48]

In order to address this stubborn question more productively, it will be necessary to gain a thorough understanding of the perspectives both of those who join in the prevailing get-tough view and of those who dissent from it. We need to know why those in the dominant group believe what they do and why they do not believe what the dissenting minority believes. Conversely, we must ask what motivates or explains the views of those few who buck the tides of public sentiment and formulate a picture of the influences in their lives that distinguish them from the dominant group.

My Research

When the pressing need is to understand why people hold the opinions they do, and how they put those opinions together, no methodology has an edge over the technique of intensive interviewing. Thus, seeking answers to these questions about consensus, I spent roughly five hours each in interviews with two dozen Americans. Participants were chosen in a stratified random sample of Oakland, California. Each was guaranteed anonymity; in what follows, their names and certain of the details of their lives have been changed in order to disguise their identities. In two or more interview sessions, respondents were asked open-ended questions not only regarding crime and criminal justice, but also about their broader political and personal philosophies. Each interview was tape-recorded, and the analysis that follows is based on verbatim transcripts of the tapes. The reader will find a description of each participant in appendix A, a list of the interview questions in appendix B, and a more detailed account of the methodology in appendix C.

The depth that has been missing from survey-based research can be amply supplied by the use of intensive interviews. Many dozens—even hundreds—of questions can be asked, along with appropriate probe questions when answers are vague or incomplete. Open-ended questions and a general atmosphere in which thinking aloud is encouraged offer the opportunity to understand how participants put their thoughts together. Interviewees describe not only what they think, but also why they think it; and, both spontaneously and under specific questioning, they make connections between their thoughts on different issues. In short, we can draw from such interviews instructive portraits of whole, complex, unaggregated individuals. The figures that survey research offers, important as they are, reside in charts and graphs; but the figures that arise from intensive interviewing are three-dimensional.

The task of intensive research is not one of simply presenting a set of detailed attitudinal biographies. What will be found in the remainder of this work will not read as twenty-four life tales, told one after another—although this is precisely what undergirds it all. Instead, the focus will move among several major aspects of the participants' beliefs, at each point seeking patterns of belief shared by various interviewees. Thus, at any given time the concentration will be not only on a particular aspect—the values by which criminal justice opinions are motivated, for instance—but also on selected individuals as exemplars of a certain pattern of thought regarding that aspect.

Of course, intensive interviewing is no be-all and end-all. Certainly I make no claim that these interviews will provide information about proportions of Americans who hold particular views. Instead, I turn to this method for its ability to generate new hypotheses, to enrich the bare data of mass polling, and to produce a comprehensive analysis of the beliefs of individual Americans. This is a methodology that serves not to supplant the large sample survey, but to complement it.[49] When all is said and done, these interviews should provide not only the additional data needed to suggest answers to the central questions of this study, but also a depth of understanding about the way people put together their criminal justice views that has not been available elsewhere.

Believers and Dissenters

Among my interviewees, there were thirteen persons who, in varying degrees and manners, aligned themselves with the get-tough movement. I have chosen to call these individuals *believers*. Nine others were persons who questioned the wisdom of a get-tough policy. I will call them *dissenters*.[50] Oversimplification is an ever-present danger in selecting any one descriptive term to characterize a group of study respondents (or a segment of the American public). The terms believer and dissenter are by no means immune from this criticism. I selected them for their implication that there is a broad American ethos—Scheingold has called it "the myth of crime and punishment"[51]—that most of our citizens have bought into, but a few refuse to endorse.[52]

Thirteen believers; nine dissenters. This is a disproportionate division, for, of course, dissenters are rare in the American population. I have selected a substantial number of dissenters as interviewees, quite simply, to get a decent look at them. I wanted to be able to understand both the dominant and the minority positions on this issue; but in a small, intensive study of this type, to have taken a proportionate number from each category would have yielded far too few dissenters to make possible a reasonable comparison. Including a larger number of dissenters in the group will not damage the findings: this is not a quantitative study. But it will allow me to examine the thoughts of a large enough number of persons in each category, to be able to seek patterns and draw comparisons.

The Setting

To help to set the stage, a word should be said about the location and time in which the interviews took place. Oakland, California is "that other city" across the bay from San Francisco. Its population is racially very diverse,[53] and a 1980 University of Wisconsin study found it to be the most integrated city in the United States.[54] After many generations of dominance by a white Republican establishment, Oakland has in recent years had a power structure that is predominantly black and Democratic.[55] When my interviews were conducted in 1987, an ambitious (if sometimes financially troubled) downtown redevelopment program was well under way, the city's Chinatown was booming, and the Port of Oakland had grown into the second largest container port in the nation.[56]

But Oakland is also home to drugs, crime, and poverty. Like many other cities, it has suffered an epidemic of crack use, with its accompanying violence and despair.[57] Oakland has a bad reputation for crime, and at the time of the interviews had the tenth highest reported crime rate among major U.S. cities.[58] At least 25 percent of the city's population then lived in poverty.[59] And only 30 percent of the new jobs that had thus far been created by redevelopment had been filled by Oakland residents.[60] This is the home of my twenty-four interviewees—a city of both problems and possibilities.

Sundry and conflicting arguments might be made about whether or not Oakland is a representative U.S. city. But since this study is not based on a representative sample, it is essentially a moot question. More important is that the Oaklanders I spoke with hold criminal justice beliefs that span the spectrum to both extremes. The use that I make of these people's beliefs will never be to suggest figures or proportions that would quantify public opinion. No doubt there are people in other cities who hold patterns of opinion very much like the ones I discovered here. My task is not to say if there are more or less of them in Oakland than elsewhere. It would have been folly to have conducted a study of this nature in Lancaster, Pennsylvania, Salt Lake City, Utah, or any other area in which vast numbers of persons hold beliefs influenced by specialized moral or cultural conceptions. But it could have been conducted just as well in Portland, Los Angeles, or Wilmington. I chose Oakland.

When I spoke with my twenty-four interviewees in the spring and early summer of 1987, the conservative political tide that had swept through the decade was very much in evidence. Ronald Reagan was in the White House and Republican George Deukmejian sat in the governor's chair. Crime had shown a decline, but prison populations continued to rise steeply. In the previous November, Rose Bird, the chief justice of the California Supreme Court, along with two of her more liberal colleagues, had failed to win reconfirmation in a hotly contested election. Criminal rulings, particularly those that had blocked implementation of the death penalty in California, were the focal issue in the campaign to unseat these justices. Interestingly, however, only two of the interview participants even mentioned former justice Bird, despite the fact that I asked a number of specific questions about crime and voting.[61]

Also of note is that during the period of the interviews there arose a considerable public furor over the parole of Lawrence Singleton, a man who nine years earlier, in a nearby town, had raped a teenage girl and chopped off her arms. (She survived.) An article announcing this man's impending release from prison appeared in the *San Francisco Chronicle* on the day I conducted my first interview, and that newspaper subsequently ran forty-five more items on the subject before the interviews were completed.[62] Still, only a quarter of my interviewees even mentioned the case during our conversations. A gruesome multiple torture-murder in Philadelphia, which came to light a few days before the interviews began, was mentioned by no one.[63] As discussed above, past research on the effects of media crime coverage on public perceptions has reaped conflicting results. And if these particular events had any special effect upon the interviewees' views, it was too subtle to be discernable.

The Organization of This Book

This book has two major sections, corresponding to the two stages of my search for answers about consensus: examination and explanation.

Examination

In order to offer a reasonable explanation for the development of this amazing tide of public sentiment, it is essential first to examine and understand the views of both the believers and the dissenters. I seek this understanding from three perspectives.

Content. At a much more detailed level than is reached by large-scale survey research, just what are the views that respondents express about crime and criminal justice? Are some individuals uniformly harsh and other strictly mild? What kind of role do mixed views play? What specific policies would respondents have our government pursue in the "war against crime?" What is the content of their thought on this complex topic, and most importantly, what distinguishes the content of the believers' thought from that of the dissenters? I undertake to answer these questions in chapter 2.

Motivations. What are these Americans trying to achieve with the policies they support? What leads them to support capital punishment over life imprisonment, prison over probation, or victim restitution over a court fine? What spurs them to place punishment before rehabilitation, or incapacitation before a more general deterrence? What values or deep concerns are they responding to when they express particular views? In short, what are the motivations behind their many opinions? Chapter 3 addresses this question.

Structure. What is the structure of participants' beliefs? To what degree are the criminal justice views of the interviewees logical and internally consistent? Beyond this, do the participants have coherent general political belief systems? If so, are their criminal justice views grounded in and consonant with these larger belief systems? Experts in the field of public opinion have taught us to expect a significant degree of incoherence within the responses of the public regarding most policy questions.[64] Yet views about crime, a topic that can certainly be classified with what Philip Converse has called "doorstep issues," may prove to be an exception.[65] People tend to have more clearly defined and better organized ideas about matters that concern them most closely, and certainly the specter of crime looms physically close to many, and emotionally close to nearly all.[66] Perhaps, for these reasons, we will find that views about crime also are more closely tied to individuals' fundamental political beliefs than are views about less emotional issues. The area of criminal justice (as with other doorstep issues) should mark one boundary on the continuum of public belief crystallization and coherence. And viewing these attitudes from a structural perspective should further enhance our understanding of how Americans put their criminal justice views together. Chapter 4 addresses these areas.

Explanation

Only after thoroughly examining the views of the believers and the dissenters on the three levels just discussed will it be possible to offer an explanation for their opposing views—and for the strange phenomenon of consensus.

Dissent. Chapter 5 takes up the task of explanation with a special focus on those persons whose unpopular views are so much in the minority. What makes the dissenters dissent? With national opinion so strongly skewed in one direction, why are these people not believers like everybody else? What makes them different from those who share the dominant view?

Consensus. Drawing on all that has gone before, chapter 6 takes on the big question: why such consensus? In an era of falling crime rates and increased tolerance toward other forms of deviance and social change, still the vast majority of the American public supports harsh penal policies that they themselves acknowledge have been powerless thus far to reduce crime in our nation to an acceptable level. Why? How can we understand the formation and maintenance of this consensus?

Ultimately I will argue that Americans look at incarceration like some old-time patent medicine: although they know that the first few tablets have had little effect, they are certain that just a few more will bring relief. And I will offer a detailed defense for what I make now as a simple assertion: that Americans have become harsher on crime not in spite of becoming more liberal on a variety of other social issues, but at least in part because they have done so.

Clarifying Key Terms

Before moving on to the core of this research it is essential, with the reader's indulgence, to discuss a set of key terms that will appear often here. These are terms that describe various possible goals and objectives in the struggle against crime. Most are used repeatedly in the literature on criminology and appear in everyday conversation as well. In one sense, they are virtually self-explanatory. Yet the shades of meaning that they receive in different contexts vary widely. I want to state precisely what meaning I have attached to them, both in the interviews and in their subsequent use here.

Punishment is an approach that I described to my interviewees as "making criminals suffer because of their crimes." Although this word is bandied about with ease, its meaning may vary greatly in different contexts. Even persons who advocate quite mild responses to crime may still speak in general terms of "crime and punishment" or casually refer to "punishing" an offender for whom they have suggested an entirely compassionate treatment. In the chapters that follow, I have attempted to avoid the casual use of the term punishment, reserving it only for those times when I mean to indicate that the purpose of a criminal sanction is to cause the offender to suffer as he or she "deserves." Of course, the meaning my interviewees have attached to this term does vary; this is reflected in the quotes that I draw—unaltered—from their conversations.

Rehabilitation I described to the interviewees as "teaching offenders how to become productive citizens." Contained within this goal might be such specifics as a basic education, job skills training, psychological counseling, treatment of substance abuse, or the inculcation of ethical values.

Deterrence was explained as "setting an example to discourage future crime." This might mean the specific deterrence of an offender who, having received harsh treatment for one crime, decides that it is not wise to risk committing any further offenses. Or, it could mean the general deterrence of potential lawbreakers who, seeing the harsh treatment that others have received for crimes (and perceiving a genuine risk of capture), decide to refrain from pursuing illegal activities.

I described *isolation* to the interviewees as "removing criminals from society." In this case the intent is to protect potential victims from new crimes that offenders conceivably might have committed during their period of incarceration had they been left within society. This approach is sometimes called by the more descriptive term, *incapacitation.*

Compensation was described as "repaying victims for their losses." This might either mean repayment coming from the criminal justice system or from individual offenders who work in order to repay their victims for property stolen, medical bills incurred, or other expenses.

A final term is *prevention,* which involves actions aimed at alleviating problems such as substance abuse, child abuse, inadequate education or parenting, substandard housing, unemployment, and so forth—actions through which some crimes might possibly be prevented before they are even contemplated. Generally speaking, these are not activities of the criminal justice system, but prevention is still a possible objective for society as a whole. Indeed, it is an objective that some participants repeatedly invoked—although they may not have called it by this name. The distinction between prevention and deterrence is an important one to clarify. With deterrence, we are talking about influencing persons not to commit crimes that they *want* to commit. With prevention (as with rehabilitation) we are talking about altering people's lives in such a way that they will *not want* to commit crimes. Many of the traditional activities of policing— patrolling the streets, organizing neighborhood watch groups, and the like—are devoted in large part to what often is casually labeled "crime prevention." Under closer examination, however, we can see that this function actually is deterrence: these activities strive both to increase, and to make more obvious to potential offenders, the risks of being caught.

This introductory chapter has laid out the questions and assumptions that undergird this study. As outlined above, the quest to understand attitudes toward crime and criminal justice should begin with an exploration of the range and substance of individual beliefs. In the next chapter I let some of my two dozen diverse interviewees speak in their own voices in order to illustrate the critical distinctions between the believers and the dissenters— distinctions that will inform the remainder of this study.

Part 1. Examination

CHAPTER 2

Believers and Dissenters

Drew Snowden

Drew Snowden, a bank executive, is Oakland born and bred. An enthusiastic man with a striking zest for life, he is forty-nine years of age, white, and gay. Drew is the father of a teenage son from a former marriage. He lives with Patrick Johnson, a management consultant who is his long-time lover.[1]

Of my twenty-four interviewees, Drew unquestionably holds the harshest views on criminal justice. He sees the causes of crime in "permissiveness . . . mostly by the legal system"; in giving people too much ("the wonderful word is *coddle*," he remarks); and in "the economic policies of inflation" that have forced women to have to work, thus breaking down the family order ("A little strange, my talking about family order, perhaps").

It goes without saying that Drew feels that the courts are not harsh enough on crime. I asked him what would happen if tougher sentences were handed out to more criminals: "It would make an example. People would remember." He tells about a relative of a friend—an Alaskan Eskimo—who had committed a murder in the process of a robbery:

> He was taken up on the hill and he was hung. And everybody knew it. Everybody remembered it. You killed someone: you hang. It's a public spectacle. And you know maybe it should happen. It's barbaric, certainly. Why is there no crime in the Arab countries? You get your hands cut off. You get killed. And I—people get tired of it. They get tired of crime. That guy in the subway in New York . . . Goetz . . . he sits and he says these preposterous things like, "I could have shot him if I'd have had twenty rounds," . . . I understand him completely.[2]

Drew feels that deterrence should be the number one goal of the criminal justice system, although "punishment and deterrence are pretty much the same thing." And when he says punishment, he means serious business:

> There are countries in which they cut off the hands of somebody who steals. I might give it a try. . . .

21

I hate to sound so redneck, but I think when it all comes down to it, these criminals are staying at the Hilton ... And they talk about we need to build more prisons. Are there rats crawling in and eating them while they're asleep? No. Well [then] I'm not too terribly concerned about it.

A self-described "libertarian conservative," he favors decriminalizing victimless acts: "The legal system runs around trying to protect people against themselves. I don't understand that either—such as prostitution, suicide. Let people do what they want. Just don't let them hurt other people." Drug use by adults would be legal in his system of choice, but "if you are doing that kind of behavior ... you should not expect the government to provide your existence." And, "selling or giving drugs to a minor is a death penalty offense as far as I'm concerned."

Who belongs in prison, I ask him: "If it's important enough to make a law, and the person breaks the law, they deserve to go to prison." I try to clarify whether he's talking about even minor thefts:

DS: What, for instance?
KTG: Shoplifting.
DS: Go to jail.
KTG: ... Where's the line? ... A candy bar ... a dress ... a stereo? Even a candy bar?
DS: Candy bar ... Go to jail.
KTG: How long? ...
DS: OK, maybe a public whipping. I mean, there should be some punishment ... Stealing a candy bar—go to jail for two weeks.

Confronted with hypothetical scenarios describing a robber, an embezzler, a triple rapist, and a pair of habitual burglars, Drew calls for incarceration for each.[3] The burglars draw life sentences: "I don't see why they should ever be released to society again. I've had it with burglary! ... Something has to be done, and you never make an impression until you go to the extreme. The extreme has to be done and it has to be public."

Drew feels that our current prison system is not very effective in preventing released convicts from committing new crimes; he estimates the recidivism rate to be 70 percent.[4] And at present the threat of prison sentences is not at all effective in preventing people from starting a life of crime:

I don't think the average person who starts that ever thinks he'll go to prison. Because he'll get off. If he thought he would go to prison, I think it would be effective. ...

Most people think they are not going to go to jail, so the deterrent is not there. But then the idea is, if I do go to jail, is it that bad? No, it's not that bad. So there is no deterrent... Now if a person came out of prison and talked about being tortured, now, maybe, that would be a deterrent.

Drew Snowden grounds his deterrence philosophy in what he calls "impersonal justice": "If the crime is defined and... there is a punishment laid out, that's what should be adhered to. Because that is the only way you'll get fear." We all, he says, react to fear. Although Drew supports this position because he believes it is the only thing that will work, he mentions several times during the interview that the idea of a more personal justice is very appealing to him. As in a family dispensing discipline, the backgrounds and differences among offenders would be considered in determining penalties. But he doesn't think it feasible for our government to carry out such a policy justly, and so his desire for an effective deterrent wins out. As he says in another context, "if it's not predictable, then it's not a deterrent."

It is clear that Drew Snowden holds extremely harsh views on crime. In fact, his views are *so* harsh that he doesn't much care for them, himself:

I sound like George Wallace. That is not the kind of person I am. But I am frustrated. . . .

I don't particularly like my opinions. They are not fashionable. They are not intellectual. But they are realistic.

Yet, even this man's views, while overwhelmingly harsh, are not unremittingly so. Even he gives the occasional nod to an alternative approach. When discussing possible goals for the criminal justice system, Drew grudgingly remarks, "And then there's rehabilitation, I suppose comes somewhere in there." Indeed, for the juvenile justice system, he believes rehabilitation should be the number one goal. When I pose a hypothetical murder by a teenage boy of the guardian who has for ten years abused him, Drew sentences the youth to counseling: "He's a minor!"

Drew says he generally favors the type of prison work release program I describe. He manages to think of one offense (graffiti) for which a sentence of restitution or community work-service might be an appropriate alternative to incarceration. And the idea of working alongside an ex-convict or of having a relative bring one home to dinner doesn't phase him. About a (crime of passion) murderer who was at a party he attended, Drew says: "He went to prison, and the book says that you go to prison and you come out a free man. That's the way it should work."

But these remarks are the rare exception among the views Drew expresses. It is difficult to imagine a citizen more tough on crime than he. Drew Snowden is a believer—and in the extreme.

Defining Believers and Dissenters

Drew Snowden presents a stark portrait of a believer—a useful place to begin. But he and his fellow believers are not carbon copies of one another. What ultimately defines a believer or a dissenter? What is it that the believers believe? From what is it that the dissenters dissent? For that matter, what do the dissenters believe? In this chapter I will endeavor to answer these questions about the content of participants' views, both in general terms, and by providing detailed portraits, such as that above, for several more of my interviewees.

When we look at those interviewees whom I have called believers, we see, for the most part, a group of people whose harsh views dominate their mild views.[5] Most do support (if in varying degrees) measures such as aid to the underprivileged, alternative sentencing for certain nonviolent offenders, and rehabilitation for those imprisoned. But by and large, these views are overshadowed by their desire for measures like handing down longer sentences, increasing prison capacity, making prison conditions tougher, or increasing our use of capital punishment.

When we look at the participants whom I have called dissenters, we see, in the main, a group of persons whose mild views dominate their harsh views. These are not people who would leave ax murderers to roam the streets. But by and large, they would have us halt the practice of capital punishment,[6] greatly reduce the use of incarceration in favor of various alternatives, and concentrate a far greater portion of our resources on solving the human problems that they feel lead to crime.

This is the surface-level picture, but when we turn to examine those people who are at the margins, it gets a bit hazy. I have placed Aram Isaac among the believers; but how do we decide whether it is his harsh views or his mild views that dominate—he seems to feel each with nearly equal fervor. I have placed Olivia Hassan among the dissenters; but can I fairly report that the balance of her views is so very different from that of Aram's? There must be something that can distinguish the believers from the dissenters better than a mere surface-level calculation of the relative strength or number of each participant's mild and harsh views. Indeed there is.

There is a critical difference in the way in which the believers and the dissenters conceive of the basic aims of the criminal justice system. Each and every believer holds that harshness toward certain criminals is appropriate in order to serve the purposes of punishment or deterrence—or both. The dissenters disagree. Many announce outright that they hold punishment to be an inappropriate aim, and deterrence a bankrupt one. Others indicate their disapproval with silence: in the many hours of our conversations, never do they choose to defend a harsh sanction with the language of punishment or deterrence.[7] Dissenters may on occasion advocate measures that are inherently and unfortunately harsh, but they never advocate them *because* they are harsh. For a dissenter, the only justification for a harsh sanction— incarcerating a murderer for a lengthy period, for instance—is to protect the public from further harm. This is the principle of isolation, or even more aptly, incapacitation. Most believers support this aim *along with* their beliefs in punishment and/or deterrence. For the dissenters, this is the only room allowed for harshness, amid their otherwise mild views: it is a policy of last resort.[8]

This, then, is the most critical distinction between the dissenters and the believers. It is the criterion that allows me, with reasonable confidence, to classify participants like Aram and Olivia, whose views are such that to have judged them on the surface level alone would have yielded far shakier determinations.

Now that this framework has been set out, we can return to the examination of some real-life believers and dissenters, which was begun with the sketch of Drew Snowden. The views that these individuals express, and the cases they make for their views, should demonstrate more fully how the distinctions between the two groups are played out. Two more believers and three dissenters will be presented here in some detail. Included among them are some who like Drew are clear-cut examples of their type, and others who stand nearer to the margins. The former should establish the pattern. The latter will test it.

The Believers

Gladys Jones

Gladys Jones, at sixty-two, is looking forward to retirement from her job as a clerk at an Oakland hospital. A native of the industrial Midwest, where her family was active in early struggles for civil rights, she moved to Oakland in the late 1960s. She is black and is married, but separated. Gladys is a high school graduate; her only child holds a degree from a prominent university.

For Gladys Jones, there seems to be little question but that the courts are not dealing harshly enough with criminals. I ask her why we should be harsh on them:

> Well I say, not being harsh, they just take it for granted you not gonna do anything ... But if you're more harsh and more firm, I think [they]

would think twice before they just—see, a lot of the crime is done by people over and over again. They let 'em out and they do it over and over. And I think if they keep them longer—they don't have to be that harsh . . . but keep them in longer.

When shown a list of possible goals for the criminal justice system, Gladys selects punishment as the most important, but indicates that deterrence and victim compensation are also important aims. The current system, she says, doesn't "make them suffer enough . . . for what they do. And don't repay the victims. They very seldom talk about the victims. Mostly, it's just the criminal."

Asked to propose sentences for some hypothetical offenders I describe, Gladys Jones suggests terms of at least twenty years for a triple rapist and of five years for a pair of habitual burglars.[9] She supports capital punishment for murderers who "really intend[ed]" to commit their crimes and has this to say about murderers in general:

They know [if] they kill a person . . . they'll spend no more than between five and ten years and get right back out. So they don't care. They don't care much for life. But if they know they had to stay . . . at least twenty years, twenty-five, I think there'd be less killing, myself. You don't have to give 'em capital punishment, but they'd have to stay in prison at least twenty to twenty-five years . . . 'Cause a lot of killers, they kill a second person, too.

To describe Gladys Jones as tough on crime would be perfectly fair. She supports harsh penalties for the perpetrators of crime. But this is only half the story. When the time comes to discuss the causes of crime, she reveals a second layer to her views. Gladys sees the causes of crime in unemployment, especially among minorities; bad schools; and inadequate parenting. This last she considers the most important cause:

The parents don't seem to care about them, a lot of 'em. . . .

A lot of blacks, they don't have but one parent. Their mother works most of the time. They don't see a father. It's kind of hard on the . . . children. They start crime very early.

When I ask her who she thinks is more to blame for crime, individuals or society, she replies: "Oh, society, definitely. I really do." She certainly does not regard this as an excuse, however. At another point in our conversation she speaks negatively of some co-workers who "don't seem to think people should be punished . . . They [say] the way society is, that's why they do it."

This two-part perspective of harsh punishment for individual offenders, alongside broader sympathy for the social causes of crime, is a common thread throughout the conversation. Thus, while Gladys believes that the perpetrators of crime deserve punishment whatever their social circumstances, she repeatedly endorses measures that she hopes will reduce crime by addressing these broader causes. Asked to choose from a list I show her containing ten possible solutions to the crime problem, she selects *increasing educational and employment opportunities for all* and *working harder to end racism and discrimination* as the most important. And as she talks about why she wanted greater harshness toward criminals,[10] she moves easily from a call for longer sentences into a discussion of the need for rehabilitation:

> And while they in, give them some kind of education . . . so that they have something to do when they—usually when they get out they don't have anything to do. That's why they go do the same thing over. If they had a job, or something to do, I don't think they would do it over. While they in prison you should teach them some kind of skills, I think.

This example of a smooth transition from punitive remarks to an emphasis on rehabilitation is typical of Gladys. Several times during the course of our conversations, she makes a similar shift of gears, as in this interchange, in which she has just asserted that at the present time the threat of prison sentences is not effective in preventing people from starting lives of crime:

> *KTG:* But now, thinking back to some of your comments earlier, you thought maybe if we were stricter, that it might be a more effective threat?
>
> *GJ:* Um-hum. If they were stricter, but they're not strict enough— too lenient, we're being.
>
> *KTG:* Now, are we talking about stricter in terms of longer time, or more certain that you would actually be punished, or both, or . . . ?
>
> *GJ:* Both. Longer term, well, they, prisoners don't have nothing to do. If you gave 'em something to do in prison. Teach them more things to do. I think that would help them. But they don't do anything, the way I hear.

Gladys Jones's policy prescriptions for crime are firmly grounded in the use of confinement, but she has little respect for our current jails and prisons: the conditions are awful, she says, and they throw everyone together so that the lesser criminals end up learning new tricks from the more hardened convicts. She proposes creating rehabilitation centers for nonviolent first- and second-time offenders; still, these would be fenced-in facilities to house offenders on a twenty-four hour per day basis.

Asked what's the point in sending so many people to our current prisons, if they don't do very well at discouraging recidivism or providing a general deterrence, she replies:

> I don't see anything. It really isn't doing them any good, I mean, it's not helping them any. There's a lot of them that come out, they're in worse shape than when they went in.

Then, after going on to dwell again on the importance of rehabilitation during incarceration, she moves the discussion back to the underlying sources of crime:

> What caused them to do it? ... There's always a cause to it when they do it ... You should teach people, like in school. You should prevent things before they happen, you know what I mean? Always prevent, not wait till it happen, then want to put 'em in prison. There's always things that cause people to do these crimes. They need some kind of prevention program.

Gladys favors the prison work-release and conjugal visitation programs that I describe. She approves the use of victim restitution and community work-service programs as alternatives to confinement for minor nonviolent crimes. And she supports sending some offenders with substance abuse problems to treatment-oriented halfway houses instead of to prison.

Gladys Jones gives a clear demonstration that a believer can hold more than one layer of views about criminal justice. She supports the concept of punishment and doesn't cringe at making criminals suffer. She holds that harsher penalties for crime would provide an effective deterrent. Yet, she places the source of our crime problem in socioeconomic causes, and her desire for preventive and rehabilitative solutions is strong and sincere. Even in describing a situation in which she felt considerable personal jeopardy, she is able to maintain this perspective:

> GJ: I went to a funeral last year—a co-worker of mine's son died of an overdose. You see the whole gang, teenagers, coming in—it's a whole gang of drug ... pushers ... It took the whole side of the funeral hall. They had beepers. And they said they were very violent people. And they were mostly teenagers or

early twenties. And I say, five years ago you wouldn't see that... They just sprung up in the last two or three years, they said.

KTG: Where did they come from?

GJ: They come from regular family, and they say they make easy money. Quick money, *'cause they couldn't get a job anyplace.* So they start selling drugs... That's the first time I seen a gang like that... And I feel so awful. They all had on jackets alike. There's about fifteen of them. I mean, they weren't afraid or anything. And I heard they have guns in their cars and things. (Emphasis added.)

Still, no quantity of sympathetic views about the ultimate causes of crime can erase the fact of Gladys Jones's deep convictions about punishment. These extend through her past and permeate her conception of even the brightest future. When I ask this lifelong Baptist whether her religion has any special teachings about criminal justice, she says, "Well, when you do wrong, you're supposed to be punished." And asked what would be done about crime in the utopia she's described for me, she replies, "They have to be punished, the same way they are now." Gladys Jones is a believer.

Aram Isaac

Aram Isaac came to the United States a decade ago as a refugee from North Africa and became a U.S. citizen just a few months before our conversations took place. A Catholic by birth, he is thirty-seven years of age and married; his wife is at home with their two small children. Aram is a college graduate, but is currently employed as a delivery truck driver. He is black and has lived in Oakland for four and one-half years.

Aram sees the causes of crime in America as grounded in "the system." People are allowed to take advantage of the freedom to work or not to work, to go to school or not to go. Instead, he asserts, each citizen should be required to be contributing something to our society, and our leaders should be creating the opportunities necessary for each to do so. "So the cause of crime is not keeping busy the individuals... not creating... incentives and initiatives so people they have something to eat... dress." Instead, they sit around idle—drinking and smoking—and then commit crimes out of boredom.

Asked what solutions he would suggest for the crime problem, Aram proposes that we "create many means of hav[ing] a better life, easy life." Even in this superpower nation, he says, there is a lot of unemployment, ignorance, and illiteracy. "This country have immense wealth. It is the first on the planet, and it should spend a lot of money to create jobs, to create education, to create [health care]." Later he returns to this theme:

If you don't eliminate these crimes, if you don't eliminate this big difference of classes, we will all suffer, no matter who. Even the upper classes, they don't feel comfortable; they don't feel proud when they have ghetto in front of their skyscrapers.

And many times he reemphasizes how little excuse he feels there is for having failed to achieve such social change:

I feel sad because in a powerful country like this . . . it [crime] could be eliminated easily . . . If you have money, you have everything. If you have money . . . you can solve all these problems we are talking about . . . And we know how much money have the American government. Why it not relieve us of this problem?

Even as we turn to discussing appropriate responses to those crimes that have already taken place, Aram continues to hammer home his insistence on fundamental change:

We talked already—that is not a solution, eliminating the criminal from the street is not. The main job should be through aid centers, eliminate the unemployment through education and reconstruct the society. Only by that means, not by prisons, can we eliminate or diminish the crimes.

But while prisons may be no solution, they are, for Aram, an absolutely critical stopgap. As we discuss the use of incarceration and other penal sanctions that he supports, it becomes clear that there is more to Aram Isaac than just the enthusiastic social reformer. Like Gladys Jones, he has another important side.

Asked the standard survey question about the courts, Aram answers without hesitation that they are not harsh enough. Why should they be harsh on criminals?

Well, now, the teenagers, they know that whatever crime they commit they are not going to jail or nobody's going to kill them. And the [adult] criminals, they know that they are not going to be killed. "So what? I try to get this five hundred dollars from this man. If I get it, OK; if I don't get it they will catch me, so I will go to jail. So what? I will eat. I will have a place to sleep. Then I'll come out and start all over again. Big deal." That's the way they say.

Essentially, he says later, there are two alternatives. Either criminals must "understand that crime is not good for society or for themselves," or they must be "scared of jail."

Fear of capital punishment, he feels, could provide an additional deterrent. Here he continues his explanation of the need for harsher sentences:

> And when they stop you they say, "Man, I killed a lot of men—you might be the last, and then I will go to the jail." The jail is a place where you can pass your time, temporary time, and then come out and establish another similar or different plan. So if they know that who kills is going to be killed... we wouldn't have all this homicides.

Aram would use the death penalty for murderers who kill "indiscriminately"—"for the sake of killing"—and for drug dealers. But he might spare some who killed "in time of madness" or of "financial or emotional crisis."

Besides this belief in the deterrent value of harsher sentences, Aram also supports punishment as a legitimate purpose of the criminal justice system. But punishment alone is not enough, he says, and in this he returns to strike some of the same notes he struck earlier in discussing the means by which we might prevent crime at the source. He calls for a long period of incarceration for the hypothetical burglars I describe, but then he adds:

> What I am scared of—what if they put them in jail ten years, fifteen years—or six months, two years—if you don't give them really a humanitarian way of treatment, humanitarian way of teaching to rehabilitate them, that doesn't help. Ten years or fifteen years or five years in jail is nothing. In fact they become more criminals, more crude. So when I say put them in jail, I don't mean just punish them. Punishment is just stay in jail without freedom. You don't have any connection. That is the worst thing from my view. And the same time, rehabilitate them.

In fact, Aram wants rehabilitation to be the number one goal of the criminal justice system, and he feels that it should be sincerely tried at least twice with each offender.

> I don't disagree with put many people in prison. If I disagree, it should be in the way they are handling the prisoners. Just put them, feed them, and let them vegetate like trees. I don't agree... Give them education... and let them work—as I say, they might help you to pay the expense of the state—they might learn for themselves a skill.

If rehabilitation has not succeeded after two attempts, Aram would have the offender incarcerated for life.

Aram is adamant that, by and large, confinement in one form or another is an essential accompaniment to rehabilitation. While confinement cannot be the ultimate solution to crime, it is still critical to remove as many current offenders from the streets as possible, in order to insure that they will commit no further crimes while they are being rehabilitated. Thus, he proposes rehabilitation centers instead of prisons for some offenders but would have them housed there twenty-four hours a day. He grudgingly approves the use of prison work release programs, but only if we can "certify" that the offenders chosen will not use this opportunity to commit new crimes. And he opposes outright the use of drug treatment halfway houses as alternatives to incarceration: "You don't have any guarantee. Keep them in jail and ... use them for useful things, to rehabilitate them." An Italian proverb that Aram cites elsewhere succinctly expresses his basic outlook: "To trust is good, but to not trust is better."

Aram would approve of restitution and community service as alternatives to incarceration in some cases, but only if they could be administered in the style of his native country. There, before offenders can be released on alternative sentences, relatives or friends must sign for them, agreeing to take the punishment upon themselves if their charge should commit a new crime.

Aram Isaac is a man of many approaches: it seems that he would have us wage the battle against crime from every possible angle. Prevention through social change and rehabilitation through education and vocational training are prominent among his beliefs. Incapacitation, mainly through isolating as yet unrehabilitated offenders, holds an equally critical position among his views: the personal-guarantee approach described above demonstrates the extreme to which he is willing to go to ensure that captured criminals will not be allowed to quickly repeat their crimes. Finally, Aram supports the concept of punishment, and he advocates harsher sentencing because it would serve the purposes of deterrence. Because of these last, he is a believer.

The Dissenters

Kate Fontana

Kate Fontana is a nurse-midwife at a municipal clinic and holds a master's degree in her field. She is white, thirty-three years of age, and married. Her husband is self-employed as a cabinetmaker. Kate was raised in a rural town in Delaware, but her adult life all has been urban. She moved to Oakland in 1980 and lives by choice in an area of the city that most of her race have shunned.

I first met Kate Fontana and Drew Snowden on the same very

stimulating day. From Kate springs forth immediately the same vibrancy, the same striking love of life that I found in Drew. Yet, in their views on criminal justice, there could hardly exist two more diametrically opposite individuals.

Kate places the underlying cause of crime in the state of family life in this country:

> There are people who are parents that obviously have not the ability to parent and therefore raise children that have a lot of problems with security and self-esteem. And crimes are committed—they are just a manifestation of a problem with a person's sense of self.

This is the root, she says, and from this grow problems like dropping out of school and therefore not getting jobs. Even if more jobs were available, she continues, many people couldn't handle them, because they have never been taught responsibility in a family, nor learned that responsibility brings self-esteem.

> So, therefore, if there is high unemployment and there is no sense of community ... people turn to whatever way that they can make themselves feel good. It could be an escape with drugs and alcohol, or it could be ... robbery or selling drugs or whatever to get the money ... that is going to make them feel good and get ahead and buy big cars and some nice clothes, and all that stuff, because that is where they will get their self-esteem.

Further, inequity of economic resources is an important and related cause of crime:

> I don't think the current welfare system works, and therefore we have a lot of perpetuating cycles—third and fourth generation of people on welfare. People who have not, who want to have, and don't have a mechanism to have, revert to selling drugs and crime ... Well, it's kind of like we put them in that position, in a sense, and how are we going to deal with that?

To Kate's mind, the number one goal of the criminal justice system should be rehabilitation. Punishment she doesn't approve of: "I don't go in for the eye-for-the-eye business, so I don't think that that should be any kind of goal of the criminal justice system." The problem with our current system, she says, is the limited means we have for dealing with crime:

What we have is ... either long or short prison sentences, or life, or we have ... capital punishment ... Are any of those means that we deal with crime substantial? I mean, is locking somebody up in a prison cell without any kind of rehabilitation [substantial]?

Recidivism rates among teenage criminals are at 60 to 70 percent, she says, and "obviously what we are doing is not working ... That's because there is [not just] that crime that is the problem; the problem is what happened long before that, and how do we change that, and can we change it?"

I ask Kate what she would propose that we do to solve the crime problem. First, she says, she would require parenting classes—something much more real than the current courses in family life education that are offered in the high schools. "Developing family and parenting skills" would be "the ultimate deterrence of crime." Then, from the list of possible solutions to crime that I show her, Kate selects the following as top priorities: *increasing educational and employment opportunities for all* ("That gives people alternatives to criminal acts"); *working harder to end racism and discrimination; programs to reduce child abuse* ("Abused children turn out to be abusive adults. And they not only abuse their kids, but they abuse everybody else."); *fighting drug and alcohol abuse;* and *making more use of alternatives to prisons.*

For those who have committed crimes, Kate insists that there must be rehabilitation—counseling, not just authoritarian supervision. She would have them contribute to society in some way, perhaps turning a jail into a big farm, so that

> there is kind of a community spirit versus a jail where just everybody sits around and does nothing ... And that they are given rewards for accomplishment in a rehabilitative setting ... I believe in the philosophy of like, chop wood—carry water; I think that it's to get back to the simple routine of basic living, growing, having vegetables and planting and kind of taking care of basic human needs. There is a good place to start in a rehabilitation program—for people to learn to depend on each other and to trust.

Also, the criminal justice system should offer offenders the opportunity for more education if they wish it—"having them decide for themselves goals that they would like to achieve and accomplishing those. I don't know, maybe this is all too ideal and we would never have enough money for all of it. But we could just dismantle one Trident submarine or something!"

Kate completely opposes the use of capital punishment: "Life is sacred, and ... human life has much potential; and I don't believe that killing a person makes any sense at all." Initially, she states that incarceration (with rehabilitation) is appropriate for murderers, drug dealers ("take them out of their network and try to show them another lifestyle that can be rewarding"), and for other violent offenders. For nonviolent and victimless crimes, she proposes alternative sentences such as victim restitution, community service, and drug treatment programs. I ask her if it is worthwhile to imprison as many people as we now do:

> No! What ends up happening is it just overcrowds the prisons. Even the people who are there don't get adequate shelter, and it doesn't allow for enough supervision, and there's more crime in jail, and it leads to the never-ending revolving door for the people who are in there. Because it's like they never experience a different way of life. So it doesn't work.

Kate's responses to the hypothetical crimes I describe demonstrate her strong desire to limit the use of prison sentences. For the triple rapist, for example, she proposes a sentence of therapy (including family therapy) and nonmonetary victim restitution. And despite her earlier general statement that violent criminals should be incarcerated, she wrestles over whether this offender needs to be isolated in any way, or if he might live at home and be supervised by a probation officer and a therapist. Finally, she decides he should be in a "jail or some place where he stays in a supervised setting" and has to check in at night, but can go out to a job during the day. In a similar softening of her earlier position, she comments later that having drug dealers live in a supervised setting in the community, work "at the local Wendy's," and give part of their earnings back would be a better penalty than sending them to jail.

One has to listen hard and long to pick up a few harsher elements in Kate Fontana's views about criminal justice. She does believe that isolation should be the second most important goal of the criminal justice system, and she advocates the incarceration of murderers and at least some other very violent criminals. She also is unwilling to conclude that our current system of incarceration is worse than doing nothing at all. But these ideas represent a tiny portion of her thoughts about crime and justice.

Most importantly, Kate rejects the concept of punishment outright; and she finds no defense for a policy of deterrence:

> We're spending too much money on incarceration and stiffer sentences that are ineffective...Recidivism shows us that it's not working, but we continue to spend our money. It's kind of a crazy thing.

Isolation in order to protect the public is the only justification that Kate finds for a limited use of harsher sanctions—and these would be *very* limited. In Kate Fontana we find, beyond a doubt, a clear portrait of a dissenter.

Burt Ruebel

Burt Ruebel, thirty-four, is a freelance photographer who holds a bachelor's degree in philosophy. He is white and single. Originally from the East Coast, Burt moved to Oakland in 1982. A thinking man who says he gets some of his "biggest thrills . . . from bashing ideas together," he also admits to the "bad habit of beating ideas to death." Indeed, he requires four sessions totaling more than ten (often exasperating) hours to meander through my questions.

Burt believes that the most fundamental cause of crime lies in the very nature of our society. Ours is not a classless society, he says, nor a true democracy. We have all these theories that don't apply to the actual situation in which we live. In fact, we have a hierarchy, and the people at the top, he asserts, figure that they are above the law. So the people down below see this, and they want to "grab" some of the "goodies," too. Other causes that Burt mentions are poverty, hunger, and psychological imbalance (which, he says, might be brought on by child abuse, drug abuse, or illness).

Asked about possible goals for the criminal justice system, Burt places the greatest importance on rehabilitation (although, he remarks, it may be more a matter of "habilitation"). Isolation, he says, is absolutely necessary in extreme cases; the examples he gives are Idi Amin, Adolph Hitler, and Charles Manson. "There is not a whole lot you can do with these people," he explains, but "I don't think that there are all that many." Victim compensation, he feels, should be another important goal. But Burt has nothing positive to say about either punishment or deterrence. "The whole point of the penal system," he says later, should be "to strengthen the individual who is being quote unquote punished, to make them viable in society."

When I ask Burt what he would propose we do to solve the crime problem, he calls for "sweeping educational reforms"—extending the school year, and creating a new type of curriculum. He also suggests initiating a jobs program somewhat on the order of the WPA; improving the quality of television programming ("A lot of it spends so much time promoting the easy way out"); and trying to find some means of heightening the sense of community in urban areas.

From among the list of possible solutions I show him, Burt focuses on *increasing educational and employment opportunities for all, programs to reduce child abuse, improving conditions in slum areas, fighting drug and alcohol abuse* (he would legalize, regulate, tax, and attempt to "deglamorize" drugs), and *making more use of alternatives to prisons.*

Burt opposes the use of capital punishment. He challenges the notion that it is a deterrent: "Just because you kill the son of a bitch doesn't mean that somebody else is not going to kill somebody else. Matter of fact, it almost heightens the thrill for some kind of psychotics." Further, he feels that he is not qualified to decide who should die, and if he is not, who is?

As we move into a discussion of incarceration, Burt touches first on what he feels prisons can do:

> Now when you're dealing with the notion of prison, in my mind you're dealing with the notion of isolating an individual from society basically for the purpose of keeping them away from everybody else. As much as I would like to see prisons become ... habilitation centers, they're not. Incarceration is a form of torture. It's not necessarily productive. Effectively, you're being brutalized by your system. You're probably going to be raped by your fellow inmates ... [But] there are some people out there who are really weird and really bad off that really should be kept away from the rest of the population. This is unfortunate, but it's true.

Later he discusses what he feels prisons do not do:

> I don't see it as a disincentive to criminal activity ... Prisons as they are, are just really nasty places. And they're not serving the function that I think would be ideal to the situation. Lots of people in prison need better education. They need better skills. They've got to develop awareness. A lot of them need therapy ... But they're not going to get that kind of help in prison. Effectively prisons are just going to produce more of a malicious criminal element. I think they should be reorganized. I think that a lot more attention [should be] paid to education, medical help, psychiatric, philosophical, whatever.

A prison, Burt contends, "is someplace where you stick somebody so you can forget about them. We don't need more prisons, we need ... more progressive places where people can learn to deal with themselves and their environment effectively." He suggests that we might explore the notion of work farms or kibbutzes staffed with counselors as possible alternatives: "It's not incarceration. It's not like being locked in a cell nonproductively." Later, though, he adds that he is "nervous about any institution. Obviously the potential for abuse is monumental."

Burt supports work- and educational-release programs. He feels that victim restitution is a good idea for property offenses and advocates community service sentencing long before I bring it up. The sentences he prescribes for the hypothetical offenders I describe illustrate his sincere desire to seek alternatives to incarceration:

Burt would send the young robber to a rehabilitation-oriented halfway house. Dry him out and teach him to read, he says. Try to teach him some job skills. "Incarceration will not help this person."

About the pair who have repeatedly committed burglaries, Burt says, "I need more qualifiers. Why are they stealing? Who are they stealing from? . . . I imagine there would be mitigating circumstances." These circumstances should be taken into consideration, he insists. But he also considers the possibility that they are "just being obnoxious and stealing stuff from people that can't really afford it" and that they are aware of the situation of the people from whom they are stealing. In this case, "for your general rank-and-file, basic bad guys—Bonnie and Clyde ripping off Ma and Pa Kettle—send 'em to a kibbutz."

About the triple rapist who lured his victim away from a night school class, Burt says "obviously, therapy is indicated . . . Incarceration does have a bit of appeal in this setting, but I think that it would only tend to make the problem worse." Depending on the individual, he would think that intensive therapy (including group therapy) for about six months to a year, followed by weekly sessions, would be appropriate. Such an offender would be under fairly strict monitoring to begin with and would reside in a halfway house. "I can't really see taking them out of the workplace, if they were in the workplace to begin with," Burt muses. "I can see taking them out of music appreciation classes for a while."

Clearly, Burt Ruebel is another dissenter. What little harshness he would mete out is strictly limited to the incapacitation through incarceration of a small number of extreme offenders. He places no faith in a policy of deterrence. And he will not sanction a policy of punishment. As he says at one point, taking the focus back four thousand years to Hammurabi, "This is where I think the whole notion of justice as balance came from. Eye, eye, tooth, tooth, balance, balance. I think the notion is invalid."

Olivia Hassan

Olivia Hassan, thirty-six, is head teller at a local bank. A high school graduate, she has also completed some college coursework. She is black and is the divorced mother of three children. Olivia was born in Los Angeles but has lived in Oakland since she was a small child. She recently moved from a nicer area of the city back into the neighborhood where she grew up. This is one of the highest crime areas of Oakland, but rents are also lower, and she hopes that because of this move she will be able to afford to purchase a home sometime in the future.

Asked about the major causes of crime, Olivia replies that it seems to her that crime is always committed out of some kind of frustration. The person couldn't think of a better way—couldn't cope. It could be, for instance, the frustration of feeling that you have to have something that others have—feeling bad about yourself and your situation and not having the money to buy the "solutions" that we're taught that money can buy, and, so, just stealing them. "So, it's just, not knowing how to solve problems . . . just not having a good idea about life." Society, Olivia says, is primarily to blame for crime, but individuals are also responsible. Even when people have everything they need, she explains, some may still make destructive choices.

I ask Olivia the standard question about whether the courts are too harsh or not harsh enough on criminals: "I think that they don't deal with it enough, but it's not necessarily harshness, it's just not dealing correctly with it, not dealing with, sometimes not with it at all." The justice system gets into the act too late, she says. "After this long, progressively worsening situation of someone getting more and more destructive, then they come in and put them behind bars or what have you. But when the problem first starts . . . a lot of times, there's no help there." There isn't enough available in the way of support systems at the preventive stage, she asserts. "I guess they kind of see . . . it as a black-and-white situation of first one day you're good, and the next you're a criminal! I don't think it works like that."

As goals for the criminal justice system, Olivia advocates isolation, rehabilitation, and victim compensation. Unless an offender is "really dangerous or really destructive," he or she should be helped "within society," because "if you start removing everybody that has something wrong with them, you're going to have a lot of people." When necessary, however, the offender should be isolated while the attempt at rehabilitation is made. To Olivia, "crime is some kind of sickness." We don't want to reward offenders for what they have done, and we do want to "try and make them understand what they're doing to another person." But we also want to help them to become healthy again.

From the list I show her of possible solutions to the crime problem, Olivia selects *increasing educational and employment opportunities for all* as the most important.

> Until a person gets in a real desperate situation where their mind isn't working anymore, if you can kind of educate them so that it sinks in that choosing drugs or choosing crime or violence will only make the situation worse . . . Increasing education about life instead of the empha-

sis that we had in school I think was on getting jobs, making money. But it has to be more, because that—it's just not enough to cope now.

It is a "spiritual, moral type of education," she says, that we need to provide: "How, when you get under pressure ... how do you get yourself out from under pressure, so you don't find yourself being carried away doing things ... How to get some kind of self-control." If, through this, we can "get a person to take care of himself better," then many of the other items on my list—employment, preventing child abuse, improving slums, fighting substance abuse—"just kind of fall into place."

Olivia opposes the use of the death penalty. To her, it makes no sense to punish an offender for a murder by doing the exact same thing to him or her. However, she is not as critical of the use of incarceration as are most of her fellow dissenters. When I ask her what kinds of criminals belong in prison, her reply is roughly in line with theirs: "People that can't or won't stop themselves from ... hurting people or animals, or destroying property." But when I ask whether or not it is worthwhile to imprison as many people as we now do, she says: "Yes. They try to not imprison as many people as possible, so I suspect the ones that they do imprison must be pretty—for the most part, there is a reason that they are in prison." Although Olivia feels that California doesn't necessarily need more "traditional" prisons, she does believe that it needs more "rehabilitation centers." Some of these would provide twenty-four hour per day confinement, while others would be operated on an outpatient basis.

Olivia approves of the use of prison work release and conjugal visitation programs. And she feels that restitution and community service sentences are appropriate alternatives to incarceration in nonviolent, not-too-serious crimes—in cases where "there isn't any danger of the person hurting someone or something." For instance, she suggests sentencing prostitutes or drug users to go around to schools to speak to kids about why not to get involved in these activities.

The sentences Olivia suggests for my hypothetical offenders demonstrate the high priority she places both on rehabilitation and on protection of the public. She would send the young robber to a rehabilitation center where whatever is wrong with his life would be worked on: drug treatment, preparation for employment, education, and so on. He would stay there under full-time confinement until his drug problem was licked, because "that's probably what set off that desperate situation." About the habitual burglars, she exclaims at first: "They should put the people that keep letting them out in jail!" Then, more seriously, she insists that these offenders should be isolated because "they can't stop." "They're inside other people's houses while they're sleeping, which is a dangerous situation." They should be taught skills that they can use in confinement, and they should remain there for a longer period of time. The rapist should also be confined, Olivia says. He is a repeater and committed a premeditated offense. An attempt should be made to figure out what makes him commit rape, and to rehabilitate him. "It's something real deep that he's going to a lot of trouble to act out, so, he should really be watched, confined."

When we have covered all the hypotheticals, I ask Olivia what she would do with those whom she wanted to incarcerate if, for some reason, no places existed in which to confine them. She can think of no acceptable alternative to imprisonment:

> The whole thing would be to keep them from hurting another person ... The only way that you can control a person besides locking them up is to kill them. I mean, once a person starts—especially like the rapist ... or the person that was on drugs that might really get out of control—there's really nothing I can think of ... besides confinement, that would keep them from hurting someone else, or doing something worse.

Still, Olivia is no fan of our current prison system. To her mind, prisons today are not effective at discouraging convicts from committing new crimes when they are released: "If people change, I think ... something happened to the people—they did it ... I don't think the prison helped them change." I ask her how effective the threat of prison sentences is in preventing people from ever starting a life of crime:

> By the time a person gets to the point where they're even *considering* committing a crime ... they're beyond being reasonable and thinking about prison and prison sentences. Those are reasonable types of thoughts that I don't think—people [who] are thinking about committing a crime—they're not being reasonable.

Olivia contrasts her own beliefs to those of others: "Most of the people that I'm around think that people should be punished; they're into punishment and/or they think that retaliation does some good." But to her, punishment "just seems pointless." The only point in using our current prisons at all is that they isolate offenders. "It's better than having them all killing other people or destroying other people's lives and stuff."

This is where the rubber meets the road. True, Olivia supports the heavy use of incarceration made by our current penal system, and at times her tone is both colder and more desperate than most of the other dissenters'. But in the most critical matter, she joins them absolutely: she will not justify any harshness on grounds of punishment or deterrence. Further, they join her in endorsing at least some element of harshness: with one exception, they insist that those offenders who seriously threaten the public safety must be isolated.[11] The difference is that Olivia sees this threat as larger than do most of the other dissenters. This may devolve primarily from differing perceptions of the current state of affairs. In endorsing our present, wide use of incarceration, for instance, Olivia may be unaware that a large proportion of those behind bars in America have been incarcerated for nonviolent offenses.[12]

Near the end of our conversations, Olivia summarizes her own philosophy:

> My basic belief is that people do something criminal, it's because in some way they're unhealthy, they're sick; and that's the best that they could do at that time... To me, that's how it should be treated. I don't want them hurting me while they're sick. They should get well... And if they're going to destroy other people with their sickness, they should be isolated until, or if, they get well.

If Olivia had a slogan to explain her harsher views, it would not be "get tough," but rather, "play it safe." She is a dissenter—a frightened dissenter, but a dissenter, nonetheless.

Summary

The stories of these Americans are fascinating to reflect upon: they express a level of reality that no secondary analysis can approach. Certainly a major goal of this chapter is to allow the reader simply to immerse him- or herself in the raw content of some participants' views. But we must not lose sight of the broader purpose of identifying a critical distinction between the two groups. As these descriptions have illustrated, this distinction lies not only in the fact that there generally is an obvious difference in the overall harshness or mildness of their views. More importantly, we find that there is a fundamental difference in the way these believers and dissenters conceive of the basic aims of the criminal justice system.

The believers maintain that harshness toward certain criminals is appropriate to serve the purposes of punishment, deterrence, or both. The dissenters march to a different drummer. Although they may occasionally advocate measures that are inherently harsh, they never advocate them *because* they are harsh. For the dissenters, the only justification for a harsh sentence is incapacitation—the protection of society from further harm by the offender in question. Of course, most of the believers support the aim of incapacitation as well, alongside their convictions about punishment and/or deterrence. But for a dissenter, this is the only allowance made for harshness: it is a least-of-evils choice.

Having established and illustrated this essential difference between the believers and the dissenters, we can move on now to examine the motivations for their differing views. To what values or deep concerns are they responding when they express the opinions they do? In this chapter, we have examined what participants want our government to do to respond to crime; in the next chapter, we must consider why they advocate these policy directions.

CHAPTER 3

Motivations

Over the course of the many interviews I conducted, participants advocated dozens of different policy directions. These included highly specific policy changes, such as making drug dealing a capital offense or removing prostitution from the criminal code, and broad policy objectives, such as rehabilitating offenders while they are in prison or providing compensation to crime victims. Now we must ask why they support these policies: what do they hope to achieve? In what sorts of language do they cloak the raw opinions they present? To what sorts of underlying values or deep concerns are they responding? What are the motivations of these Americans—and in what ways do the motivations of the believers and dissenters among them differ? Developing an understanding of these motivations is a critical step toward explaining the emergence of the existing public consensus about criminal justice. It should be useful as well for illuminating the complex foundation upon which future policies—be they innovation or continuation—must be built for successful presentation to the public.

In this chapter I will identify the various motivations displayed by the study participants, discuss broad patterns of motivation exhibited by the dissenters versus the believers, and then allow these Americans to demonstrate in their own words how these values influence their views on criminal justice. The chapter concludes with a discussion of its implications for an explanation of public consensus.

Four Underlying Motivations

From the noise and confusion of so many dozens of hours of conversation, there emerge just four deep, underlying motivations for the criminal justice views that the interviewees express. Importantly, these motivations are not preconceived standards against which I tested each of the interviewees' statements: no formulation of such values was even attempted until all of the interviews had been completed. Rather, they emerged very clearly and powerfully from my reading of these many conversations. The first motivation is *security,* the basic human desire for protection from loss or harm to self, family, or community. The second is *desert,* a sense of what is right or proper, expressed especially in a striving for balance on the scales of life (as in "just deserts"). The third is *compassion,* a concern for the welfare of other human beings. Finally, there is what I will call *social critique,* the conviction that a major change in our social, economic, political, or cultural arrangements is essential to the achievement of "the good society."

Note that the term compassion will be used here only to describe a concern for offenders and potential offenders. My decision to limit the use of this term is in no way intended to obscure or degrade participants' expressions of concern for victims and potential victims. Rather, two of the terms already include this focus. Security denotes a concern for potential victims—self and others. And desert often reflects a plea that justice be rendered for the victim's sake. Thus, we would have no need for the term compassion at all were it not for the necessity of describing a concern for offenders and potential offenders. Reserving it for this use alone should contribute to analytical clarity, by helping to distinguish between the various forms of concern.

How are the four underlying motivations related to the various goals described in chapter 1, some of which played such a key role in the last chapter? Essentially, the goals—deterrence, rehabilitation, and the like—are policy objectives pursued in varying degrees and manners by our society in its fight against crime. The four motivations, however, are broader values and concerns that may guide our hopes and actions in many spheres of life, not merely in the area of criminal justice. The policy goals, then, represent possible means through which the ends embodied in these underlying values might be served in the sphere of criminal justice. Table 1 lists beside each broader motivation those specific objectives that might conceivably spring from it.

TABLE 1.   Participants' Underlying Motivations and Related Policy Goals

Motivations	Criminal Justice Goals
Desert	Punishment
	Compensation
Security	Deterrence
	Isolation
	Rehabilitation
	Prevention
Compassion	Rehabilitation
	Prevention
Social critique	Rehabilitation
	Prevention

Several of the goals listed in table 1 clearly are expressions of only one of the underlying motivations. A policy of punishment, of course, would be pursued in the service of desert; so too would the compensation of victims, a policy that seeks the restoration of balance that the notion of desert demands. Deterrence and isolation, on the other hand, serve the ends of an underlying concern for security. However, prevention and rehabilitation each appear under the heading of three out of the four larger motivations; at different times, they serve entirely different ends. Under the heading of security, prevention and rehabilitation serve the end of creating citizens who will be disinclined to commit crimes. Under the heading of compassion, they serve the end of ensuring that all individuals are treated with respect and dignity, and that all are encouraged to develop to their full human potential (which, as a result, may create citizens who are disinclined to commit crimes). Under the heading of social critique, they serve the end of contributing to the changes necessary to bring about "the good society" (which, as a result, may create citizens who are disinclined to commit crimes). The differences between these three motivations are subtle but important and will be further illuminated when we turn to the statements of the participants.

Table 1 illustrates, as well, how two persons can begin from the same motivation—security, for instance—and arrive at policy prescriptions that differ significantly in their degree of harshness. One person may begin from security and advocate a policy of deterrence and isolation only; another may be moved by a concern for security to support prevention, rehabilitation, and isolation; a third, deterrence, isolation, and prevention—and so forth. Understanding how, and why, they are led to such different opinions is the central task of this chapter, for it bears directly on the questions about consensus with which this book is concerned.

Patterns of Motivation

In chapter 2 we saw clearly that both believers and dissenters actually hold a combination of views—some harsher, some milder. Naturally, each also holds a variety of motivations. Let me emphasize that the motivations I will be discussing here are the *primary* motivations influencing each interviewee. Thus, to say, for example, that a believer draws the primary motivation for her mild views from a concern for security is not to say that at no time during our hours of conversation did she utter a mild word motivated by desert, compassion, or social critique. Some or all of these influences may indeed have entered her conversation at a few points, here and there. What this does say is that any other values were clearly subordinate to her primary motivation, security. The notable exception to all this is in the harsh views of the dissenters, where to talk about primary motivations is tantamount to talking about sole motivations: none of the dissenters (who by definition eschew the pursuit of harsh policies for any purpose other than incapacitation) allow any value other than security to influence them toward harshness.[1]

Beginning with the dissenters, we find two major patterns of motivation. In the first pattern, the harsh views of the interviewees are motivated by security, while their mild views are primarily motivated by compassion. In the second, the harsh views are motivated by security, and the mild views are primarily motivated by social critique.

Among the believers, there also are two major patterns of motivation. In the first group of interviewees, whom I will call the *traditional believers,* no motivation other than security or desert plays a primary role in their views, harsh or mild. In the second group, the *complex believers,* security and/or desert provides the primary motivation for their harsh views, but values other than these play an important role in motivating their milder views.

Let us turn now to examine the role of these motivations in the statements of some individual dissenters and believers.

The Dissenters

A majority of the dissenters demonstrate the first pattern of motivation outlined above. Sketches of two participants will reveal how these motivations are played out.

Abby Edwards
Harsh Views: Security
Mild Views: Compassion

Abigail (Abby) Edwards is forty-seven years of age and is the mother of five grown children and stepchildren. She has lived all her life in the western states, and Oakland has been her home for the past twelve years. Abby teaches courses on meditation, stress reduction, and first aid at a community college. She is white and married. Her husband is a plumber.

Abby's views on criminal justice are overwhelmingly mild, but not exclusively so. The few harsher views that she expresses all are held in the service of security. Like her fellow dissenters, she is willing at times to support policies that are inherently harsh, but only when she deems them essential to the protection of the public. Thus she does accept the temporary incarceration of some offenders. I ask her who belongs in prison:

Those who ... we feel are going to turn around and knock someone else off the minute they hit the street, or rob again—be violent towards someone, that way. They need to be removed from society. But then just to lock them up and throw the key away is not the answer either. People who are going to continue their violence, whether to themselves, which is very often the case, or someone else—they need to be under supervision until someone feels that they can function normally again without hurting someone.

Abby's answer to the hypothetical I pose about the habitual burglars expresses both her sense that a harsh response is sometimes necessary to protect the public, and her regret that it must be so:

> *AE:*   I would like to again say that they pay it back. But I don't think that is the right answer in this case ... You can't just let them free, because they'll probably continue this. We don't have the kind of supervision for someone to follow them around twenty-four hours a day ... Each time [they've been in prison] I suppose their sentence got harder and harder, but it didn't help them any. That's a very hard question ... They need help, and just putting them in prison and throwing the key away is not the answer. Because eventually, no matter how many times they've done this, they'll get out again, probably.
>
> *KTG:*   So am I hearing you saying, you'd like not to put them in prison. And you're struggling for some other way to help them and stop them?
>
> *AE:*   Yes, but I don't know if there is another way.
>
> *KTG:*   And if you couldn't think of it, you'd say, "Well, I can't think of it, I guess they have to [incarcerate them]."?
>
> *AE:*   That's right, that's right, if I, you know.
>
> *KTG:*   But you'd like to think of it?
>
> *AE:*   Oh, I would.

Security, then, is the only motivation behind Abby's few harsh views. Her mild views, also, are primarily motivated by a single value: compassion. Her fervent belief that every individual should be allowed and encouraged to develop his or her full human potential comes through time and again in our conversations. For Abby, this includes the offender, however serious the crime. For instance:

If someone has murdered someone, I'm sure most people would not want that person back out on the street. I wouldn't either—temporarily.

But I don't believe in capital punishment, nor do I believe in life imprisonment. Because I think people can change, and people can grow and better themselves.

Abby explains that watching a change take place in the life of a family member has had a significant influence over her views about the potential for change by offenders:

I have a brother-in-law who has been in and out of prison for a long, long time . . . His third or fourth time in prison he—and this was done by himself—picked up some books . . . on yoga, and started reading them, and practicing yoga in prison. And I had been corresponding with him for many years, and I could see the change in his character after awhile. *And so I know people can change.* And then, when he got out, he's now a different person . . . [Before], he had a slightly violent nature; he would blow off the handle; and he had a bad opinion of prisons and himself and government and everything. And then he began to take responsibility for his own actions, by whatever it was—reading these books, or changing his thought. And I think we can help people do that. Just how, I'm not sure. (Emphasis added.)

This is what is behind Abby's predominantly mild beliefs about criminal justice—this conviction that "everyone changes," that "everyone has that right, and they do change." It fuels her strong beliefs in prevention and rehabilitation and her desire to see alternatives to incarceration implemented wherever possible.

We can see her motivation in compassion plainly in some of her other remarks about offenders and ex-offenders. When I pose the traditional question about the courts, she argues that after the first offense, sentencing is often too tough. "I think sometimes that the first offense is handled all right, but then it's what happens to the person after they're put into prison or whatever happens to them. I don't think there is enough care in that area about what happens to a person after they are sentenced." She continues: *"Why* they did it needs to be looked into a lot more than that they did do it."

Sometime later, I ask Abby how she would feel about having a halfway house in her neighborhood: "I would welcome it!" she exclaims. "I would go volunteer some of my time." When I ask about how she would feel if a member of her family brought home to dinner a friend who was an ex-convict, she says: "I would probably try to make him feel more welcome than just his ordinary average buddy, or whoever." Clearly, it is compassion that enables Abby Edwards to hold the overwhelmingly mild views about criminal justice that she expresses in our conversations. When she looks at offenders, she see lives filled with problems we may help to solve, lives filled with potential we may help to encourage. To wit, this interchange:

> *KTG:* Some people think that *government* will never be able to solve the crime problem. They insist that if change is ever to come it will have to start from some other source—moral or spiritual change in individuals, for example. Others are convinced that if government would finally enact the right policies, the crime problem could be brought under control. What do you think?
>
> *AE:* I like both those ideas. I think the government can help, but I also think it's a very individual thing—spiritual, moral. I think people need to take more responsibility for that themselves, but everybody needs help. A lot of people just don't know how to pick themselves up by their bootstraps and move on. They get a little help and it makes all the difference in the world ...

We find in Abby Edwards a clear example of the first pattern of motivation among the dissenters: harsh views held in the service of security; mild views held primarily in the service of compassion. The sketch that follows add a small variation to the basic pattern: the participant holds mild views for which *both* compassion and desert are primary motivations. I take the space to examine this variation carefully—despite the fact that it was demonstrated by only one interviewee—because it provides an opportunity to consider the influence of desert in motivating views about compensation, a role that this value plays in a secondary way for many of the other participants. It will also serve to further illustrate the dominant role of compassion in motivating the beliefs of this group of dissenters.

Anne Girard
Harsh Views: Security
Mild Views: Compassion/Desert

Anne Girard aspires to make her living as a writer, is studying to become a nurse in case she cannot pull this off, and, meanwhile, supports herself with part-time work in a department store. She is white, forty-five years of age, and the divorced mother of two grown children. A native of the Bay Area, she lived for years in Spain and Brazil. Anne moved to Oakland five years ago.

Just as it is for all the other dissenters, security is the only motivation for the few harsh views that Anne expresses. In the first passages of chapter

1, we heard her injunction against treating offenders "like they're bad—with disrespect." This, she says, is "only going to make them angrier and more lacking in self-esteem, and thus ready to go out and do more lawbreaking. To be harsh," she continues, "is just not going to work. So any harshness would be too much."

Still, Anne does consider isolation an appropriate goal for the criminal justice system "if somebody is killing people or raping people." She would put in prison those who "do physical violence . . . to people . . . [and who] can't be trusted, really, not . . . to harm other people." She opposes capital punishment but wants to be certain that "really dangerous" murderers—the example she gives is Charles Manson—are isolated for life. "It's kind of scary to think of the system not protecting the innocent from that kind of thing," she explains. Clearly, the sole motivation for the limited use of isolation that Anne advocates lies in security. As she says early on, "isolation may feel like punishment, but [that's] not the purpose."

In her mild views, Anne is strongly motivated by two values: desert and compassion. Before we consider the specific ways in which these values have influenced her views, a few general comments about the notion of desert are in order. As a motivating value, desert may exert its influence in two quite different directions. When a crime is committed, the victim is *hurt,* physically or otherwise. Honoring desert, we could say: now it is right that the offender must also be *hurt* in some way (punishment). But, honoring the same value, we could also say: now it is right that the offender do something to *help* (compensation—through victim restitution or community service work). Both policies are pursued in the service of desert; each attempts to restore the balance that the offense has disturbed. But the paths by which this is attempted are very different.

Anne responds strongly to the value of desert in formulating her mild views about criminal justice. She speaks of the importance of "changing from punishment to consequences . . . instead of just punishing and locking people up, giving them work . . . meaningful work." This theme of consequences that involve some form of compensation to society is one she consistently emphasizes. It can be seen most clearly in her comments about the hypothetical offenders I describe. About the young robber, for instance, Anne says:

> . . . I don't think he should just be let go. I think he should have to . . . come before an evaluation or court case or whatever and be charged with what he'd done. And then have to serve the consequence. But it doesn't sound like going to prison or to jail or anything like that would be a good idea . . . He would need to enter a drug program to

clean up. He would need support for that. And then I think, to do meaningful work to make up for—you know, to pay off in a way, to society, [for] what he'd done. So that he could be forgiven and have it all over with and start new. And in the process build up some good feelings about himself in a new direction. So, do some work that other people can appreciate, and get cleaned up about his drug abuse.

And about the embezzler:

> ...He should have to pay it back. Again, he should have to face the consequences—be told: "Okay, we know you have done this; it's not okay...Make it up by...just working it off in a meaningful way...for the well-being of others, and gain some self-esteem for doing that.

At times, Anne's motivations in compassion and desert appear very much intertwined with one another, as can be seen in her comments about the habitual burglars. They are to be giving something back to society, but it is also through this same process that they may be healed:

> *AG:* They should be on a work farm, or something, and just kept busy. Doing, again, something useful—but where they're not going to be out on the streets.
>
> *KTG:* So you would be confining them in a twenty-four hour a day situation?
>
> *AG:* Well, for a while ... So that there's hope—so there's some way for a new direction to take place. But a new direction's *only* going to take place if ... they really can feel good about the work that they're doing, with people who really appreciate it, and are good models. If such a new direction can even happen, that's the way I think it would happen. And then, after time, maybe they could have a part—go out into the world and do it [their work] and come back, possibly.

Indeed, even Anne's most basic conceptions of rehabilitation and compensation are interwoven with one another. Rehabilitation, she says, should not be lecturing, but "just ... giving people meaningful work so that they can feel good about themselves."

This equally strong influence of compassion on Anne's mild views comes clear early in our conversations, as she discusses the causes of crime. She places the cause of crimes of all types in a lack of self-respect and self-worth. Street crime, she says, also stems from the fact that some people are "being deprived of what they need" and are expressing a "real anger." I ask her why so many people lack self-esteem:

> I think because they didn't get the respect as they were growing up, the love, the care that they want. And so feel an emptiness inside themselves and don't really know who they are ... So it has to do just with people not knowing how special and unique they are ... They're out of touch with that because ... their parents didn't know it either— didn't know how to give it to them....

> If a person really feels a love for himself—the basic self inside—then he's also going to feel that for other people and not want to rip people off [but] want to treat them with real care, real respect ... And it seems to me that's the only thing that will ever prevent crime. That it has to come from deep inside, not from rules out here.

Thus, she proposes that we attempt to deter crime not by *setting a* (harsh) *example to discourage future crime,* as that criminal justice goal was defined on the list I showed her, but by "just setting an example, period":

> Being—all of us—being the kind of people who—like starting with parents—being able to give that love to their children. And treat them with such respect that ... [it] wouldn't occur to them to commit crimes. Starting from the very beginning ... we all live in such a way that we're examples for each other ...

Even once crimes have already been committed, she proposes that we "give everybody an opportunity—treat everybody with respect—including the people who have broken the law." From her own life experiences, especially in working with children, Anne says that she has come to see that "it doesn't work to punish, to criticize." Instead, we should create "an environment that's inspiring and supportive and loving, and when something is off" we should "just [be] aware of it, rather than judging it as a bad thing. That's what works ... just to notice what is. To be aware, and then to see that by doing that, change takes place. Whereas criticizing and judging and blaming doesn't make for change but makes for defensive behavior and more of the same."

Of Anne's many expressions of compassion for offenders and potential offenders, the most telling is found in these words about the man who broke into her daughter's apartment one night and raped her at knifepoint:

Here I have a personal experience with my daughter—very personal experience . . . I can't . . . imagine anything worse than that whole thing happening. I wouldn't want it to happen to me, or to anybody that I know, and that makes me angry, that such a thing could happen . . . It just pisses me off . . . It makes me angry that . . . the world is in such a state that that can happen. And at the same time, the guy who did it, I don't feel the anger directed exactly at him . . . He's obviously screwed up. He's obviously a miserable person. He obviously needs a lot of help. Punishing him isn't going to help her. I don't want him out where he can do it again . . . [But rather than punishment] whatever can be done to change him ought to be done . . . I think we need love. I think that we really need it. And we all need it. He needs it as much as I need it. And I feel that I have a lot of it in my life. And I feel he probably doesn't. And if he did he wouldn't be doing what he's doing . . . What my job, and I'm going to do, is to spread that around as much as I can. And that just to be angry with him, and to make him suffer, will only—it puts the focus, you know—it's what we pay attention to that we become . . . And the world just needs to be filled with love and caring for each other. For ourselves and for each other . . .

Having heard the love and concern that this woman can express even for a man who has brought so much pain to her life, we can have little doubt about the influence of compassion on her many mild views about the treatment of far lesser offenders. Compassion and desert, then, work closely together as motivations for Anne Girard's mild views. Security, however, works alone to motivate her harsher views.

This combination of motivations found in Anne involves a variation on the first major pattern observed in the dissenters. Investigating it in detail here has not only served the purpose of conveying Anne's individual style of motivation, it has also demonstrated the manner in which desert can operate to engender mild instead of harsh views. Anne is the only dissenter for whom this motivation plays a central role. But for many other participants, dissenters and believers alike, desert wields a secondary influence over the mild views they express.

Before moving on to examine the second major pattern of motivation among the dissenters, it may be helpful to consider briefly the distinction between compassion and social critique. Certainly these two concerns are not without similarities. Each plays a secondary role in influencing the views of some of the participants for whom the other motivation is dominant. But there is an important difference between the two. Participants for whom compassion is the primary motivation are those who express a central concern for the well-being and fulfillment of *individuals*—offenders and potential offenders—even if they may also express an accompanying belief that crime is to a large degree socially caused. But participants for whom social critique is the primary motivation are those for whom the social etiology of crime and a social responsibility for its abatement are the overwhelming theme. They may (or may not) at times speak compassionately of individual offenders, but their central focus is on *society*.

Daniel Steinbach
Harsh Views: Security
Mild Views: Social Critique

Daniel Steinbach, forty-eight, is a licensed clinical social worker employed by the Oakland Public Schools. He counsels youths in two inner-city high schools. Daniel is white and is the father of three grown children from a former marriage. An urban dweller all his life, he has lived in Oakland for the past ten years. Daniel holds his harsh views on criminal justice in the service of security. His mild views are motivated primarily by a wide-ranging social critique. His story will serve to illustrate the second pattern of motivation among the dissenters.

Daniel rejects punishment outright as a goal for the criminal justice system: "Making criminals suffer because of their crimes...God, it's terrible...I'm not into people suffering." Deterrence he holds in no higher regard: "This doesn't work. This has never worked in any society ... Yeah, it has worked in some societies. But what you have when it works is a bunch of robots, and so I don't want to be a robot."

He does, however, support the limited use of isolation. This is appropriate "if they're very violent criminals." "But," he emphasizes, "where you remove them to is very important—the conditions."

Daniel is so critical of our current criminal justice system that I ask him at one point whether he feels that prisons do more harm than good:

> ...Given the context of the society we live in...putting someone in prison that has committed certain crimes absolutely serves a purpose. It gets 'em out of society, and as long as that person is in prison, they're not going to be out there committing violent crimes. So, in that sense, that one person is removed from society, to not commit violent crimes, so you could say that's a positive thing ...

Indeed, there are some extreme cases in which he would even like to see lengthier incarceration than is given under our present system:

> I don't like it, I don't like it, but if you have somebody that, like Singleton, who just got out, who cut off someone's arms, gets out four years, five years, and put that person out on the streets—that's insane, absolutely insane . . . There's certain people like him—other people that are just psychopathic killers and so on, and rapists, and so on. Until you have another system, I guess you got to keep them behind bars for a long time and not let them out. . .

Here we see both Daniel's willingness to use isolation in some cases and his distaste at having to do so. This then is the only justification for the use of a harsh sanction that Daniel will support: protection of the public. Like his fellow dissenters, he is motivated in his few harsher views about criminal justice solely by a concern for security.

The primary motivation for Daniel's mild views is his wide-reaching social critique. He is by no means without compassion for offenders and potential offenders, but this motivation is secondary to his central concern that our society is phenomenally "screwed up." Here he speaks about the causes of crime:

> I think the basis of all crime, including white collar crime, is that our society is so into objects and external things, that people . . . are not in touch with who they really are, their true selves, their spiritual selves, or whatever you want to call it. And our whole society is geared toward this kind of philosophy, separation, and so on . . .

> And I think another major cause . . . is the way we raise children in this country . . . Most parents use their children to fulfill needs they never got from their own parents, and it's a very unconscious thing, and they can do it with love. And as a part of that process, what happens is the child—you cut off the spontaneity, the spiritual—you cut off their sense of who they really are . . . [They] grow up and are walking around with what you might call false selves . . . We're totally out of touch [with] who we really are. I think that has a lot to do with crime too, and child abuse, and so on.

When I ask Daniel what he would propose that we do to solve the crime problem, he shows that he is critical, as well, of our socioeconomic arrangements:

I think one of the first things I would do is redistribute the wealth in this country on some levels ... Create job programs that work ... Create tax incentives for private industry to work with ... job programs ... Economics, and so on, is very, very important. It's like, I don't think we'd have the amount of crime we have in this country today if we didn't have people living in ghettos and poor people and so on. I doubt it ... Also, have some kind of guaranteed income in this country ... Also, to make it advantageous to work ...

The economy has to be changed—absolutely. The distribution between the rich and poor in this country is getting wider and wider ... In terms of what we spend money on—weapons, war, the possibility of war— we have to change our whole priorities ... Change our priorities, where social values, human values, become very important ...

One might say that Daniel's broad social critique provides the motivation for his mild views about criminal justice because it leads him to the attitude that we must not choose responses to crime that, so to speak, blame the victims (who, from this perspective, include the offenders). For, in his view, "the government's created these problems." We can see the parallels to this attitude about crime, in his attitude about poverty.

Sure, I can say some poor people deserve to be poor, because they don't want to work. But ... it's like, why don't they want to work? Something's out of kilter ... So I don't think anybody deserves to be poor. If society wasn't screwed up on so many levels, I think everybody would be contributing—want to contribute. There may be a few individuals, but ...

Daniel's essential belief is that "as long as we have the system geared around progress [and] profit ... we'll have crime." Thus, he cannot see harsh treatment of those who merely express the sickness of our society, except where this is absolutely essential to protect others from violence. And this belief leads him as well to seek milder responses to crime that are in tune with the broad changes he feels are essential to the creation of a healthy society: counseling, education, skills training, treatment of substance abuse, and other alternatives to incarceration.

Two major patterns of motivation have been found among the dissenters. In Abby Edwards and Anne Girard we saw the first pattern: harsh views motivated by security; and mild views primarily motivated by compassion (in Anne alone, joined by desert). In Daniel Steinbach we have seen the second major pattern: harsh views motivated by security, and mild views primarily motivated by social critique. Let us turn now to the believers.

The Believers

As was the case with the dissenters, two major patterns of motivation also can be observed among the believers. The *traditional believers* are those for whom no motivation other than security or desert plays a primary role in motivating their views, harsh or mild. The *complex believers* are those who draw a primary motivation for their mild views from a source other than security or desert.

The Traditional Believers
The traditional believers are a varied lot, their common thread being that they reach no further than security or desert to draw the primary motivation for their views, both harsh and mild. Some draw only upon security, others upon certain combinations of security and desert.[2] We must turn once again to the stories of individual participants to observe the workings of these values up close. Because the specific combinations of motivations are so varied, here it will be simpler to take examples from the harsh and then the mild side, one at a time. The most important thing will be to observe how the two motivations—security and desert—can work to exert a primary influence on either harsh *or* mild views.

Violet Taylor
Harsh Views: Security

Violet Taylor is a retired waitress with a tenth-grade education. She was born and bred in Louisiana, but Oakland has been her home for the past thirty years. She married late in life and has no children of her own. Her husband, a retired gardener, also did not complete high school. Violet is black and is sixty-three years of age.

As is so common, Violet Taylor holds mixed views about criminal justice. But when she is harsh, she is very harsh. The sentences she suggests for my hypothetical offenders make this clear. The embezzler gets fifteen years; the habitual burglars get life sentences; and the triple rapist gets twenty-five years. Once or twice, she tosses the word "punishment" into the conversation, but desert does not appear to be a significant motivating factor for Violet. Instead, it is a concern for security that lies beneath the harsh views she expresses. Early on in our discussions, her remarks reveal this motivation:

KTG: Why should we be harsh on criminals?

VT: ...I would say because they do a crime—which, I know that the facilities and things are very crowded—but they do a crime, and they go and spend a few weeks in jail some place, and the next thing you know they're back on the streets doing the same thing. And so I think they should keep them longer than just a week or so and then let them out to do things all over...

KTG: And what would happen if we kept more people for longer?

VT: I think they would be a better person when they got out... [Now], they [say], "I'll be out in a few weeks," and they do the same thing over again. But if they keep them longer, maybe it would give them time to think.

Here, she has made a security argument from two perspectives. She wants offenders *isolated* from the public for longer periods—directly increasing our security during the period of time in which they are imprisoned. And she hopes that the very experience of long incarceration will influence them to think twice about engaging in further criminal activity—*deterring* them from threatening our security in the future. She repeats these arguments in similar terms several more times in our conversations: in supporting a policy of stiffer sentencing as a promising solution to the crime problem, in defending why it is worthwhile to imprison as many offenders as we now do, and in justifying a lengthy sentence for the hypothetical rapist I describe. In the last case, she debates with herself over the primacy of isolation versus deterrence; ultimately, it is all a question of security:

[He] raped her and two others. I would give him life imprisonment. No. I would give him twenty-five years, and that would probably stop him. He would think next time, before he tried to rape someone.

Barbara Damon
Harsh Views: Desert/Security

Barbara, thirty, has risen through the ranks to become a midlevel manager at the California Department of Transportation. A native of Oakland, she has lived in this city all but four years of her life. She attended college for several years but did not graduate. Barbara is white and married. Her husband is a high school graduate who is self-employed as a plasterer.

    In the opening lines of chapter 1, we heard Barbara's views on the traditional question about whether or not the courts are harsh enough. Right from the start, we can see her joint motivation in security and desert. If the courts were harsh enough, there wouldn't be as much crime; if you merely threaten criminals, they'll turn around and commit crimes again; if tougher sentences were given, some people might think twice about committing crimes: these are deterrence arguments—arguments motivated by a concern for security. But she shows her motivation in desert, also, when I ask her why we should be harsh on criminals: "They have done something wrong. Nobody said that punishment was supposed to be nice."

Over and over, Barbara states her harsher views in phrases that express these twin motivations. Take, for example, her comments on capital punishment, which she supports for deliberate, premeditated murders. "You took someone else's life," she says. "Who gave you the right?" And later, "He gave up his right when he took someone else's life. He gave up his right to life, at that point in time." Desert. But she also says, "Who is to say that it is not going to happen again?" Security.

Or let us consider her response when I ask her what kinds of criminals belong in prison: "I'm not sure. Ones that are going to do it again, OK?" We return to this subject shortly:

KTG: How do we figure out who's going to do it again?
BD: True. Read minds here, folks! Okay, let's go back and change it to, they belong in prison if they are actually convicted of doing what they're accused of doing, and then the sentence being comparable to what they did ...

The punishment has to be equal to the crime. Where do we say that the crime is bad enough to go to prison? That I don't know.

Here again we see the joint motivations. When she has a little trouble with views expressed in the service of security, she can quickly retreat to those held in the service of desert.

Lastly, let us consider the subject of prison conditions. Here, her motivation in desert is very clear. When I ask how much she would guess it costs to build a maximum security prison these days, she complains that the costs are high because "they have to have deluxe accommodations."

KTG: What do you mean when you say deluxe accommodations?
BD: I get upset when prisoners riot or they refuse to eat, because they don't like the food. What comes to my mind is that they want steak every night for dinner. Prison is supposed to be a punishment. It's not supposed to be deluxe, and wonderful ... So when I hear that they are holding a ... hunger strike, I just sit and go, fine, don't eat, nobody ever said you had

to—that's just one more thing we have to pay for. That's just probably cold and cruel, but like I said, they're not supposed to be in prison to be having fun.

But Barbara also would like to see prison conditions toughened up because she feels that this would serve the purposes of deterrence. When I ask what she thinks an average day in the life of a prisoner might be like, she admits that she doesn't know a great deal about it. But, "it doesn't sound like a real rough life." "There has to be something in there to discourage them from doing it again," she says a few moments later. "But I don't know what it could be." "I mean, if it's not real comfortable, I wouldn't want to come back." Barbara's views about appropriate prison conditions, like the rest of her harsh views, are importantly influenced by security, as well as by desert.

Clarence Peters
Mild Views: Security

Clarence Peters, a seventy-three-year-old white businessman, has tried several times to retire from the glazing concern he founded but is still at work part-time. A native Californian, he has lived in Oakland since the Depression. His formal education ceased after one year of junior college. Clarence is a remarried widower and has three grown children. His wife is a retired elementary school principal.

On balance, Clarence's views on criminal justice are quite harsh. He feels that the courts—with their hands tied by prison overcrowding—are generally "far too ... easy, too liberal, and allow the criminal back out on the street much sooner than he should be." He supports a limited use of capital punishment and would incarcerate all of my hypothetical offenders. But he has some milder views as well.

Clarence feels that rehabilitation—along with deterrence—should be the number one goal of the criminal justice system. But unlike the dissenters and the complex believers, in this and other of his milder views he is not significantly influenced either by a sense of compassion for offenders and potential offenders or by a critique of criminogenic social conditions for which we bear some collective responsibility. Clarence does express some compassion for juvenile offenders, and for drug addicts and alcoholics who commit crimes, and he mentions unemployment as among the causes of crime. But these small influences are subordinate to his primary motivation: security.

Clarence describes in detail just what he has in mind in the way of rehabilitation for criminals, and as he does so, it gradually becomes clear that his chief concern is not with help for offenders, but with the alleviation of a social menace:

> *CP:*   Our penitary [*sic*] system has not been able to deal with ... the criminal as I would wish they could.
>
> *KTG:*   How would you wish they could?
>
> *CP:*   ... It's a matter of reaching that person—finding out what makes him tick—why he ... is a criminal in the first place—and then replace that desire with something else. Perhaps a religious training, and I know that has corrected an awfully lot of people. To take up religion and in effect learn how to love the other man, love your fellow man, instead of fight him or try to get the best of him ...
>
> I'm sure that the criminal who learned that crime does not pay would come out and be a good citizen. And we'd have, then, fewer criminals. ...
>
> *KTG:*   What would teach them that crime doesn't pay? ...
>
> *CP:*   We would have to change the thinking of the person—the criminal. The length of the sentence really has nothing to do with it ... The person themself could rehabilitate in a week's time, or a month's time, if he so wanted to ...
>
> *KTG:*   Is there a way that we can help people to do that, or do we just have to wait until they decide that they want to do that?
>
> *CP:*   Oh, no, no ... you cannot just wait ... A criminal that's in there is perhaps very surly and perhaps very much against society for having picked on him and mad at somebody else for having caught him or snitched on him or something. He's very adamant at first, I'm sure, and only till he realizes that he is against his fellow man, his family, and that he is against society in general, going against the laws of nature and of—let's say the laws of God ... He has to be led, however, and taught by superiors, perhaps—I wouldn't even say superiors—but by others who were trained to cope with people like that.

In this entire long discussion, Clarence never once suggests that the offender might have problems—personal or socioeconomic—that it would be to his or her benefit to solve. Rather, all this effort, it seems, is just for society's sake. Not even for society's sake *and* the offender's sake—but *just* for society's sake. We are to rehabilitate the offender while he or she is incarcerated, simply because we will produce, thereby, one less criminal to worry about. To be sure, the reduction of crime is an important end result, also, for those participants whose mild views are primarily motivated by compassion or social critique. But here, it is the *only* important result. And security is the primary motivating value.

We can see further evidence of this primary motivation in security in Clarence's comments about a rehabilitative proposal that he does not like:

> *KTG:* Many proposals have been made for changes in our prison system. Would you tell me whether you think each of these suggestions is a good or a bad idea: ... Conjugal visits in special areas on the prison grounds, so that spouses and prisoners can spend a few full weekends a year together, thus helping to keep family ties intact.
>
> *CP:* That's a very disturbing one to me. I'd certainly have to agree that ... it could be good ... It's hard to say, for me. I don't like the idea to start with—conjugal visits. However, perhaps it has saved a few families. Enough effort in the first place by the criminal ... could have kept him out of that situation of being in there in the first place. I feel almost that he has lost his rights to his family. If conjugal visits was the only thing that is going to hold his family together—which I don't believe—that it could be the only thing. Perhaps to answer it: I don't like the idea at all. I wish we didn't have it. And therefore, then I wouldn't be disturbed about it—seeing it, or even having to say sometimes that I condone it. Because I do sometimes say that.

Here we have an example of a rehabilitative program that unquestionably provides direct benefit—happiness, even—to the offender. And it is this very benefit that seems most unsettling to Clarence Peters. He concedes that the program may have a socially beneficial outcome—but not a large or exclusive one. He makes no complaint that conjugal visits would expose society to any present danger, but neither does he see them as contributing very much toward a future reduction in crime. There is not enough in this proposal to satisfy his great concern for security—and too much that calls for a degree of compassion for offenders he simply does not feel.

As we can see from his earlier comments, Clarence prefers a style of rehabilitation that attempts a very direct change in an offender's character. Here, when I ask what solutions he would suggest for the crime problem, he speaks about the agents of this change:

> I think that the biggest thing ... it's a matter of rehabilitation, and perhaps that is done by psychology, and therefore I would train

criminal psychologists to try to cope with the problem of rehabilitating the criminal...

Several other times he makes mention of the psychologists who would be responsible for the rehabilitation of offenders. Nowhere is there any word about tutors and literacy, teachers and high school diplomas, instructors and skills training. Rather, it is almost as though he were speaking of a medical problem and calling upon doctors to attend to it. But instead of being concerned to bring offenders from sickness to health—a perspective that might reveal a strong influence from compassion—he seems essentially to desire to change them from bad to good. Even when he speaks of penalties for offenders who commit victimless crimes—among them the drug addicts for whom he does have some compassionate feelings—there is no mention of treatment or healing. The emphasis is still on teaching them to do right by society:

> They're not prison offenders, but they have to be taught to accept the fact that they are doing things against the community and against society as such. They have to realize that, and just how that's done— counseling, perhaps...I don't know whether that would do it—counseling classes. See, psychology is a big factor, to me, in dealing with people. A good psychologist.

For Clarence Peters, in short, we need doctors to perform "surgery" on offenders' characters. This accomplished, we will have fewer criminals. Such a policy could be pursued in the service of only one value: security.

Adam Perlman
Mild Views: Desert/Security

Adam Perlman is the director of a speech therapy program at a Bay Area medical center. He is thirty-three years of age, white, and single. He came to Oakland in 1984, having lived most of his life in large cities on the East Coast. A careful man, he prides himself on seeing both sides of every coin.

Adam is a believer, and of course he holds a significant array of harsh views. He supports deterrence, isolation, and punishment as goals for the criminal justice system; he believes that "a lot of criminals need to be incarcerated"; and he advocates capital punishment for "incorrigible" offenders who have murdered or "severely disabled" their victims. These harsh views, like those we saw in Barbara Damon, are primarily motivated by a combination of both security and desert. But it is the motivations behind his many milder views that will be the focus here. In these also, he is primarily motivated by both desert and security.

Whether Adam is speaking of harsh or mild responses to crime, the concept of "accountability" is a critical one for him: "There has to be something to let people know that they've done something wrong. And that they can't just keep doing something wrong. They can't keep on violating other people's rights ... If you violate somebody's rights, you forfeit some rights." This applies on all points of the criminal spectrum: "Maybe we're talking about degrees of seriousness of crime and therefore degrees of loss of rights." Halfway house or other partial incarceration programs that somewhat limit an offender's freedoms are the type of milder loss of rights that Adam often advocates.

He also advocates broad use of restitution and community service programs. He feels that these could be used without incarceration for any nonviolent, nonrepetitive form of stealing, and he would add some form of victim compensation on to most incarcerative sentences as well. He makes it clear that accountability is a major purpose of this policy: "I think people should learn that they have to take responsibility for what they've done, and I think they should be responsible to the person that they've violated."

We can see both forms of accountability played out in the sentence that he suggests for my hypothetical young robber. Adam proposes that he pay back the money and more and that he live in "some kind of structured environment" where he "cannot come and go as he pleases." We should "not penalize him severely." But "he has to be accountable for what he's done ... It has to be impressed upon him that he's done something wrong, that it's a bad thing to do."

Both policies—mild loss of rights, and victim compensation—bear the stamp of a strong influence from desert. The offender has hurt someone, even if not physically. Now the offender will suffer hurt as well. Now the offender will have to help the victim. Either way, we are talking about an attempt at balance. This is what lies beneath Adam's consistent pleas for accountability.

Adam acknowledges the role that poverty sometimes plays in crime, and he occasionally expresses compassion for certain offenders—most notably those who have been the victims of child abuse. But the vast majority of the time, it is the value of desert that wins out over these concerns: "No matter what kind of oppression society are imposing on people, I think people are still—have to take responsibility for their lives and can't blame it on everything or everybody else."

There is, however, a second value that joins desert in wielding a dominant influence over Adam Perlman's mild views: it is security. This influence can be seen even in the policies that have just been discussed:

If you do something that violates somebody's rights, you have to pay some kind of price...The punishment may involve compensation. It may involve some kind of loss of rights...I don't think people should go on like it's okay to do, *then you don't learn anything from it.* There's gotta be some...kind of effective way to teach people. (Emphasis added)

Here he is saying that not just harsher punishments like prison, but even milder sanctions such as victim compensation, may have a deterrent effect upon future criminality—a security argument.

The influence of a concern for security can also be seen in Adam's attitude toward rehabilitation, which, he says, "would be great" as a goal for the criminal justice system. Although not to the extreme of Clarence Peters's, still Adam's approach to rehabilitation appears predominantly to be aimed *directly* at teaching offenders not to commit criminal acts, rather than at finding individually and socially beneficial solutions to their problems. Here he speaks about the rehabilitation of juveniles:

It would be nice to try to get some kind of education going early on. 'Cause that's when you make the most change. It's hard to change people as they grow older...As they're younger you can make more changes, expose people maybe to more things. Maybe even set up situations where their rights...have been violated—kind of play out situations. So people know what it feels like. And maybe from experiencing it—maybe not on an irreversible level, but on an artificial, reversible level—but still something that's real enough so that they can feel it—perhaps that would make more of a difference.

We might also consider one remaining element of the sentence that Adam proposes for the young robber discussed earlier. In addition to placing limits on his freedom of movement, and having him pay victim restitution, Adam also calls for rehabilitation. In the description of this hypothetical crime that I read to the interviewees, I stated that the offender is a high school dropout, unemployed, and a drug addict. And, indeed, Adam mentions "all those other disadvantages of life" when he speaks about this man. But still, when he proceeds to discuss his rehabilitation, he says that this "education and rehabilitation *should involve not only the crime* but should involve the drugs, 'cause the assumption I think is that he's doing this for his habit" (emphasis added). Adam's mention of the treatment of addiction is hardly insignificant, but note also the italicized language. The offender's problems in education and employment are not addressed; instead the focus, again, is more directly on training him not to commit crimes.

Last, let us consider Adam's comments about the importance of attempting rehabilitation even in the prisons: "Just taking them off the streets isn't good [enough] in and of itself, because you run out of room, and because if you don't try to change their behavior somehow, and you have to let 'em back on the street, they're going to have to do it again." Here, rehabilitation of prisoners is defended purely on the basis of effectiveness. Even with offenders who have committed crimes that are sufficiently serious that they would be sent to prison, Adam would have us try some form of reeducation. Constraints from overcrowding prevent us from keeping most of these people incarcerated for very lengthy periods; we must then also attempt through rehabilitation to alter their behavior. He seeks, through one route or another, the most effective way to prevent future crimes: security again is the underlying value.

Regarding the traditional believers, the central discovery seems to be that their primary motivations are not as mixed as their views. Their views are not all harsh: every one of them has at least some mild views. But their primary motivations for both harsh and mild views are found in some combination of the same two values: security and desert.

The Complex Believers
The complex believers (four of the thirteen) stand out from the rest. Unlike the traditional believers, these individuals draw a primary motivation for their mild views from a value other than security or desert. Three of these complex believers hold mild views that are primarily motivated by social critique. Their harsh views are primarily motivated by security or a combination of security and desert. Since these motivations for harshness already have been explored above, let us turn immediately to examine the influence of social critique on one of these believers.

Sadie Monroe
Mild Views: Social Critique

Sadie Monroe, seventy-two, is originally from Missouri but has lived in Oakland for thirty years. Sadie is a retired physical education teacher, her husband a retired optometrist. She is black and has two grown sons.

Sadie's views about criminal justice are predominantly harsh. She approves of capital punishment and would make heavy use of incarceration. Confronted with six hypothetical offenders, she suggests prison sentences for all of the five who are adults; these range from "a couple of years" for the young robber to "twenty years or more" for the triple rapist. Still, Sadie holds some milder views, and the motivation for these will be the focus here.

When I first ask about the causes of crime, Sadie says that "a lot of people commit crime 'cause they think they can get away with it." But as our conversations progress, it is clear that she places a fair bit of importance on a second cause as well:

> They should start hiring more minorities. That's why they are bein' in crime. They don't have no job, and then they are idle, and they steal and burglarize people's home, and all of that to get food to live.

Several times she repeats this theme of unemployment and its connection to crime. And she makes it clear that the responsibility for this problem is primarily social, not individual. Here I ask her why we have high unemployment:

> I think that unemployment is so great because they don't have enough jobs. They need to create more jobs for people. The people go around and look for a job—look and look—and can't find a job.

She emphasizes that minorities receive especially poor treatment:

> [Minority groups] have larger unemployment. That's because they won't hire them, and they don't get the experience. And when they go for a job, they tell 'em that if you don't have any experience—and you can't have experience if you're never hired for that type of work.

Further, job discrimination remains a problem even in the 1980s:

> In job employment it's always discrimination, and they go and go for job interviews, and they're turned down. And then a person of another race come right along and get employed.

It is this social critique, I believe, that is the primary motivation for the few milder views that Sadie expresses. Her selection of *increasing educational and employment opportunities for all* as the most important of the possible solutions to crime on the list I show her, her belief that rehabilitation is an important goal for the criminal justice system, her feeling that work release from prison is "a good program"—these follow naturally from certain of her beliefs about the social causes of crime. Sadie Monroe's is not a broad, sweeping social critique. Nor is it necessarily the only influence on her mild views. Compassion, security, and desert each enter at some point, but their influence is even more limited. Her critique of joblessness in America, its causes and its consequences, may indeed be a thin motivation for mildness of views. But neither is there much bulk to the mild views that she expresses. They play but a small part in the overall set of opinions she holds about criminal justice. This limited motivation can easily have inspired them.

Aram Isaac, the college-educated truck driver, and Gladys Jones, the hospital clerk, are the other two believers whose mild views are primarily motivated by social critique. The views of each were described in detail in chapter 2. Aram issues sweeping criticisms of the way in which our society has failed in its social responsibility to the young, the poor, the unemployed, the uneducated and the illiterate. In this, he places the ultimate cause of crime. And his mild views—broad preventive action to alleviate these social problems, and sincere attempts at rehabilitation of those who have already committed crimes—clearly follow from these most fundamental concerns.

With Gladys Jones, it is much the same, although the critique that she makes is not as broad as Aram's. She places the primary blame for crime on society, citing the problems of the black family, high unemployment (especially among minorities), and the sorry state of the city schools as prime causes. The failure of our society to equip convicted criminals with the skills and jobs they need in order to be able to turn away from further crime is an even more important theme. From these criticisms follow, first, her moderate emphasis on preventive programs in education and employment and on efforts to end racial discrimination; and, second, her major emphasis on strenuous efforts at the rehabilitation of those who have already committed crimes. Certainly other motivations—security and compassion—play secondary roles in influencing her to the milder policies she proposes or supports, but this two-pronged social critique wields the dominant influence.

There is one more complex believer. Although no other participant shares her unique combination of primary motivations (harshness from desert; mildness from security and compassion), it will still be instructive to consider the way in which these values influence her views. Most important is the opportunity to examine the workings of compassion in the views of a believer, for while she alone makes this a primary motivation, others among the thirteen exhibit a secondary influence from this value. Because her motivations are particularly complex and interesting, however, I will consider them as a whole.

Elizabeth Williams
Harsh Views: Desert
Mild Views: Security/Compassion

Elizabeth Williams is a thirty-four-year-old physical therapist. She holds two bachelor's degrees: one in art history and one in her current field. A native Californian of Anglo-Hispanic parentage, she has lived in Oakland for seven years. Elizabeth is married to an architect.

Elizabeth Williams holds something of a two-tiered set of views about criminal justice. On balance, she is probably the mildest of the thirteen believers, and for the great bulk of all crimes, she advocates responses emphasizing rehabilitation and alternatives to full-time incarceration. But for the most major offenses, she strongly advocates harsher treatment by the courts: longer sentences and, for *all* murderers, capital punishment. Although a concern for security certainly exerts a secondary influence over these harsh views, they are motivated primarily by desert.

When I ask the traditional question about the courts, she complains that they aren't harsh enough on major crimes, going on to tell the story of a friend who had been shot, and several other persons who were killed, by a convicted murderer on parole. She concludes, "To really bring justice, you know, there isn't any." It is the same when we discuss her feeling that sentencing has gotten lighter over the years: "I don't look to the judicial system . . . in the United States as really bringing about justice."

Elizabeth certainly believes that capital punishment could provide a greater deterrent against murder, but still her greatest motivation in prescribing it for all murderers seems to be that they *deserve* it:

> Now we're in the era of massaging psyches . . . we're into the whole psychological issues of people, which I believe are valid. But after someone has committed five murders and done all of that, it's like, as harsh as this is to say, I think that there should some recompense. There should be some kind of punishment for what they've done. . . .

> I guess I look at a murder as murder, and . . . it's an all-thing. If you're willing to pick up a gun and kill somebody, then I guess I'm really faced with the dilemma that you're willing to be—you know, for the responsibility of that, and that means your own life.

Toward the end of the second interview, I asked each interviewee to describe utopia. A follow-up question asked whether or not there would be any crime there and, if so, what would be done about it. The answers to this question were sometimes quite revealing about the interviewees' deeper motivations. So it is with Elizabeth. She speaks first of education and understanding and of trying to get to root of the problem. But her final words reveal the strong influence of desert: "And then, kind of go from there, in terms of punishment, that kind of thing. I mean, when I think of punishment, I think of, that the crime would have to—the crime and the punishment would have to be of equal weight."

In Elizabeth Williams's mild views, the influence of desert, although far from absent, is no longer dominant. It yields instead to primary motivations in compassion and security. Let us begin with compassion.

Just as it is for many of the dissenters who draw the primary motivations for their mild views from compassion, help for offenders is a large theme for Elizabeth. I ask her whether California needs any more prisons: "I don't think it needs more prisons. I just think we need effective kinds of ways in which to help people." This follows from her views about what happens inside our penal institutions: "It's sort of like jail . . . is . . . kind of like, you know, the hole, until you can pay your time and then get out. I don't see it as being where . . . people really have that many rehabing kinds of skills that are happening for them." When I ask what things she would propose that we do to solve the crime problem, Elizabeth emphasizes this theme of help and stresses, as well, the basic human dignity that she feels belongs even to offenders:

> One of the things that I definitely see as a problem in our country that . . . I would work on doing is the way in which we mainstream people back into society . . . I just feel we need stronger ways in which to parole these people . . . Some kind of . . . buddy system, that could live with them, to help them. I also feel definitely that these people should be asked to be going to group therapy—some kind of continuing reentry back into society. 'Cause I'm sure that they must be experiencing some type of culture shock . . . One of the greatest things that I see is wrong with our system is that it demeans and takes away the self-respect of an individual, and so that just makes it even doubly hard of getting back into society, as well. . . .

No doubt the strongest proof of Elizabeth's motivation in compassion lies in her ability to feel for an offender who has hurt her deeply. Soon after she and her husband had moved into their first home, it was burglarized and vandalized by an intruder who was never caught. In the first interview, she explains her reaction at the time:

> I was ready to go and shoot the balls off of this guy who took our [things] . . . I went through a lot of anger . . . It was while I was preg-

nant, and that . . . probably [had] a direct relationship as to my feel-ings—that they were so strong—in terms of, you know, protective . . . I didn't feel really good after we had gotten robbed . . . I felt terri-ble . . . I had contractions after that—it really just disturbed my psyche for several days afterwards. And for many weeks it was very difficult sleeping and a very difficult time relaxing.

But despite the deep effect that this crime had upon her, in the second interview, Elizabeth is able to say this about the person who has wounded her:

I was thinking about our house . . . with the vandalism that went on there. I think it would really have been very helpful if the person, let's say if they had been caught and we could have spoken to that person. It'd have been wonderful, just to say to him, we'd like to just tell you—we forgive you for what you've done. We don't like . . . the act that you performed on our home. But I think that part of the thing of why people wanta begin to act out their anger and bitterness . . . is because it's always this unknown . . . They've never gotten to fully go through the process of forgiveness with the person that did do them harm.

Compassion, then, is one strong motivation behind the many mild views that Elizabeth expresses; security is an equally important one. If programs that *help* and *respect* offenders are important to her, so also is it critical that these programs be *effective* in reducing crime. On spending:

I'm not exactly sure how much of our budget goes to spending on crime. But whatever they're spending . . . it needs to be effective, whether it's ten cents or if it's ten million, it needs to be effective at what it does. . .

About attempts at rehabilitation in our current prison system:

Also, it's just the way in which rehab programs are set up . . . I mean, what kinds of . . . rehab are they training these people for, so that they can do it when they get out? If it's making license plates for DMV and that kind of stuff—I mean, how effective is that?

And about her support for alternatives to incarceration:

One of the things that I think would be really good in someone who's doing research, is looking at the programs that are working. Oftentimes we are trying to fund things that don't work, and that's one of the problems I see with our system . . . Let's see what really is working and what is effective, rather than trying to support something that's ineffective.

In short, Elizabeth's emphasis is not only on helping the offender to overcome his or her problems but is just as strongly on the imperative to reduce crime in our society.[3] More than once, she describes how her views on crime have become less lenient in recent years, as she has had more personal exposure to it, not only through the events already described, but also in working with patients who have been crime victims. She is more concerned about crime than she ever was previously, and she wants responses that will *work:* "It's made me much more feeling just that general anger, outrage, helplessness, all of those emotions . . . It's probably, as well, made me feel like we need to do something . . . much more constructive than we have been doing." Elizabeth hasn't changed her view that poverty and other environmental influences are important causes of crime, but she remarks, "I feel like I want to come down harder on it [crime] than . . . before." She continues: "I see it kind of as a mix of the two. And you can even see that in . . . the ways in which I'd approach it . . . What I consider for a hard-line attitude for myself would be constructive kinds of rehab programs." Also critical is that people really get into these programs instead of "just falling into the cracks"—"just sort of spanking them and saying, 'Now, now, you know you need to do better.' I mean, that's not gonna do—whether that be somebody who's in politics or someone who's in . . . an impoverished state."

Elizabeth Williams has complex views about criminal justice—motivated by a varied set of values. For most offenders, she advocates fairly mild sanctions emphasizing rehabilitation without traditional incarceration. These views flow from dominant motivations in compassion and security. Desert has some influence over her mild views—encouraging, for instance, her advocacy of victim compensation—but it is decidedly subordinate here. Only in the case of crimes that have passed a critical point of severity does this value rise to the forefront: here, it leads her to the conclusion that these offenders *deserve* the pain inherent in harsh sanctions like lengthy incarceration or execution.

Elizabeth is a devout and active Christian. When I ask whether her religion has any special teaching about criminal justice, her response sheds no light on her concern for security, but it does sum up nicely the intertwining influence of her other two motivations:

People have taken an eye for an eye and a tooth for a tooth and ... drug that one through the millstone, so to speak. But the thing that I think ... that oftentimes people fail to see is that there were a lot of thieves ... and robbers that Christ came to ... and revealed himself to them, where that, they felt quite at home with him ... And you also look at Jesus as being someone who didn't miss a party if he was invited. He was not somebody who put himself in a sterile—and just encapsulated himself ... I see Christ as someone who has forgiveness, but he also—there were repercussions for our wrongdoings. There were definite things that ... do happen to you because of certain choices that you make ... I do believe that there are certain laws that have been set out for us, and it was for our good that we had those constraints ... I do believe there's a point ... where that, if our hearts are right, and we're willing to say, "Please forgive me for having done that," that there's a ... lot of room for mercy and forgiveness ... But what happens is that when we go beyond that and just say, "Screw you, God, I'm gonna do what I want," I think that what we've done is ... we've brought it to a place where that we have to accept the repercussions for our actions. And for some people ... that can be to the point of death.

Questions about Motivation

In this chapter, I have examined the primary ways in which the harsh and mild views of the interviewees are influenced by four underlying motivations: security, desert, compassion, and social critique. Let me stress again that these motivations were not pre-conceived notions against which I tested the thoughts of each interviewee. No formulation of such motivations was even considered prior to conducting the interviews. Rather, I listened for these Americans to teach me something about what was motivating them in their formation of opinion about crime and criminal justice: the four deep values examined here sprang very clearly from the statements of the participants. In the preceding discussion, the reader may have sensed an underlying assumption that these citizens are ordered, coherent thinkers who rationally derive their specific opinions from well-considered values—a position that has been called into question by cognitive and Freudian psychology, postmodern analysis, and the dominant tradition in public opinion research.[4] Certainly it is not my aim to take issue with the findings of these scholars. I am well aware that the average American would have difficulty in making a coherent connection between underlying values like economic independence or community solidarity, for instance, and specific issues like the prime interest rate or congressional redistricting. Rather, as will be discussed in chapter 4, I present these interviews as evidence that the incoherence of American public opinion is not all-encompassing, that coherence in fact varies across a continuum of issues, and that, as Converse has suggested, the most coherent sets of opinion appear on those issues closest to home and heart—for instance, crime. Whatever the state of opinion on other issues, the fact is that these interviewees, chosen in a stratified random sample of an average urban area, present remarkably coherent statements of their views on criminal justice and, in the vast majority of cases, defend these views with clear, if not necessarily sophisticated, references to the values highlighted here. I do not assume that the average American is an ordered, coherent thinker when it comes to most issues of public policy; on the other hand, I cannot ignore the evidence that *these* Americans are highly coherent when it comes to *this* issue.[5]

With both the dissenters and the believers, we saw two major patterns of motivation. While all of the dissenters draw the motivation for their harsh views from security alone, they are divided among those who find the primary motivation for their mild views in compassion (in one instance joined equally by desert) and those who find it in social critique. The believers also are divided into two groups. Among the *traditional believers,* none reaches beyond security or desert to draw a primary motivation for their views, harsh or mild. Among the *complex believers,* security and/or desert still provides the primary motivation for their harsh views, but values other than these play an important role in motivating their milder views.

For all but one of the participants—dissenters and believers alike— security exerts a primary influence over the harsh views they express. But in the dissenters, of course, the application of this value is much more limited in scope: it is reflected in incapacitation only. In comparing the dissenters with the traditional believers, the reasons for this seem fairly clear. The traditional believers derive their primary motivations from security and desert alone: these values motivate both their harsh and their mild views. But the dissenters bring in additional primary motivations: compassion and social critique. It is reasonable to presume that these additional motivations work to regulate the acceptable application of security. Because they respond so strongly to social critique and compassion, the dissenters arrive at either one or both of two positions: that purposefully harsh sanctions are an ineffective means of seeking security; or that purposefully harsh sanctions are an unconscionable means of seeking security.

But what about the complex believers? They, like the dissenters, respond to additional primary motivations beyond security and desert. Why then do they not place the same limitations on the expression of security as do the dissenters? Why are these four individuals even believers at all? In looking at Gladys Jones, the hospital clerk, and Elizabeth Williams, the physical therapist, the answer obviously lies in the presence of one other primary motivation: desert. Even given the counterbalancing effect of social critique or compassion, this strong influence is sufficient to lead these women to advocate the use of purposefully harsh sanctions (to serve both desert itself, and security).

The question becomes more difficult when we turn to Aram Isaac, the college-educated truck driver, and Sadie Monroe, the retired physical education teacher. These two complex believers respond to primary motivations that are identical to those exhibited by several of the dissenters: harsh views in the service of security; mild views in the service of social critique. Why are these two not dissenters? We must look at the conversations with Aram and Sadie in more detail, to answer this question.

In the case of Aram, I suspect that the answer lies in two factors. First, unlike the dissenters, Aram moves from his strong concern for security not just to endorse the incapacitation of certain offenders, but also to support the use of harsh sanctions for purposes of deterrence. Given the pervasive influence of social critique on his thinking about crime in our nation, where does this attitude come from? The answer may lie in his cultural roots. Aram reports that although he was raised a Catholic, he has thrown off all spiritual belief. But what of the influence of his North African heritage: has he thrown this off as well? Aram's comments when we speak about the concept of vengeance are illuminating:

> Vengeance means, the individual commits crime—that he pay . . . And I think it would work. I don't know how much, but it would work. Of course, it is against all our analyses . . . according to the rules—you know, justice, court, constitution, rules—all these things. But in Saudi Arabia,[6] the rule is according to the Koran . . . whoever steal something—cut his hand. Not any hand—the hand that he steal with . . . See, the Constitution deals [with] who did, how he did, why he did . . . in which situation, for what purpose . . . all these questions must be answered, when you go to court. But in this case it is eyes to eyes, teeth to teeth.
>
> So in this civilized society, it should go according to the court . . . The court gives you this kind of analysis—pros, cons, and this, this, this. But the Koran law—venge—it is blind . . . So, if it was under the rule, whoever kills must be killed, then I am sure all these teenagers, they are going around with the gun . . . they would put away their gun. They do it because . . . the court might give them a lawyer—they have a

chance ... if they pay good money to the lawyer, he might create many reasons ... justifications. I mean, there is a chance to survive and to be free. But if there was the other one—if I kill, they will kill me—so I don't want to kill myself ... it is not that he doesn't want to kill you—he doesn't want to kill himself. So, he would think many times before taking on an action.

Here it becomes clear that whatever other moderating forces may be present within Aram's motivations, he is also influenced to some degree by a tradition of tit-for-tat justice and that he draws from this tradition a belief that harsher and more consistent penalties could work. He is by no means urging the Saudi Arabian extreme, but this underlying influence may provide some explanation for his willingness to support harshness in the pursuit of deterrence.

As a second factor in explaining the fact that despite having primary motivations identical to those of some dissenters, Aram is still a believer, we might consider the likelihood that even a small motivation from desert can go a long way. Aram's harsh views are primarily motivated by his very strong concern for security, but as we saw in chapter 2, he also supports punishment as a legitimate purpose of the criminal justice system. This secondary influence toward harshness, from desert, is one not present in the dissenters; they eschew the goal of punishment as a justification for the use of harsh sanctions.

In the case of Sadie Monroe, an explanation is less clear. Several factors should be considered. First, recall that both her mild views about criminal justice and her motivation in social critique are quite limited. Her views are predominantly harsh. Then, it is important to consider the general scantiness of the interviews with Sadie. She was quite reluctant to participate in the study and almost backed out when I arrived for the first interview. In general, her answers were very short, and, during the second interview particularly, she appeared quite preoccupied with several personal problems. The two interviews required only a little over two hours total to complete—the shortest period of any interviewee. A related problem was that Sadie was somewhat offended by the more personal questions at the end of the second interview, questions that probed for the interviewees' religious and personal philosophies. She revealed that she was a churchgoing Protestant and that religion was important in her daily life. But had we discussed these and related questions in more detail, it is possible that some deeper understanding of her motivations and how they make her a believer might have come forth. (For Gladys Jones, another of the complex believers, for instance, the section on religion was revealing.)

There are two other pieces of evidence that might explain the fact of Sadie Monroe's being a believer. First, her comments about liberals and conservatives are of interest. When I ask whether she would describe herself by one of these terms, or as "something else," she says, "I guess a liberal." Upon further questioning she states that she is a "very strong" liberal. But then she acknowledges that she does not know the difference between liberals and conservatives. The conversation continues:

KTG: When you say that you're a liberal, what does that mean to you?
  SM: Your ideas, your way of thinking and all is—I don't know—I can't think of the word I want to use. Whether it's going along with the majority—their way of thinking and all.
KTG: Going along with the way the majority thinks?
  SM: Yeah.

Here, we have some small evidence that the simple fact that the majority of Americans support the get-tough movement, and believe that harsher penalties would more effectively deter crime, might be a very powerful influence over the way in which Sadie applies her motivation from security. Most Americans are not like the security–social critique dissenters, who will condone the use of harsh sanctions only for purposes of incapacitation. And Sadie Monroe—a believer despite sharing the same combination of primary motivations as those dissenters—is quite like most Americans.

Second, there is the issue of additional motivations, primary or secondary, that may also influence an interviewee. Sadie Monroe seems a more difficult case than Aram Isaac because nowhere during our brief interviews does she invoke the concept of desert to justify the use of a harsh sanction. But interestingly, in the mailed screening questionnaire that she completed several months before the interviews, she did make use of this justification. Indeed, in answer to the question regarding what should be the most important purpose of our criminal justice system, she checked *punishment: making criminals suffer because of their crimes.* (In the interview, she said that isolation was the most important goal and did not mention punishment either positively or negatively.) Further, she answered this mail question by indicating opposition to alternative programs:

Some people feel that many nonviolent offenders should be placed in alternative programs, such as community work-service or victim repayment projects, instead of being sent to prison. Others are concerned that such programs *do not adequately punish offenders* or protect the safety of the community. Generally speaking, how do you feel? (Emphasis added.)

(In the interview, she said she approved of such programs and stated that they could be used for "burglary and some fraud—those especially."[7]) If we can take Sadie's answers to the mail questionnaire—particularly the first of these—as evidence that she has at least some secondary motivation in desert, it should become even easier to accept that despite the nature of her primary motivations, she is a believer.

Implications for Consensus

The influence of security is omnipresent. In examining the motivations of these interviewees—believers and dissenters—I found that each and every one of them draws upon this value as a primary motivation for some portion of their views. So in searching for a distinction between the believers and the dissenters, it is the tension between the other values—desert, on the one hand, and compassion or social critique, on the other—that seems to make the most important difference. Desert, when combined with an extremely strong motivation in compassion, as we saw in Anne Girard, appears powerless to influence views of harsh proportions. Instead, we saw it undergirding Anne's firm views about victim restitution and community work-service. Among the traditional believers, where compassion and social critique are consistently absent as primary motivations, the presence or absence of desert is of little consequence as well: there is nothing pulling these Americans away from traditional views on criminal justice anyway. Finally, among the complex believers, this *tension* plays an essential role in the formation of these participants' criminal justice views: where motivations from desert are very strong, or those from compassion or social critique are relatively weak, a believer emerges.

   Why do the believers believe? Either, it seems, because no strong motivation in compassion or social critique prevents them from accepting the traditional answers, or because even if they hold significant motivations from these two concerns, desert exerts an overpowering influence. A further layer of questions naturally follows: Why *do* compassion and social critique have so little influence on these believers? Why *does* desert have so much? And if these interviews have discerned values at work among the broader public as well, then why have the relative levels of these influences changed in recent decades, resulting in this startling consensus of public opinion? We have examined here the inner motivations that the interviewees' own words suggest, but what may govern these very motivations? In chapter 5, I return to these questions, searching for characteristics of background or outlook that may coalesce in the lives of each group of interviewees, leading them to respond to these values in the manner in which they do—and to respond so differently from those in the other group. In chapter 6, I will draw heavily on the findings of the present chapter and those that follow, as I address broader social changes that may have brought us to the point of such consensus.

Meanwhile, in the next chapter, we will stay within the realm of personal ideology. Perhaps some readers were surprised, in the present chapter, to find that the underpinnings of the interviewees' opinions, in broad values and concerns, could be so easily dissected and discussed. In fact, the primary motivations of all but three of the twenty-two interviews considered here were in fairly plain view. In contrast, we are accustomed to the findings of scholars of public opinion, who in studying so many other issue areas have stressed the presence of distressing levels of disorganization and incoherence among the views of the American public. Based on the material presented in this chapter and the one preceding, we have convincing evidence that the issue of criminal justice is an exception to this rule. Let us take this proposition one step further. The following chapter explores the relationship between participants' attitudes on the issue of criminal justice and their more general political belief systems. Will this exceptional level of internal coherence be borne out when we take the analysis to the next level—and what can this tell us about our underlying questions about consensus?

CHAPTER 4

Structures of Belief

We have looked at what the believers and the dissenters think should be done about crime and at the motivations that they reveal in speaking about these views. Now we can broaden the framework to consider how participants' views about criminal justice are related to their more general political beliefs. Centuries after Thomas Hobbes suggested that the primary justification for government is to preserve each citizen from the war of all against all, crime is still a central *political* issue. We need to know where attitudes about criminal justice fit in with the fundamental assumptions about political concepts that are held by everyday Americans—if indeed they fit in at all. Three questions will be addressed in this chapter: (1) To what degree do the criminal justice views of the interviewees comprise logical and internally consistent sets of opinions? (2) Do the participants have coherent general political belief systems? And, if so, then (3) are their criminal justice views grounded in and consonant with their more general political belief systems? While the connections between crime views and fundamental political ideas that will be discussed here are not necessarily *conscious* connections, the mere fact of their presence or absence should reveal a lot about how Americans structure their attitudes about criminal justice.

Criminal Justice Views

The very fact that in earlier chapters I have been able to suggest meaningful interpretations of the criminal justice views of twenty-two of my interviewees is the best demonstration that these individuals hold sets of opinions about this subject that are reasonably logical and, for the most part, internally consistent. I have been able to discuss two broad perspectives toward criminal justice—the differences in which divide the dissenters from the believers—and I have been able to identify various patterns of motivation that underlie each perspective. The views of the twenty-two are by no means devoid of contradictions or inconsistencies, but these are scattered and occasional and have not stood in the way of a meaningful interpretation of each person's overall set of views. Certainly, there are among these individuals some whose views about criminal justice are neither deep nor broad and others whose approach is quite eccentric. But all of these people say what they think in words I can understand: at the most basic level, these people "make sense."

The remaining two of my twenty-four interviewees did *not* make sense. In the five to six hours I spent with each of these individuals, often I found myself struggling to understand what they were saying. Even among the more comprehensible views that each expressed, contradictions were plentiful. At other times, the answers were truly unbelievable.

Consider Paul Bongolan, a thirty-year-old native of the Bay Area whose parents were immigrants from the Philippines. He is a high school graduate and is currently attending a community college while supporting himself making deliveries for a florist. Paul's past occupations include a short period of work as a jail guard in another Bay Area city; he was asked to resign when he failed to pass a necessary exam. Paul is divorced and has lived in Oakland for one year.

One sizable excerpt will demonstrate the rambling incoherence that characterizes many of Paul's replies to my questions. Here, he speaks about the concept of rehabilitation.

> *PB:* ... The program that they have for people that are in jails—it's a fairly good program, but again, you're gonna have to think if that person that you're teaching, if that person is gonna learn anything. I mean, you could, unless you want to, then you'll actually learn, and that's in all phases, but in the jails ... my personal feeling is that I don't think it'd really work. Because in a jail is that they have—I'm sorry to say, but they actually know more than any person ... If a person's staying there for a month, for whatever crime, that person has actually twelve hours to think, to do, to plot, for a whole month, than a person who is actually going to school only has—or if he's going through the program—only has like only hour. Somehow that doesn't pop in my head. ...
>
> *KTG:* Are you saying, what's the good of one hour a day of job training if you've got eleven hours a day of plotting diabolical deeds, or ... ?
>
> *PB:* Yeah, diabolical. Actually, that's all that they—actually one hour of ... actual working your brain toward an education that you have this person that—he has to ... want to do that. What he actually has in mind is what he wants to do, and—they have the expression "jail house slaughter," or "jail talk," whatever—is that he can—let's put it like this: actually he can find out everything about you if you were a teacher, for one

day—everything—and he's in jail for twelve hours. I mean one month, or whatever. But it's actually what he wants to do. As far as the teachers that are coming in there that try to do something, I think that's nice, but I don't think it will get them anywhere, because they already know what they want to learn when they go out on their own.

Besides the many incoherent answers, there are also the preposterous answers Paul gives. How much do you think it costs to build one maximum security prison cell: five or six hundred dollars. How often do the courts convict innocent persons: about 40 percent of the time. How would you describe the average criminal: age twenty-five, upper middle class, about two years of college.

Finally, there are the contradictions between answers. Paul says that the courts are not harsh enough, that alternatives to incarceration should not be pursued, and that rehabilitation should be the lowest priority goal for the criminal justice system; but at other points he also expresses the view that we incarcerate too many people, that we shouldn't build any more prisons, and that we should spend our money on new nonincarcerative programs and more probation officers instead. Paul remarks that prisoners are the "escape-goats" [*sic*] of society, and, as noted above, he indicates that frightening numbers of innocent people are being convicted; but he also suggests court reforms that amount to conviction without guilty plea or trial. Paul thinks that being incarcerated feels like having your whole body "submerged into ice" with a "black pillowcase put over your head"; but he also suggests that there are people who get arrested on purpose in order to get three meals a day and "service by the [guards]," and that we ought not to teach skills in prisons because then even more will want to get in.

Besides Paul there is also Evangeline Reed, sixty-eight, who has retired from her job as an administrative assistant for the Department of Defense. An Oakland native, she is a high school graduate who dropped out of nursing school in order to marry. Evangeline is divorced and has three grown children. She is black.

Two quotes will illustrate the confusing style of free association that often characterizes her answers. Here, she responds to a question regarding her feelings about the treatment of crime victims by the criminal justice system:

...I think this is an area where they can really treat the victims of crime a lot better. But I can well imagine that when you're in a job of their type that you get hardened to things and you just don't have enough compassion, and so this is why I think that police ought to have to go to school—it should be much more rigid. We need a lot more of them. We need a lot more of like these little vigilante kids ... [*KTG: Guardian Angels?*] The Guardian Angels, yes. And I think they should have—like neighborhoods, such as this one—they should get some kind of a little marshall or something and have them all—like Boy Scouts—all our children should be taught law and order and all this sort of stuff, and know and become a part of it. And when they see each other, do. I think they should have these reform places, in juvenile halls, just like they do in the prison, and that they should do this so that there's more self-esteem to everybody should be taught, and particularly to police officers...

And here, I have asked what sorts of things she would propose that we do to solve the crime problem—if she were in a powerful position in our government:

Just what I have been talking about. I'd try to get some reforms in the prison, and outside of the prisons with the policemen and everybody. I think all of this Democrat and Republican and all these different parties—there'd be one party ... if I was powerful ... May the best man [win], but it would be all of us—it would be for America. There wouldn't be two sides and the richest one would get this and the poorer one would not ... We would be a voting system that would work. And it would have to be somebody. And everybody would vote. We don't need all ... that money going to that. That money could go to reform our people that are in jail or that do things is wrong. Or could go to our schools and our colleges, to make ourselves super human beings, and to make ourselves—gee—just love. I think it takes this in your heart to really—'cause nothing is impossible. I really believe that it doesn't have to be like this. This must be the days of revelation or something like that I hear so much about. I really believe that it could work nice if we didn't have to. It takes so much money to have all this ... the two-party system. It's more than that, I know—different parties—but we don't need all of that. I wish I was in power!

Then, as with Paul, there are the contradictory statements Evangeline makes. Several times, she speaks out strongly against harshness and punishment. But she also uses an argument that sounds like desert to support the execution of some murderers, suggests that the hypothetical rapist I describe be castrated if he cannot be rehabilitated, and proposes that for my habitual burglars there should be "no leniency whatsoever" and that they should serve "a very steep penalty." Asked who belongs in prison, she says, "Incorrigible people." But during the course of the interview, her comments range from those that imply that most offenders would be dealt with behind bars as a matter or course, to those that indicate that the use of incarceration should be quite limited. She brings up the notorious rapist Lawrence Singleton twice within a short period of time—the first time saying that he should not be released, but the next suggesting that he should either stay in a hospital for the rest of his life, *or* be released to get a job and pay restitution.

Interestingly, both Paul Bongolan and Evangeline Reed were very willing—even anxious—to participate in this study. Both were likeable individuals, and the rapport we established was good from start to finish. Moreover, they are not uneducated persons; indeed, Paul was the only person I interviewed who considered himself to have some specialized knowledge and expertise in the field of criminal justice. I have no reason to think either person crazy, in any clinical sense. And yet, at bottom, their views on criminal justice do not make sense: too often they are confusing or downright incomprehensible, and taken as a whole, the opinions of each individual are internally inconsistent. Against the backdrop of the incoherence that has been demonstrated by these two, we may appreciate more fully just how reasoned and consistent the criminal justice views of even the least intellectual among the other interviewees really are.

That two of the twenty-four interviewees presented incoherent views about criminal justice should not be interpreted as detracting from the validity of this study. Scholars of public opinion have shown us that in studying American attitudes about most policy areas, we should expect far greater levels of incoherence than was found here. The fact that so little incoherence was uncovered is no doubt directly connected to the nature of the crime issue, as will be discussed in the following section.

Political Belief Systems

The second of the questions with which I began this chapter asks whether or not participants have coherent general political belief systems. My conclusion is that almost all of these twenty-four individuals do. The exceptions are Paul Bongolan and Evangeline Reed (as might be expected), and Thelma Winters, an eighty-three-year-old former home health aide. The belief systems of the remaining interviewees, while coherent, do vary in degrees of sophistication. Some are noticeably *un*sophisticated. But a substantial majority (all of the dissenters and half of the believers) have general political belief systems that are not just coherent but are also fairly sophisticated: that is, they are reasonably detailed and wide-ranging, and largely conscious.

When I speak of a political belief system or ideology, I am referring to a set of attitudes centered on foundational political concepts such as freedom, equality, authority, democracy, and justice.[1] And when I say that an interviewee has a coherent political belief system, I mean that he or she conceives of an arrangement of such fundamental concepts that—given the benefit of the doubt—can be considered reasonably logical and internally consistent.[2] I do not necessarily mean, however, that the individual makes use of the standard liberal-conservative organizing device to assist in arranging his or her beliefs about these concepts.[3] I also do not mean that this person is necessarily consistent about the *operationalization* of his or her political ideology into opinions about the world of everyday politics. Thus, a person who holds a belief system in which a broadly defined liberty plays a key role may not necessarily endorse the provision of a specific real-world liberty—say, the right of an atheist to make a public speech. That such inconsistencies are common among Americans is a well-documented phenomenon.[4] From Philip Converse, we derive the notion that an exception to this rule might be found in opinion about "doorstep issues"—issues that are very close to home for those whose beliefs we study.[5] John Zaller also emphasizes the significance of "a person's level of cognitive engagement with an issue" in his recent model of public opinion formation.[6] Indeed, the major purpose of this chapter is to consider whether and to what degree such inconsistencies exist when the real-world application of deeper beliefs involves this doorstep issue—crime.

Political Belief Systems—Criminal Justice Views: What Connection?

The third question structuring this chapter asks about the connection between participants' specific opinions and their broader beliefs. To what degree are the interviewees' criminal justice views consonant with and grounded in their broader political ideologies? First, let me offer a general answer. Then we can move on quickly to examine the belief systems of some selected interviewees. These examples should provide a demonstration both for my assertion, above, that almost all of the participants have coherent political ideologies and for my conclusions on this final question.

Generally stated, my conclusions are these: among the twenty-one interviewees who have coherent political belief systems, the vast majority hold criminal justice views that are reasonably consistent with, and appear to be grounded in, these broader political ideologies. Only four participants held criminal justice views that appeared in significant ways to lack a foundation in their political belief systems.

I present below portraits both of participants who exemplify and of those who lack such consonance. These illustrations are further divided to highlight in each group both those whose political belief systems are reasonably sophisticated and those whose belief systems are rather unsophisticated.

Sophisticated and Consonant

Let us begin where most of the interviewees converge. Strikingly, *all* of the dissenters, as well as four of the believers, have political belief systems that are fairly sophisticated (that is, coherent, as well as reasonably detailed, wide-ranging, and conscious) and also hold criminal justice views that appear to be consonant with and grounded in these broader belief systems.[7] To illustrate, the beliefs of one dissenter and one believer will be discussed here.

Victor Rodriguez

Victor Rodriguez, a dissenter, is an administrator with the Department of the Interior. Born and raised in the Caribbean, he lived on the East Coast for years, then moved to Oakland in 1982. Victor, thirty-seven, is the father of two teenage children from a former marriage. He and his present wife (a biologist) both hold master's degrees.

Victor's political ideology might well be described as a welfare state liberal's interpretation of a civics textbook. Individual rights and democratic values are treated with a consistent respect, as here, when he speaks to the question of what rights all people should have from birth:

> *VR:* They have the right to be happy ... I mean, pursuit of happiness is what the Constitution says ... There are some basics that I think every individual should have. Most of them are spelled out in the Constitution ... An education, enough medical care to at least insure that you are going to survive—I think that should be a right too ... I would say health, housing, and education—those three things—everybody should have them—minimum.
>
> *KTG:* Plus the constitutional rights?
>
> *VR:* Of course—freedom of expression ... that definitely—the freedom to express yourself is a must. But we have those. And those are one of the things that we should fight to keep—those

rights. Don't let them slide because of this or that. There's no need for that. No way of waiving rights. Those rights are yours—yours to keep.

Or here, on the subject of freedom:

Freedom is, I think, the chance to be what you want to be, and to do what you want to do as long as you don't interfere with the rights of other people . . . I should be free to do what I want as long as nobody else is hurt, or I don't impose an economic or social burden on others. Then I should be allowed to do as I wish. Period.

And here, on civil disobedience:

KTG: Are there ever times when laws and government authorities are wrong and should be disobeyed, or would you say that citizens should obey their government under all circumstances?

VR: Citizens should obey their conscience. Government is most of the time a reflection of the wishes of the people . . . But there will be times when government—although it will be elected . . . goes into certain aspects of control maybe, or re-striction of freedoms even, that will require that people with conscience stand up and combat that type of behavior from the government. There have been instances in this country in which civil disobedience has been exercised . . . People have deliberately gone and done it to just test that particular law, and I think it is the way it should be. That's why we have judges and the judicial system which I hope will recognize the right of the individual to protest any law—any law.

And here, on democracy:

Democracy is the will of the people. In our democracy, we basically put in power the people that we all want—collectively want. I might not like the present administration—granted—but the people of this country who want this type of government—that is democracy. Having somebody that you want to represent you . . . Democracy is basically an exercise of the right of individuals—equally.

Further, as can be heard even in these statements, Victor has a considerable concern for socioeconomic justice and is of the conviction that government should do much more to bring such justice to our citizenry. To him, "poverty is a moral crime," and justice would be

> [the] fair sharing of whatever we have ... Equal opportunity for everybody to develop and reach the goal that they want. Justice is also in the sense of balancing the needs of society with the individual needs somehow.

Asked if some groups are treated unjustly in our society, Victor speaks of "people who are discriminated against; ... people who were never given the chance maybe to improve their lives; ... people who have been punished for actions that they committed—sins or however you want to put it—when they might not be able to help it." In his reply to a later question, which asked how difficult it is for people to make their own lives better, Victor expanded on the second of these points:

> It depends on how much you want to improve. I think it's something that should be your choice. The unfortunate thing is that how much you want to improve depends on how much you have been developed to want to improve. You see—in a situation in which you have lived in an environment since you were a little boy ... maybe the dreams of your parents, or your ... role models, are so low that there is no vision ... nothing. Just—you will probably never get out of the hole, because you never have Dad to guide you. You just thought—well, that's the way life is. You never been out of the ghetto, or something. But if you are given the opportunities to see that this is something you could achieve, if you—you individual—take the certain step, I am sure that everybody will have a little bit of a more chance to improve in life—or make life more bearable...

Minority groups and the poor, Victor says, are particular targets of injustice. And when we discuss equality, he identifies women, abused children, the elderly, and the disabled as groups who are still not treated equally. I ask him what form of equality we should be working toward:

> Ooh ... [These] eighteenth-century philosopher[s] have been thinking about that for about three hundred years and they haven't come up with a solution. I don't think I'm going to come up with a solution ... Equality is a concept, and it is in your mind. You feel equal, and you feel you're treating everybody equally—or you don't. The goal is to ... do everything in such a way which you feel you are equal, and you are treating everybody equally. And everybody feels the same

way. How to get to that point? Still can debate it, probably. I think that as long as there are economic inequalities, there will be inequalities... Inequality in general—I think it's economic. Even the racial inequalities are such because usually the racial groups have some of the money problems we don't have. But I think if there is economic balance, soon we will find equality is just more real than when there is no balance...

However, Victor does not take economic equality so far as to endorse the proposal I mention for equal incomes across the board, regardless of the nature of individual jobs:

It's difficult because that's the idea behind communism, basically. You provide to the best of your abilities, and you receive meeting your needs. I don't necessarily agree with that. I think [you] should have the opportunity to get in the best economic position you could be—you should be given the tools to improve your life—to be given the opportunity to be promoted without regards to any type of color or whatever, based on what you do, and be compensated accordingly, but also give you the incentive to prove it, and produce it. Because otherwise, our society as we know it will be gone, because there will be no incentive to be productive...

We speak briefly about capitalism and socialism at a later point, and Victor indicates that he would seek some middle point between them, emphasizing the best of each system. "Extremes—capitalism or socialism—I don't think that they work, really."

Overall, Victor's concerns for individual rights and for social justice appear to be in balance—and it is a balance of which he is quite conscious. Indeed, in many of the excerpts above, he acknowledges both values, even when one or the other receives the primary emphasis at a given moment. Here, he addresses that balance explicitly:

KTG: Are there any ways in which freedom and equality conflict with each other?

  VR: When there are abuses of freedom, yes... See, we're all human, and what some might consider is my right to do this, might interfere with the right of the other person. In that sense, the balance is distorted, and then you will have inequalities, even in the name of freedom. But real freedom will basically equal equality...

> *KTG:*   ... Which do you think is the more important value—freedom or equality?
>
> *VR:*   They are equally important. I don't think that I can separate them from each other. Liberty, equality. I mean they are all together. They become one concept...

Another important element of Victor's belief system is introduced when he addresses the subject of human nature:

> There is such thing as human nature... The ability to think and rationalize... People are people wherever you are, and I think you have the... basic desires. And I think you put in two different persons from different countries or different regions that work together, and they'll find a way to live together ... We have some animalistic traits that we still have—we're flesh, and that also makes us be a little bit uncivilized sometimes. But that's also human nature, so the most you can do is try to control those impulses, and behave....

> I think that people are willing to give some of this impulsive behavior up—put it aside—to be able to live together with this other guy ... I think that is part of human nature too... There is the capability of improving... from the animal type of behavior to the more rational social behavior.

Some of the same convictions are implied in his comments about the utopia I ask him to describe—a place, he says, where "people will respect each other":

> Of course there will be disagreements... we're human, so there will be difference of opinion—but there will be a basic respect, understanding. There will be a minimum of differences in the sense of lifestyles— like living conditions and stuff like that. People... will have the basics. They will be able to exercise their freedom in a meaningful way so that they can be happy.

Such a place, Victor says, is an ideal that he does not expect to see in his lifetime, or in his children's. Still, he continues, in an expression of optimism about this point that is unmatched by any other interviewee: "My grandchildren might—I don't know."

From all of the above we can identify three key elements in Victor Rodriguez's political belief system: the importance of individual rights and democratic values, the imperative to seek socioeconomic justice, and the belief that humans are not mired inextricably in strife and iniquity but rather are capable of growing into healthy relations with one another.

Victor's opinions about criminal justice appear to be consonant with, and well grounded in, this broader ideology. His criminal justice views are predominantly mild, and while compassion is certainly an important secondary influence for this dissenter, a biting social critique is the primary motivation for his views. This critique has two themes. First, it is primarily social circumstances that lead persons to crime:

> ...It has to be, necessarily, society. We cannot really in honesty, I think, blame the individual for what we as social entities are given—you know, this is your circumstance. You are born within this environment. You are raised within this constraints or parameters—either you are poor, or racial makeup. They have no choice about it. You grow up, and you become the citizen that we, society, let you become...

And second, prisons are criminogenic institutions:

> It is difficult to be in prison and not become a criminal yourself—if you are not already hard enough to be called a "criminal"—and survive this life, unless you go crazy. I think in order to survive the conditions of the prison you have to think and act many times as a criminal.

This two-pronged social critique inspires his conclusion that "it's a disgrace to have prisons" and his desire only to make use of incarceration as a last resort. And it leads him to advocate responses to crime that focus on the alleviation of the many social problems he views as so importantly causal.

Plausible connections between Victor's broader ideology and his policy views about crime can be found without difficulty: He has an enormous concern for socioeconomic justice, and this undergirds his view that responses to crime should take into consideration the position of disadvantage in which so many of the perpetrators of crime have lived. He considers human beings to be capable of growth and improvement, and this supports his strong convictions about rehabilitation. Finally, he honors individual rights, a reasonable foundation both for his advocacy of rights to subsistence and opportunity even for most criminal offenders, and for his support of harsh responses when they represent the only means of protecting the rights of innocent citizens from offenders who cannot or will not control their impulses to do harm.

James Morton

James Morton, a believer, is a masonry contractor who has lived in Oakland for all of his sixty-two years. Still, he wants out now. His feeling is that this city, which was once "a very problem-free, beautiful place to live," has gone irretrievably downhill. James is a high school graduate who greatly regrets having passed up the opportunity to go to college. He is white, married, and the father of three grown children. His wife is a homemaker.

Like Victor, James Morton has a coherent and fairly sophisticated political belief system. The content of that belief system, however, is considerably different from Victor's. A central conviction involves the notion of limited government:

> I don't think that the government can do an awful lot to answer for all the problems for all the people, and I don't think that's government's responsibility ... The government's responsibility is to protect us in the case of a horrendous war ... awful diseases. See that we get pure food, pure air, water, or whatever and an opportunity to do what we do. A decent education ... The rest I think is pretty much up to the individual, and if he can't cut it, I feel sorry for him. But if he has equal opportunity ... somewhere along the line he will have to stand up and do what he is supposed to do.

Intertwined with James's ideas about limited government is a second pivotal conviction: individuals should be self-sufficient. It is a theme he returns to often, as here, when he describes the ideal citizen in a democracy:

> [He] would be reasonably well educated—enough to make good decisions for himself ... He would vote. He would probably do something to influence his fellow man about basic concepts in some little way ... He would pose no problem to the community from a crime standpoint whatsoever. He would hopefully be a harmonious individual who would be able to work well with the community and never cause social problems. He would be self-supporting. He wouldn't have to ask government for a lot.

It will come as no surprise then, to find that James Morton rates the value of freedom as higher than that of equality. Freedom, in fact, is the essence of his personal definition of democracy, while any notion of equality of voting or representation is left unmentioned:

> [Democracy means a] society where people are essentially free to live the life that they want to live, whether it's as a bum on a park bench or a multimillionaire on his yacht. A person who controls their own destiny, who is free to get the education, pursue the business, live the life, enjoy the benefits, the way that they wish—unregulated. Mostly unregulated. We all have a few shackles here and there.

And as to the proposition that "all men are created equal":

> Of course they are born equal. They are born naked and crying and kicking and screaming, and that is about as far as it goes. Past that I don't think that they are born equal. They are supposedly born with equal opportunity, and I don't think that that is really true. It would be a very nice thing to contemplate, but it is impossible.

James's sense of the lesser importance of equality is underscored by comments that suggest racist sentiments. For example:

> I hope I don't come across as a racist, and I don't think I discriminate. I try not to. It's hard sometimes when you see the effects that race has had on a place such as this. I said it was a beautiful place to live, and it has gone downhill so badly. And that doesn't do anything to make me love them.

Or these thoughts, on the subject of interracial marriage:

> Now this is a personal opinion—it has nothing to do with anyone else. But I personally oppose it. I don't think that it benefits anyone. I don't think that it's a necessary step . . . I just don't see that we are broadening the base here. Ultimately I suppose we will be one big gray race. I'll be glad that I won't be here.

James Morton's emphasis on freedom is complemented, also, by a fairly rigid sense of authority. Indeed, when I ask him to define freedom, he sums up his remarks with the assertion that it means "to be free to do whatever it is that your heart really wants to do, so long as you break no moral or legal law." The limits on freedom are described in terms of morality and legality—as opposed, for instance, to the need to prevent harm to, or preserve the rights of, others. Elsewhere, he makes it clear that he doesn't "believe in civil disobedience" and that he agrees "absolutely" with the proposition that "too many people in this country just don't have the proper respect for authority anymore."

James Morton, then, draws a mostly unswerving conservative line in describing his political ideology. Limited government, self-sufficiency, freedom before equality—but freedom strongly constrained by moral and legal authority. Moderating these beliefs are only his feelings about the pivotal role of education and parental guidance in the development of children and the sympathies he sometimes expresses for those children who do not receive adequate care:

> Blacks—I could cry for them—I really could—because I don't think they have anybody. I think that a lot of those kids are left to their own devices to get their own dinner, take care of themselves, and they don't see the same guy in the house three times in a row. . . .

> I never had to make my life a heck of a lot better. My family was not rich, but in moderate circumstance. And it has always been relatively easy . . . I am afraid if you're a black and born in the wrong section, or if you're a Puerto Rican or a South American . . . and you don't have the right exposure to people and maybe not the right education, it could be extremely tough. Very tough. . . .

> One of the biggest reasons [kids drop out of school] is that there is instant entertainment out there—whether it's the poolroom on the corner, or video games, or the television at home—and nobody's at home—or just the gang on the corner. There is something that is more appealing than the school. Left to their own devices without any kind of supervision from parents, I don't think many kids would stay in the classroom and study U.S. history, which is pretty boring to a kid at twelve or fifteen years old. . .

By and large, though, James places a pretty strict statute of limitations on his sympathies. Kids may need help to overcome inadequate parenting or education, but there is little allowance made for the possibility that some adults may still need assistance to overcome deficits that, from childhood, have never been addressed. To say that, upon reaching adulthood, each person starts over with a clean slate of responsibility is to exaggerate his sentiments—but not by a great deal.

James Morton's views about criminal justice are consistent with, and appear to be grounded in, the broader political beliefs I have outlined. He is a traditional believer: his harsh and mild views, both, are primarily motivated by security. The few milder views he expresses involve support for alternative sentences and rehabilitative efforts for youthful, nonviolent, first- and second-time offenders, as well as for limited preventive programs for potential teen offenders—a position entirely consistent with the restricted sympathies described above. Beyond this point, he is extremely pessimistic about the ability of the criminal justice system to meet goals of either rehabilitation or deterrence. At times, he uses the language of both punishment and deterrence, but, from a practical standpoint, he would have the system focus primarily on providing temporary security from criminal offenders—isolation. Such an emphasis is consistent with his broader views about the limited role of government and its unsuitability for the role of social nursemaid. Adult citizens are expected to be free and self-sufficient actors, and when they abuse their freedoms, they have no ground for objection to a loss of citizens' privileges. Social equality is not a high goal, and social inequalities imply very little communal responsibility—thus they are no excuse for transgressions against legal authority and do not alter the freedom-authority equation.

James Morton refers to himself as a "close" or "firm" conservative, and I see no reason to dispute his self-designation. That a man as conservative as he is would also hold primarily harsh views on crime cannot be taken for granted, but it comes as no great surprise either.

Victor Rodriguez and James Morton have served as examples of the single largest group of interviewees—those whose political belief systems are fairly sophisticated and whose views on criminal justice appear to be consonant with their broader ideologies. About half (thirteen out of twenty-four) of the interviewees fit into this category. This includes all of the nine dissenters, but only four of the thirteen believers.

Why are all the dissenters in this first group? Two pieces of an explanation come to mind. First, the dissenters as a group have a higher educational level than the believers.[8] Second, it is reasonable to suppose that individuals who form policy views that go against the grain of popular opinion may have to think out those views quite carefully—in the process weighing them against (and reconciling them with) deeper political beliefs.

Of course, on the latter point, the causality could run as smoothly in the opposite direction. Possibly it is the case that individuals who have coherent, sophisticated political belief systems and whose specific views about criminal justice are logically linked to these overarching ideologies are more likely than others to hold dissenting views on this topic. This possibility will be discussed further in the following chapter. For the present, let us move on to consider the remaining believers.

Unsophisticated, but Consonant

Several of the believers present political belief systems that are not especially sophisticated. Their beliefs are reasonably coherent but are not as detailed and wide-ranging, nor as consciously held, as those of the individuals discussed above. Like the two men above, however, most of these individuals hold criminal justice views that seem consistent with, and reasonably grounded in, their broader political beliefs. Four believers fit this description—among them, at least one whose belief system could only be described as shallow and scanty. But let us take as an example an individual who is less extreme.

Miriam Madamba

Miriam Madamba, a fifty-six-year-old secretary, emigrated from the Philippines to the Bay Area in the mid-1970s. She has lived in Oakland for eight years. Miriam is a widow and the mother of six grown children.

Miriam Madamba's political belief system is anchored by her firm support for civil liberties and democratic values. Asked what rights all persons should have from birth, she mentions "civil rights" and is able to offer a list containing freedom of speech, assembly, the press, and religion. "Freedom," she says elsewhere, "is to be able to come and go as you please and speak your mind. To worship wherever you want to worship, and to be able to read newspapers—free newspapers—that's not censored—and to be able to lead your life as you please." I ask what limits there should be on people's freedom: "If a person uses his freedom to ... if it encroaches on other persons' rights—that would be defeating the freedom of the other persons ... If freedom's not controlled, you'd have chaos, too." Asked about the case of too little freedom, she cites the example of her homeland—the Philippines—during the Marcos regime. Further, she is a supporter of civil disobedience in instances in which laws become "oppressive."

Here, Miriam discusses the meaning of democracy:

> *MM:* Democracy—what they learn in school—government for the people, by the people, and what else? For, by, and?
>
> *KTG:* Of. Of, by, for.
>
> *MM:* Yes, the people. For the people.
>
> *KTG:* And what does that mean—in real life—how does that work?
>
> *MM:* Having a president that has been elected by the people, and also a legislative system that has been elected by the people ...
>
> *KTG:* What are the advantages of democracy compared to other systems?
>
> *MM:* Democracy has checks and balance on the power of each branch, so I think it's the best kind of system of government.

Miriam Madamba's emphasis on freedom and democracy is joined by a fair degree of concern for social justice and equality. When asked if persons are entitled to any rights that are not included in our Constitution, she mentions "the right to education" and "the right to a good job." On the question of whether there are any groups or types of people who are treated unjustly in America today, she mentions "minorities." "Even in the workplace white people are given more privileges... Like promotions, in management—while most of the minorities stay in clerical jobs. There are very few of the minorities in the management's level." What would the best form of equality look like?

> ... There would be no segregation, and there won't be a particular area where only certain color people can live safely and be accepted. It will be mixed, and one will be welcome. And you can see everyone represented in every community. You don't have to look any farther than your own neighborhood to see these people work together and live together in the same place.

Miriam sees no potential conflict between freedom and equality and thinks that "they should go together." To her, freedom is the more important value, but "if everyone has freedom, I think equality would follow."

There are two other important elements of Miriam Madamba's political belief system. Both are evident in her conception of human nature:

> What's human nature?... Wherever you go, no matter what country you go to, or no matter what people you get in touch with, you will find people ... you find that there are good ... mixed in with the bad. I think that's true in every country and every race....

> Parents are prone to want to give their kids a better life than they had. I think that's one of the [elements of] human nature prevalent among every nation... Also it is in the nature of people to want to have good jobs, so that they can support their families. And have their own home.

One important idea expressed here, then, is that although most people are good, some people are not. We can hear this theme, also, in her answer to my question about whether there will always be poverty in the world: "I think it would be, because people think differently, and some people are either lazy or are not ambitious enough to get to somewhere where they can be self-supporting and be useful citizens." It can be heard even more strongly in her response to the question of whether there will always be crime: "I think there will be ... There will always be bad people."

The second important conviction involves the high value of self-sufficiency: good people want to be self-supporting. Indeed, when I ask Miriam what have been the most important lessons of her life, she says,

"The best lesson is not to depend on another person." She reports that she has worked since before adulthood and has always been very independent. And it was a good thing, too, she notes, because her husband deserted her and their six children, leaving her as the sole breadwinner for her family. The same conviction can be heard when, after discussing her conception of utopia, Miriam sums up with this:

> I guess I have really a very simple lifestyle. I only wish that I have this for my kids too. Get better jobs—better paying jobs. *So that they can stand on their own*—probably have their own houses. (Emphasis added.)

Miriam Madamba's views on criminal justice appear reasonably consonant with and grounded in her broader political ideology. Her convictions about rights to education and employment and her sense that we have problems of social injustice in this country are reflected in her proposed solutions to the crime problem: creating jobs, increasing educational opportunities, improving living conditions for slum dwellers and others, fighting drug and alcohol abuse. She is also a reasonably enthusiastic supporter of rehabilitative efforts with convicted criminals and is willing to sanction a number of alternatives to incarceration for certain offenders.

On the other hand, her feeling is that, in general, the courts are not harsh enough on criminals. She supports the goals of deterrence and punishment and feels that for certain offenders, prison sentences are the appropriate response—fifteen to twenty years, for instance, for my habitual burglars. These harsher views, in turn, seem to be undergirded by her broad belief that some people are not just maltreated or misguided, but bad. Likewise, when she at times assigns the blame for crime expressly to individuals—counterbalancing her nod to social responsibility—this may find a natural foundation in her high regard for personal self-sufficiency.

Neither Miriam Madamba's views on criminal justice nor her broader political belief system could be said to be especially sophisticated. There is every appearance, however, that they are reasonably "in sync" with one another.

Sophisticated, but Not Consonant

Three more believers hold political ideologies that are as sophisticated as those of Victor Rodriguez, James Morton, and the group they represent. But in these instances, the criminal justice views of the participants do not seem fully consonant with their broader political ideologies. In each case, their milder views about criminal justice seem well grounded in their overall belief systems, but their harsh views do not appear to have a sufficient foundation there.

Adam Perlman

Consider the case of Adam Perlman, the speech therapist whom we met in chapter 3. Individual rights and democratic values play a very prominent role in Adam's political ideology. Here, he speaks to the question of what rights all persons should have from birth:

> You'd think they should have the right to have education. And the right to pursue interests that they have, as long as whatever they intend to do isn't going to infringe on somebody else's rights. And I think that people should have the same possibility of employment, given the same background, the same qualifications. I think people should ... all have access to the same basic liberty.

Here, on the definition of freedom:

> Freedom is the right, the access, to privileges, to bettering your life—to try to do anything you can to make you happy and successful without imposing on somebody else—without infringing on somebody else's rights. Freedom to enjoy yourself, and freedom to support yourself.

Here, on civil disobedience:

> I think governments make mistakes, because governments are made up of people. I think though that we have the channels to compensate for that ... to correct the mistakes, rather than everybody just taking the law into their own hands ... You can take things into your own hands, but you do that to effect change at a national level—on a policy level—rather than ... being anarchical about it. Do it so that there's control on it—so that there's organization to it. Organized change, rather than just haphazard disobeying of something, even if it's wrong. And there are a lot of things that have come up from time to time that feel wrong. That means that sometimes the government ... didn't take everything into consideration ... you have a mistake—how do we go about correcting that? That's the way I think it should be done. The problem is that it often takes too long to do that ... If ... the way you're correcting it is *just,* or is not doing harm to somebody—you're preventing harm from being done to somebody—that should be protected. Then I think it's okay to act out and do that and to present it

afterwards ... The assumption is that you're disobeying a rule that is unjust—that's causing somebody to be violated unjustly, and thereby by intervening you're preventing that from happening.

And here, on democracy:

> Democracy to me means situations where people's rights will be protected, and everybody has the right to have their opinion count—their preference. And not that ... everybody's going to get their way, but everybody has the right to express it and have it considered—i.e., in voting.

A second important set of beliefs involves the conviction that social justice and equality are values to strive for—and are values that have not yet been fully realized. Here, he discusses the famous phrase from the Declaration of Independence:

> [People] are created equal [in that] they all have the same basic needs. And they're created unequal in their ability to pursue opportunities. They're unequal as a result of biases of their fellow humans. Ideally they should be equal in their ability to pursue their basic rights. That's the ideal—that they're equal and they should be equal in freedom and in rights. And in reality, I don't think access is equal. I think the law—the way it's ordered—is to be equal to everybody. But I think in practice it doesn't work out that way, for some people can have access to better representation and have better understanding, more education, and just better ability to manipulate the situation to their end. ...

Later, we discuss the question of how difficult it is for persons to make their own lives better, and Adam asserts that "if you really want to do something you can do it. You may have a lot of obstacles, you may keep on getting knocked down, but if you really want something bad enough, I think you can do it. I just think it takes a lot of motivation—a lot of persistence." But a minute later, as he answers another question, he interrupts himself to return to this subject: "You can do whatever you want to do ... It isn't really true. There are some people that aren't able to do that ... Yeah, there are a lot of groups that are discriminated against." At various points during the interview he mentions such groups: minority groups, senior citizens, the disabled, even the middle class (sometimes, he says, the government tries to overcompensate for injustices done, and since the "upper strata" can always arrange for preferential treatment, those in the middle get squeezed).

Adam's response, when I pursue the question of basic rights, sheds some light on his conception of social responsibility:

>   *KTG:*   What about these three other things: food shelter, and health care? Should any of these be rights from birth, or would you say not?

>   *AP:*   ...I think people should have the same chance to be able to attain those. I don't think necessarily that it's something that everybody should get for free. Then government would have too much control over our lives ... And I don't think that's the responsibility of government. Individuals are responsible for taking care of themselves. But I think they should have [the] right—equal right—to attain those things. I do think education, though, should be available to everybody that wants it. And that is going to enable people to pursue these other things. . . .

>   But things aren't ideal, and people get shortchanged. And I do think that there need to be provisions for people like that . . . It's good that people who don't *have* can get food, can get clothing, can get shelter. I wouldn't want people to not have those things, even if, [were they] more responsible, perhaps they could [get them] . . . I do believe that it's our responsibility to care for people. Our responsibility is limited, though. I don't think we should take responsibility totally for other people's lives, but I think that we should be willing to help people out. So I think part of our taxes—it's okay to go to things like that. But I think it's also good to maybe have some kind of educational and job training programs for people like that to get them to be productive members of society. I don't think that there's any reason for people to be consistently dependent on society for [their] basic needs. I think people should have the same access to obtaining those basic needs . . . That's what we should be gearing our society for, is making those people productive somehow—giving them a job that needs to be done . . . Perhaps that could be a government job—or government subsidized . . . I think people should be willing to help other people, but I don't think they should be taken advantage of, is what I'm trying to say.

Adam sees the concepts of freedom and equality as complementary: "One depends on the other . . . If equality isn't there, then freedom isn't equally accessible ... The way I defined the two of them, they go hand in hand." As to which is more important: "They're so close to being the same thing ... One is the process by which you attain the other, so I can't say one is more important ... If I denied one, it would negate the other. If I allow one, it allows the other."

Adam Perlman's belief system contains one more important set of values. When I ask him what are his most important religious or spiritual beliefs, he says:

> *I think it's probably the same beliefs that I just said that I agree with—over the entire interview* ... Respecting other people and their rights, and trying to see the other perspective. Tolerance, and forgiveness, and compassion ... Just being responsible, period, I think is part of that. ... (Emphasis added.)

The same theme emerges when, at the close of the interview, I ask him what have been the most important lessons of life for him:

> That communication between people is very important. That it's important to see other people's perspective, and not be too quick to judge. ...

And also when I ask, "What is the point of living? Why are we here?"

> I think we're here to do good by each other, and to try to be happy. And to learn—learn all there is about living together. Learn about tolerance and patience and forgiveness ... What makes ourselves and other people tick. We need to learn how to interact, basically.

Earlier, I noted that throughout the interviews, Adam seemed to pride himself on considering both sides of every coin, as he worked his way through my questions. And indeed, this is the sort of value he stresses here, as he talks about the really important things in life.

Adam Perlman's mild views about criminal justice—his firm support for preventive and rehabilitative measures, and his advocacy of alternatives to incarceration for nonviolent offenders—seem basically consistent with his broader political ideology. We have heard his beliefs about the importance of seeking a still-elusive social justice and equality, as well as his vow to try to live his life with tolerance and forgiveness, and to check out the view from the other person's shoes. Perhaps more importantly, there is also his great concern that the rights of individuals be respected by others around them—a point he makes again and again in our conversations. As we saw in chapter 3, it is *primarily* the values of security and desert (rather than compassion or social critique) that influence Adam toward the mild criminal justice views he expresses. And it is this conviction about personal rights that most undergirds these concerns: efforts that effectively promote security from crime ensure respect of such rights, as, for instance, do compensatory penalties that require offenders to tangibly acknowledge others' rights to property, through restitution.

We must inquire, also, about the foundation for the many harsher views that Adam voices—advocacy of capital punishment and long sentences for certain offenders; support for the goals of punishment and deterrence. Again, his great concern for respecting individuals' rights comes into play. Of course, such a fervency leads no more naturally to harsh than to mild responses to crime, so long as the speaker is convinced of the *efficacy* of whichever avenue(s) he or she advocates. Thus, in Victor Rodriguez, for instance, such a belief undergirded criminal justice views that combined prevention, rehabilitation, and—when absolutely essential—isolation. Conceivably, in Adam Perlman, the same conviction might undergird a combination of prevention, rehabilitation, and compensation (as we have seen)— and in addition, isolation and deterrence. But this leaves out his extremely important views about punishment—his conviction that offenders *deserve* to suffer some loss of rights (to possessions, to freedoms, or even to life itself) because of their crimes. What is there to undergird this? Missing from Adam's political ideology is the belief of a Miriam Madamba or an Elizabeth Williams that some or all people just are not inherently good. Gone is the rigid sense of morality and authority, and the great intolerance for deviance, of a Clarence Peters. Absent is the fervent belief in individual responsibility of a James Morton or a Drew Snowden. And what is there to take their place?

Adam Perlman is an educated man: he holds a master's degree in his field. Certainly he is no less articulate or intelligent than any of the interviewees—believers or dissenters—in the first grouping. And yet unlike all of them, his views on criminal justice do not seem *fully* grounded in his broader political belief system.[9] His mild views have an ample foundation there. Not so, it seems, for a major portion of the harsh views that he expresses with equal conviction. I could find nothing to undergird his advocacy of punishment, nor its motivation in desert.

Neither Sophisticated nor Consonant

Only one interviewee fits the final description: neither sophisticated nor consonant. Like Miriam Madamba and the others in the second grouping, her political belief system is not especially sophisticated. Her beliefs are reasonably coherent but are not as detailed and wide-ranging, nor as consciously held as those of the individuals in the first and third groups. And, like Adam Perlman and the others in the section above, her criminal justice views do not seem fully consonant with her broader political ideology.

Sadie Monroe

Sadie Monroe is the retired physical education teacher introduced in chapter 3. The importance of seeking social justice and equality is the most consistent and most emphasized theme in Sadie's political belief system. Justice means "being fair," and it is her opinion that minority groups are not being treated justly in our society. "They have larger unemployment," and this, she says, is due to discrimination. Indeed, she reports that she has felt such discrimination personally. For more than a decade she sought a full-time teaching position in the Bay Area and watched as others with less education than she had were hired for openings that she had been told did not exist. Finally, after years as a substitute, she was hired to a regular position.

I asked Sadie what kinds of rights all people should have from birth: "People should have a decent job, place to live, average salary." Later, we move on to the subject of equality:

> KTG: The Declaration of Independence states that "all men are created equal." In what ways would you say that all people are created equal? In what ways are they unequal?
>
> SM: They are unequal in that all people can't exercise the same things. For instance, they never have had a black president. Course, Jesse Jackson is running, but ... that position usually has to be a white male—certain age—to be president of the United States. Course, they may change that—he may go out there and win—but that's not equality there.

Sadie doesn't feel able to describe just what sort of equality we should be striving for. But she finds a subsequent question both manageable and amusing:

> KTG: How would you feel if everyone received the same income, whatever his or her job was? Would people act any differently than they do now?
>
> SM: I'm sure they would. Those that have wouldn't always be wanting to take from the have-nots.
>
> KTG: Would it be a good idea, or not?
>
> SM: That would be a good idea—if everybody had the same salary.

Later, I ask her how difficult it is for people to make their own lives better, and her answer is much more optimistic than one would expect from her earlier appraisal of our society: "Some instances it's not too bad. You prepare yourself for a job. You get a good education, and you go on to higher things." Still, with the next question, she returns to her dominant theme:

> KTG: Some people's lives don't ever seem to get any better, or sometimes even get worse. Do you think that happens very much? Why do you think that happens?
>
> SM: That's back to your poverty and freedom. Freedom of places to live—to buy where you want to...Like twenty years ago I couldn't live up here where I am now. You could live only in the flatlands....

Beyond this central theme of social justice and equality there is also a bare-bones sense of individual liberty and democratic values:

> Freedom is just the ability to do things you please within the law. Like we said, the freedom of speech. Being able to speak out, whatever you feel—free to do it.

Freedom and equality, Sadie says, "go hand in hand." But freedom is the more important value: "If you're free to do these things, you can get equality." Here, she addresses some of my questions about democracy:

> SM: Democracy—what does it mean? Democracy is a way of life in this democratic situation where people are free to have certain laws. When they abide by them, they uphold democracy of our nation. That's all I know.
>
> KTG: What are the advantages of democracy compared to other systems?
>
> SM: It gives people the freedom to vote and change things that they don't agree with. And independence that they otherwise wouldn't have if they didn't have democracy.

Sadie draws the individual-liberty line at the point of civil disobedience, however:

> KTG: Are there ever times when laws and government authorities are wrong and should be disobeyed, or would you say that citizens should obey their government under all circumstances?

SM: I think from time to time, they change laws—that's why they put them on the ballots and vote on them—because to give people a choice. And that way they don't be just set with one set of laws.

KTG: But should people ever disobey them, if they aren't changed legally?

SM: They shouldn't disobey them. They should try to change them. . . .

[A good citizen in a democracy] would abide by different laws and rules that govern the cities and counties and state—uphold all of that. And if they wanted to change something, they would go about it in a legitimate way. And like some countries—they always trying to overthrow their government—we don't have that in the United States.

Here, as with Adam Perlman, we have an individual whose criminal justice views do not seem fully consonant with the political belief system she expresses. The few mild views that Sadie espouses—a vague belief in rehabilitation; support for increased educational and employment opportunities as crime-preventive measures; willingness to accept prison work release programs, and for certain offenders, alternatives to incarceration—these find plentiful support in her core beliefs about social justice and equality. Recall also, from chapter 3, that Sadie's limited mild views were found to be motivated primarily by social critique. But Sadie Monroe's views about criminal justice actually are predominantly harsh. She favors capital punishment, strongly advocates a deterrence policy for the criminal justice system, and considers incarceration to be the appropriate penalty for all of the adult hypothetical offenders I described. Where is the foundation for these views?

We know that Sadie holds quite rigid views about the authority of law: civil disobedience is not, for her, a legitimate form of protest against injustice; and she defines freedom as being limited by law, rather than by the rights or well-being of others. But this is not enough, alone, to provide a firm foundation for a choice of predominantly harsh rather than mild responses to those who break the law.[10] And missing from her political ideology is any evidence of accompanying ideas—ideas about human evil or strict individual responsibility, for instance—that might strengthen that foundation. Instead, the dominant theme within her political belief system involves the importance of seeking social justice and equality. Sadie Monroe's quite harsh views about criminal justice form the bulk of her thoughts on that topic; yet there is just not enough of substance among her comments here to demonstrate that these views are fully undergirded by a consistent political ideology.

The Three Remaining Participants

Three of my interviewees cannot be discussed in the manner above. The first is Thelma Winters, eighty-three, a retired home health care aide whose formal education ceased after the eighth grade. Originally from the Southwest, she has lived half her life in Oakland. She is black and is the widowed mother of five grown children.

Thelma Winters's basic outlook is that "I'm not out there in the world, with the world. I'm in the world, but I'm not with the world." Earthly affairs are no longer of much importance to her, and all that matters is trying to "figure how to be a better Christian," so as to make it into heaven. Despite these protests, she is able to muster a small collection of coherent views about criminal justice, but when we come to the broader political questions of the second interview, her response is "I don't know" as often as not.

Thelma says, "I just love freedom. I really love freedom," but she is unable to say much more about its content than "Go anywhere I want to, sit where I want to." To her, freedom is more important than equality, but she can cite no more reason for this than "I just love freedom." In reply to a later question, she says that it is not right for government to force people to do things against their will. But then, with the next question—regarding when, if ever, a government is justified in using physical force to control the behavior of its citizens—she returns to "I don't know." Asked about civil disobedience, she says that the Bible teaches that persons should obey anyone who is over them: "I'm just now starting to kinda believe in it—if they're right. But I want to find out if they are right or not." However, she goes on to assert that she is in no position to tell if government is right.

As for equality, in the best case:

> I would like to see everybody be the same—treated the same, and work together, and go to churches together ... Try to get along in the world, is all I know—together—regardless of what color you are. 'Cause I think we're all human beings. God made us all. We didn't make ourselves. He didn't intend for the world to be like this—like it is now. . . .

But that is about it, as far as broad political concepts go. The scope of her beliefs is so narrow, and their content so paper thin, that it can safely be said that Thelma Winters has virtually no *political* belief system. This is not to say that she holds no broader philosophy for her life. Indeed, she expresses a quite developed personal and religious philosophy, as evidenced by her remarks about education, personal discipline, forgiveness, repentance, eschewing jealousy, love, salvation, and God's power. Age and lack of formal education may have conspired to limit the scope of her thoughts, but by no means is she thought-less.

Paul Bongolan and Evangeline Reed, discussed at the beginning of this chapter, are the remaining two interviewees. Their views about criminal justice were essentially incoherent. It will come as no surprise that the broader political beliefs Paul expresses are as incoherent as his opinions about criminal justice and that Evangeline has a largely incoherent political ideology.[11] Given all this, it is pointless to ask whether their criminal justice views are consistent with their broader political ideologies. These individuals stand as a reminder that the views of each and every member of the public cannot be understood by a logic evident to others. In a study of most other areas of public opinion, we likely would have found many more individuals who sound like these two; here they remind us to appreciate the ease with which we can make sense of the views of the other participants.

Conclusion

D. Garth Taylor, Kim Scheppele, and Arthur Stinchcombe note that

> The cognitive consistency approach to public opinion research . . . argues that what people actually do in situations of increased salience is develop coherent ideologies. When issues become salient, people think more about them. This results in the acceleration of the process through which people develop world views or general ideologies about the way the world works.[12]

Based on the evidence of these interviews, this doorstep issue—crime—fares quite well when it comes to the question of consistency between convictions about broad political concepts and views about specific policy issues. Among the twenty-one interviewees who have coherent political belief systems, all but four hold views about criminal justice that appear to be reasonably consonant with and grounded in their broader ideologies. These four are all believers whose political belief systems provide a plausible foundation for their mild views about criminal justice but seem to be lacking in the kinds of convictions that could fully undergird their harsh views. Interestingly, the reverse case did not appear: no participant held a broad belief system that formed a reasonable foundation for the harsh views, but not for the mild views, that he or she expressed.

To say that I cannot find enough in the broad political beliefs of Adam Perlman, Sadie Monroe, Gladys Jones, and Aram Isaac to fully undergird the harsh views about criminal justice that these believers express is not to say definitely that they have pulled these views out of thin air.[13] A political belief system is not necessarily the only set of overarching conceptions about life that an individual holds. When answering my political questions, some of the interviewees took the initiative to draw upon concepts that lie at the intersection of politics and religion. A few of the participants, for instance, clearly expressed views about whether or not all human beings are basically good—a highly important revelation, for the purposes of this chapter. My concern here has been with political ideology. But for the researcher interested in pushing further the effort to understand how and whether policy views about criminal justice are grounded in deep, underlying beliefs, I would suggest a more detailed look at religious convictions. Questions about good and evil, judgment and righteousness, heaven and hell—these would be among the essential elements of such an inquiry.[14] Three of the four interviewees whose criminal justice views and political ideologies are not fully consonant report that religious or spiritual beliefs are important in their lives. So too for Thelma Winters, the one participant who appeared to have virtually no political belief system. Furthermore, the reader may have noticed that three of the four believers named here because their views about criminal justice do not appear fully grounded in their broader political beliefs were named in the previous chapter as complex believers. Recall that the tension between *desert* and social critique or compassion was the defining influence on these believers. Not infrequently, individuals turn to their religion for instruction on questions of what is deserved—of what is right or just. This only strengthens the notion that a full consideration of religious beliefs would be a promising next step.

For more than two-thirds of the Americans whom I interviewed, though, there is no pressing need to look further to find a plausible foundation for their policy views about criminal justice. Their political belief systems provide ample support. Here, with a policy issue as close to the heart as crime, we find far higher levels of consonance between specific attitudes and broad beliefs than we would expect to find with important, but for most Americans distant, issues—for instance, Mexican political strife, or the use of alternative energy sources.

What can be learned from all this that may help with our questions about consensus? Certainly a striking finding of this chapter is that *all* of the dissenters, but less than one-third of the believers, are among those whose criminal justice views appear to be fully grounded in sophisticated political belief systems. But this is only a piece of the puzzle. For it is not as if only dissenters structure their views in this way: the development of a national consensus cannot be passed off as resulting from some broad desophistication and disorganization of virtually the entire public. To the contrary, those who join the prevailing consensus hold political belief systems of wide-ranging levels of sophistication and consonance.

It is the dissenters who all look alike from that angle—and this is the direction to be pursued. In what other ways do the dissenters look like each other? What other factors, perhaps of background or outlook, may be widely shared by this minority? Before making a broad analysis of this phenomenal consensus, we must make sure that we know all we can about who it is that stands against it. Chapter 5 seeks an explanation: what makes the dissenters dissent?

Part 2. Explanation

CHAPTER 5

Explaining Dissent

What enables a dissenter to become and remain a dissenter—rather than a believer? What characteristics of background or outlook coalesce in the lives of the dissenters, which may lead them to respond to underlying values in the manner in which they do and to move from the base of these values to their own particular views about criminal justice? How strongly can we distinguish between these influences and those that hold sway in the lives of the believers? These will be the focal questions of this chapter, and they will be approached from three angles: (1) a look at some possible explanations that have intuitive appeal but are not supported by the evidence collected here; (2) a look at those explanations that are most strongly supported by this evidence; and (3) a look at the explanations that the nine dissenters themselves give when asked what induced them to stand against the current of public consensus.

That I have placed a particular emphasis on understanding why the *dissenters* hold their unpopular views is partially the result of a theoretical interest in explaining what induces or enables certain people to march to a different drummer. But it is also the result of an empirical finding: where there were significant differences between the two groups, generally I found that it was the dissenters who exhibited particularly uniform or particularly unusual characteristics, while the believers proved more varied or traditional. We have seen this phenomenon already in the previous chapter, where the dissenters stood out because each and every one of them presented a sophisticated political belief system in which their criminal justice views appeared to be well grounded. In chapter 6, the emphasis will be reversed, as the focus turns to assembling a multifaceted explanation for the dominant consensus.

The style of this chapter will differ from that of those preceding. To this point, my practice has been to present a fairly detailed scrutiny of individual participants, using each as an example of a particular perspective or phenomenon. But here, my practice will be to focus on each potential explanatory factor and, where examples are given, to draw brief excerpts from several different individuals. The nature of the task demands this shift in mode: so many different elements must be considered before a more composite picture can be drawn.

A word should be said about the type of evidence I take as meaningful here—which is, in short, *striking* evidence. Anything much less, in the context of small-sample, qualitative research, would be problematic. An intensive methodology of this sort has the advantage of being able to probe deeply and widely. In the use I have made of it here, I have explored a large number of possible explanations and allowed participants room to suggest others I had not considered. But my sample, although carefully chosen, is not proportionally representative, and modest numerical distinctions that might be meaningful in survey research here may be merely artifacts of the small sample size. Where striking differences between the believers and the dissenters I spoke with do occur, it is always possible that the phenomena to which they point still are red herrings. But the chance of error will have been reduced significantly, and the issues in question certainly will be ones that bear further exploration.

Unsupported Explanatory Hypotheses

Why bother to work through a collection of reasonable hypotheses that, based on the evidence found here or elsewhere, do not work? Precisely because they are so reasonable, and because people expect that they will work. "Isn't it amazing that we now have such an enormous American consensus about crime policy!" one might say to an acquaintance. The reply: "That's easy to explain: People are just more fearful than they used to be." Or, "So many more people have become crime victims." And so on. But these are not the answers—nor are a number of other seemingly reasonable explanations. We need to look briefly at the explanations that are not borne out here, before turning to those that this study supports. In fact, an examination of the ways in which these dissenters and believers are surprisingly similar may be nearly as revealing of who they are, as an examination of their critical differences.

Fear, Victimization, and Salience
Some of the most obvious hypotheses about why certain people want harsher treatment of offenders than do others—differences in fear, in victimization, and in the salience of the crime problem—have already been tackled by analysts of large-scale polling and have not been supported by their data. The authors of *The Figgie Report Part I* report that their analysis, based on national sampling, "reveals that support for specific punitive measures exists irrespective of levels of . . . fear."[1] Stinchcombe and his

colleagues also looked in this direction as they sought an explanation for the increased harshness of the American public:

> The obvious explanation seemed to be that crime and fear of crime were increasing ... but fear of crime does not correlate strongly with punitiveness, and there are massive exceptions to that correlation. Blacks and women, who are much more afraid of crime, are less punitive than whites or men.[2]

Likewise, they found that differences in punitiveness could not be explained by differences in victimization:

> There is a significant relationship among whites between victimization and support for harsher sanctions, but it is in the opposite direction from what we would expect ... Whites whose homes have been recently burglarized are less likely than those with no victimization experience to favor capital punishment and less likely to demand harsher courts. There is no significant relationship for blacks.[3]

Further, the Stinchcombe group found that the "public salience of crime" is not strongly enough related to punitiveness to be able to explain the increased expression of harsh attitudes.[4] Several other studies have used poll data to address these three issues and have produced results that correspond with these analyses.[5]

Detailed conversation with my interviewees reveals no greater support for these obvious hypotheses than has been found in these larger but shallower studies. Based on ten questions that I asked, the overall level of fear among the dissenters looks little different from that among the believers. Most express a low to moderate degree of fear,[6] although about half of the participants in each group mention a relative for whom they are more fearful. Most think it likely that they will someday become a crime victim.[7] A larger proportion of believers than dissenters report that they are more fearful than they used to be—but the difference is not striking.

These interviews also fail to support the hypothesis that greater victimization might lead to greater harshness. Only one dissenter—Victor Rodriguez, the government administrator—and one believer—Gladys Jones, the hospital clerk—have never personally been the victims of crime. There is no noticeable difference in the frequency or severity of personal victimizations to the two groups, but in fact, many more dissenters than believers have been close to crimes of violence. All of the dissenters except Victor have experienced a violent victimization either to themselves or to someone close to them; but only half of the believers report similar experiences.[8]

This is quite the opposite from the evidence needed to support the common-sense hypothesis about victimization.

There was also very little difference in the salience of the crime problem for the believers versus the dissenters.[9] Nearly every participant expressed the view that crime is a very serious problem for the city of Oakland, and for the United States as a whole. About half of each group stated that crime is a significant problem in the neighborhoods in which they live; and again half had made quite major changes in their activities or lifestyle because of the crime problem. Interviewees were also asked about the degree to which they thought about, and talked with others about, the crime issue: there were no significant differences between the dissenters and the believers on this question.

Attitudes toward Victims

A second area to consider involves the feelings that participants expressed about crime victims. We might reasonably hypothesize that those who feel a greater empathy or concern for victims may hold harsher views about responses to crime. But based on a subjective evaluation of the level of empathy that each interviewee expressed for victims, I can report that the differences between the dissenters and the believers are not large. The great bulk of the participants can be considered "reasonably" or "normally" empathetic. If there is any surprise it comes in the discovery that the tragedy of victimization is emphasized as a major theme by very few of the participants, in either group.[10] Comments such as this, from Drew Snowden, the banker, who focused repeatedly on the pain of victimization, are an exception:

> Then we come again to political philosophy of justice from the victims' point of view—which there isn't much of. As far as the legal system goes, it's so one-sided. But there can be no justice for the eighty-year-old who is knocked down stealing a purse. The emotional trauma of breaking into someone's house and stealing memorabilia—all that through the generations—there is never any justice for that.

Information

Another interesting hypothesis aimed at explaining why the dissenters and the believers have such different views is that they may be forming their opinions on the basis of different information. Whichever group one considers to hold the wisest views, that is the group one would suppose possesses the most accurate grasp of the facts. This hypothesis is unsupported by the results of the interviews.

Sprinkled through the first interview were a number of factual questions about crime and the criminal justice system.[11] Nobody made the honor roll on this exam, and the differences between the dissenters and the believers were not significant. Only occasionally did as many as two-thirds of either group answer a question with a figure that could be considered "in the ballpark." Most often, less than half of either group gave a reasonably accurate answer. And on two questions, virtually everybody missed the boat entirely. When asked to estimate how much it costs to build a new maximum security prison—per cell—nobody came close to the $96,000 price tag that was the going rate in California.[12] Respondents did nearly as poorly when asked whether crime rates were up, down, or holding steady in the United States as a whole. Only one participant—Dexter Lane, an insurance agent with a law degree—gave the correct answer (that they had been going down).[13] Two other participants who thought they were up did mention that perhaps it was merely reporting that was up; one was a dissenter, the other a believer.

There were no major differences, either, in the sources of information about crime and the criminal justice system that participants cited. The news media and conversations with friends and acquaintances were the most common sources for both groups. Furthermore, nearly everyone felt that media coverage of crime was at least somewhat sensationalized— several in each group felt that it was considerably so.

Conceptions of Criminality

Suppose, now, that the dissenters and the believers held differing conceptions of who criminal offenders are. If one group, say, conceived of offenders as an odd, separate, and threatening minority in society, but the other group conceived of them as being just about anybody—might they not move from these differing vantage points to divergent views about criminal justice? This is yet another hypothesis that is not supported by the interview data.

Participants were asked at one point to estimate the percentage of our population who have, at some time during their lives, committed a crime for which they could have been sent to jail or prison. From dissenters and believers alike, the responses are all over the map. Dissenter answers range from 1 to 99.9 percent; believer answers from 2 to 75 percent.

Dissenters and believers also differed little in their conceptions of the "average criminal." Most in each group described the typical offender as a person under thirty, with a low level of education and income. Nearly everyone indicated that race makes no difference, except in that it is linked with poverty. There is no evidence of any distinction that would influence them toward differing opinions about penal sanctions.

Perceptions of the Courts

As Stinchcombe and his colleagues point out, "When a respondent gives a lenient answer to a question about the harshness of local courts or appropriateness of capital punishment, we do not know whether this is because the respondent thinks . . . the courts often convict innocent people, . . . the justice system assigns sentences that will have no beneficial effect, or some other reason." They also offer this hypothesis: "We suspect that people who believe that the criminal justice system is biased are likely to be less punitive than those who believe it is fair."[14] In other words, perceptions of the courts may make a difference.

Interview participants were asked how often they thought the courts convicted innocent persons for crimes they did not commit. All but one of the seven dissenters who answered this question felt that this happened pretty rarely. Richard Niederhaus, the software designer, was alone in stating that it happened "enough for it to be a problem." Most of the believers who answered also felt that the conviction of innocents was rare, but here there were more exceptions. Four believers gave answers like "it happens quite a lot," or figures as high as 25 percent. If anything, this is the opposite of the relationship which would be expected.

In addition, interviewees were asked this question: "Do you think the criminal justice system tends more to be fair, or to be biased, in regard to minorities and the poor?" All but one of the dissenters felt that the system was biased, but so did most of the believers. These interviews simply do not support a picture of the dissenters as a group of people significantly more inclined than the believers to doubt the fairness or accuracy of the convictions obtained by the criminal justice system.

Incarceration: Perceptions and Exposure

Another factor that might conceivably influence the formation of Americans' views about criminal sanctions is the degree to which their perceptions of, and exposure to, the prison or jail environment differ from one another's. Several of the interview questions offer a window on this issue. When asked about conditions and lifestyle in the jails and prisons of California, a majority of both dissenters and believers envisioned a life that (in most institutions) is quite rough. Consider these words from Abby Edwards, the community college instructor (a dissenter):

> Boring, crowded, poor sanitation, poor diet, not enough exercise, not enough personal attention. A feeling of being cut off, no one caring. Waiting.

And these, from Violet Taylor, the retired waitress (a believer):

> They say that they're very uncomfortable 'cause there's too many prisoners, and that they're filthy. And it's very crowded, and they all get frustrated. It's not very good.

Or these, from Daniel Steinbach, the social worker (a dissenter):

> Very structured ... Survival mentality, totally—I mean the whole idea when you're in prison is *to survive, in prison* ... I talk about ... men not being into their feelings, and defending themselves, and putting out these personas—be strong, survive, and all that stuff. Prison just exaggerates that to the ultimate, because I mean it's really survival time. So God ... if you become so well defended in prison, it must be a bitch to get out there and be able to feel. It's gotta be horrible, in terms of when you do get out, to be able to open your heart, to let people in—the system just perpetuates that. So it's a loser—it's an absolute loser ... I mean it's a terrible system ... God, it's like sending a bunch of—sending a military force out into society. I don't know if the word "military" is right, but—it's not the answer.

Two believers, Barbara Damon, the transportation department official, and Drew Snowden, the banker, were alone among the interviewees in feeling that prison and jail conditions are generally pretty soft.

Interviewees were also asked for their perceptions of how prisoners *react* to being deprived of "their freedom, their loved ones, and all the other privileges of the outside world." Most of the dissenters and most of the believers expressed the view that offenders find incarceration to be a very unwelcome experience. For example, from Anne Girard, the aspiring writer (a dissenter): "I think they're mostly very angry—pissed off." And from Sadie Monroe, the retired physical education teacher (a believer): "I don't know. I've just wondered—if people are all locked up and everything for all those years ... I guess they are all often very angry and despondent, I would think." Or from Clarence Peters, the glazing contractor (a believer):

"I can imagine that they feel cheated—that society's against them. They are one of the few that have been caught—that the world owes them a living, and all they can do is take some of it—and they get caught doing it."

But a few believers and dissenters expressed the view that for at least some prisoners, incarceration was little worse than a neutral experience. Take, for instance, Kate Fontana, the nurse-midwife (a dissenter):

> I think for a lot of prisoners it's probably not that terrible of a thing to be in jail. Home is probably not very secure, probably very transient, probably alone . . . not a very strong social support network. I don't think they have a strong sense of security or loved ones—responsibility toward those people. Because if they had, I don't know that they'd be criminals . . . In terms of two choices between what they had, and jail, jail might look better—in some senses.

And Thelma Winters, the retired home health aide (a believer):

> I imagine there's some that don't care and some that does. Some just get so hard-boiled.

Finally, there is the issue of personal exposure to the incarcerative environment. Although their experiences vary greatly, nearly all of the participants have had some exposure to a prison, jail, or juvenile detention facility. Some have visited friends or relatives there; others were a part of organized tour groups. A few have personally been held after arrest or conviction. But there are no major differences between the dissenters and the believers in the nature of their exposure.

Forgiveness and Vengeance

Another intuitive hypothesis is that dissenters may be more inclined than believers to place a high value on acts of forgiveness. Conversely, they may be more inclined to reject actions that are carried out for the purpose of vengeance. This hypothesis, also, is not supported by the evidence obtained in these interviews.

In the second interview, in a context removed from our earlier discussions of crime, participants were asked in some detail about their conceptions of forgiveness and vengeance. To listen to the dissenters speak of forgiveness is to be struck by how many of them have a highly worked out understanding of this act, and by the considerable importance that it holds in their lives. Consider, for instance, these words from Abby Edwards, the community college instructor:

KTG: Now I'd like to hear your thoughts on the concept of forgiveness. Think for a moment about the last time you forgave a relative or friend for something important, or the last time you remember being forgiven by one of them. You needn't go into the personal details of the incident unless you wish to, but can you describe for me the *process* of forgiveness—what happens when someone forgives someone else?

AE: ... It may be a fact of realizing there was really nothing to forgive in the first place. That you didn't even have the right to make that judgment that that was forgivable. Because maybe according to their standards, it's how everybody looks at things. ...

> If someone does something wrong to me, it's all in how I look at it, and it's probably a lot my ego. If they insulted my intelligence—even if they hit me—it's how I react to it. They hit me, and I can either get mad, or forget it ... I think everybody should just go around and spend the whole day forgiving everything and starting every day brand new. And whatever they carried over from yesterday should just be forgotten, because it is just anger.

Or these from Daniel Steinbach, the social worker:

> He who forgives, who really forgives ... can really be free. They can be in the present—now ... If you can't forgive ... then you're ... back there ... As long as you're back there, you can't be here. Those moments that you're back there, with [your] hatred, anger, hurt, sorrow—as long as you're there you can't—I can't be here with you right now. You're not living in the moment ... life is passing you by—it really is. So when you forgive someone, and you let go of that—you come back to here, now.

And these from Olivia Hassan, the bank teller:

> I've taken pains to work out a method for myself that—it's almost like I've trained myself to do certain steps ... because I consider being angry destructive ... Nature gave [anger] to me for a reason, and I should pay attention to when I'm angry, because something is going on in that area, but ... after paying attention to it, and working it out, it is destructive for me, personally—physically and mentally ... to remain angry, so I try and heal that part of me ... I ask what actually went on in the situation ... were they aware they offended me? Probably not ... So it's my own value system that I set up that caused me

to be this or that. And then, I usually will say, well, even though I can see that whatever happened, it's not really their fault, still the anger is there—I can feel it inside—so I still don't feel myself inside. So I just keep working with it until I feel like everything in it's clear . . . So forgiveness in me means that I look at the person as apart from me, and that whatever they did comes from their own value system . . . Forgiveness for me is just releasing the other person from blame from my own value system.

Alas for the hypothesis under consideration, when we turn to the believers, we find much of the same. From most, there is still the central message that forgiveness is an important and worthy act between human beings. If their comments are sometimes less intense, on the whole they are not strikingly less so. Consider these remarks from Adam Perlman, the speech therapist:

> One of the main things that happens with forgiveness is acceptance—of somebody's shortcomings—acceptance that people are going to make mistakes. And realizing that you're gonna make mistakes . . . also. How would you want to be treated? I don't think the person who's forgiven necessarily . . . has to feel remorse. They may not even be aware of what they did. I think it's a hard thing to do sometimes, but I think it's necessary for the person who's forgiving to be able to continue living—to really be free of their own frustration and anger. It's hard to live when you're angry. I don't think you can really be happy. And it takes a lot of courage to be able to forgive somebody, especially if they don't acknowledge that they've done something wrong.

Or these, from Thelma Winters, the retired home health aide:

> KTG: When you say, "I forgive you," what's happening in your mind?
>
> TW: Nothing happening in my mind . . . I keep it throwed out of my mind. Though the Devil gonna bring it back all the time, but . . . you don't have to receive it. Just throw it out—just know that's the Devil talking to you—and just go on about your business. . . .
>
> If I'm gonna forgive a person, I don't want to bring it up no more . . . When me and my husband separated—I mean, had a fuss or something like—and he apologized with me, and maybe I quit him about it—but if I take him back then—I

mean, I forgive him... I don't bring it up no more. If I'm going to go back to him, ain't no use bringing it up... And I'm like that way about anything—anybody else. Don't want to keep bringing it up. If the good Lord done forgived him... how am I gonna hold it against him? I don't believe in that.

And this response from Mary Bono, the receptionist:

> MB: It's kind of a nice feeling to forgive somebody. It makes you feel at ease. You feel like you're a kind of a human being... It makes the life easier—to forgive somebody...
>
> KTG: What kind of steps are you going through in your mind when you decide to forgive the incident?...
>
> MB: It's just the way you feel it. He's a human being. He could do a lot of things, but still there is a chance he could change, so, why not give him a chance?...I have my limits. I could forgive him two times, three times, four times, but then, until then that's it to me....

Or finally, these words from Clarence Peters, the glazing contractor:

> Forgiveness is a quality that we should all... strive to have... It's a part of good living—honest living—I'd say a Christian way of living. To forgive, and to put everything equal as if it hadn't happened, is a good trait. It puts the other person at ease, and he will be able to operate more cleanly, with more freedom of mind.

In addition to being questioned about their general understanding of the notion of forgiveness, participants were asked also whether it was possible to forgive those who are not sorry, whether forgiveness might play any role in solving our social problems, and whether forgiveness is an action that may be employed by whole communities or societies, as well as by individuals. Again, there were no significant differences between the dissenters and the believers in their responses to these questions. Nearly everyone thought that the answer to each of these queries was yes—of course with some qualifications. Only on the last question did even a small, but interesting, trend show up. Here is the complete text of the question I posed:

> Would you say that forgiveness is a concept that can only be put into effect between individuals, or could a whole community or society use it? Is it possible, for instance, for a nation to forgive another nation, or for a city to forgive the kids who cover its subways with graffiti?

Interestingly, three of the harshest believers—though they made no broad argument against the notion of collective forgiveness—took pains to distinguish between the different sections of my question. Barbara Damon, the transportation official: "It would be nice to think that a nation could forgive another nation. [But] I wouldn't want to forgive a kid for writing graffiti all over the walls. So I don't think a city would want to." James Morton, the masonry contractor: "Don't touch on graffiti! Boy, that's a sore point with me. I find no necessity for that ... I don't know if I could ever forgive anybody for graffiti ... But for a nation to forgive another one for an act—I think that maybe that's a possibility, and sure it's something we should explore more." And Drew Snowden, the banker: "I can forgive lying about Chernobyl more than I can kids with graffiti. It's hopeless! [But] I think nations can forgive other nations." So for some of the harshest participants at least, there is the tendency to back off quickly from considering even the feasibility of forgiveness, when confronted with this highly vivid image of crime.

Finally, participants were asked for their views on the concept of vengeance. Nearly unanimously, they assert that such behavior is at all times inappropriate. One dissenter and two believers do leave open the possibility that there might exist some situation in which vengeance was called for. But no one advocates it. And the believers are no less vehement than the dissenters when they denounce it. Richard Niederhaus, the software designer (a dissenter): "I think generally vengeance is an emotional act of overinvolvement and egotism and therefore really has no place in justice, punishment, crime." Miriam Madamba, the secretary (a believer): "I don't think it solves anything—doing wrong to someone who has done wrong to you. It only makes matters worse." Victor Rodriguez, the government administrator (a dissenter): "Vengeance is an irrational reaction to something that affected you. Vengeance is basically animalistic behavior." And James Morton, the masonry contractor (a believer): "It's a terrible thing. It's someone with a bunch of bottled up anger that they can't get out of their system. And then it means that they are about ready to explode, to me ... It would be nice if those kind of people could meet over a table, share a cup of coffee, ... and talk out their problems. And then the problem wouldn't exist anymore."

Clearly then, the hypothesis that the dissenters might be persons who place significantly more value in the concept of forgiveness, or who are much more repulsed by the notion of vengeance, is not at all supported by these interviews. Given their major difference in views as to the treatment of criminal offenders, these two groups are remarkably alike in their feelings about forgiveness and vengeance. This finding, though negative, is of considerable importance; it will be discussed further in the concluding chapter.

These believers and dissenters, despite all their important differences of opinion on penal sanctions, exhibit almost no significant differences in their experiences and attitudes regarding a large collection of related matters. Feelings about forgiveness and vengeance, perceptions of the courts, attitudes about victims, levels of information about crime and criminal justice—inquiries into these and several other areas produced no evidence that would suggest even a partial explanation for the divergence of opinion between the two groups.

Several other inquires proved more fruitful. Let us turn now to those explanatory hypotheses that *were* supported by these interviews.

Explanatory Factors

An explanation for the divergence of opinion between the dissenters and the believers can be drawn from the following evidence, but it is an explanation that comes in pieces. No single "chromosome" has been discovered, the presence of which would absolutely determine the criminological persuasion of its holder. Instead, the evidence points to a number of factors that in some combination may work to fertilize the ground in which dissenting views can grow and be maintained.

Before moving on to examine these explanatory factors, let me make a clear distinction between this task and those that were undertaken in the preceding chapters. In chapter 3, I sought to describe *conscious* motivations for participants' views on criminal justice: thus I focused on those values and deep concerns that the interviewees themselves invoke in order to explain what they are trying to achieve with the policies they support. In chapter 4, I looked for connections between criminal justice views and general political belief systems. There, I suggested *logical* links between a participant's broader political beliefs and his or her policy views about criminal justice—links that that participant may not necessarily have described or acknowledged and, indeed, links of which he or she may not even be aware. In this chapter, I seek to explain why these rare dissenters hold views that are so different from those of the rest of the American public. Here I will be examining influences upon the participants that are primarily *psychological* in nature—that is, they involve people's feelings, experiences, and internal defenses. As we will shortly see, distinctive patterns of this sort occur with strikingly greater frequency among the dissenters than among the believers.

Empathy for Offenders

To suggest that dissenters may to a larger degree than believers feel empathy for persons who commit criminal offenses is to propose a hypothesis at least as intuitive as any that have been discussed so far. This time, however, the evidence of these interviews supports the hypothesis. Participants were subjectively rated on their level of empathy for offenders: all but one of the dissenters was judged to have a high level of empathy, while all of the believers were judged to have a medium to low level. Given the statements of participants that have been presented in earlier chapters, this finding should come as no great surprise.

A trickier question is *why*? Why are some people, so much more than others, able to empathize with these individuals who for the most part have both hurt and been hurt? Thomas Dow, using research on Ivy League and state university students during the 1960s, has suggested that the negative attitude of the public toward offenders results from the inability of the former group to identify with the latter.[15] Perhaps this is an avenue to explore. To what degree, if any, do my interviewees have reasons to be able easily to picture themselves in the shoes of criminal offenders?

Toward the end of the first interview, participants were asked whether they or any of their family, friends, or acquaintances ever had been arrested, indicted, convicted, or imprisoned for a crime. Nearly everybody knew somebody who had been in this situation. But there was a significant difference between the dissenters and the believers when the circle was drawn in closer to home. Seven of the nine dissenters, but only four of the thirteen believers, had either been in such a situation themselves, or had a close family member who had been. These experiences are worth recounting. First, the dissenters:

> Richard Niederhaus, the software designer, was sentenced to probation as a teenager after participating in an antiwar sit-in. He is currently serving a nonincarcerative sentence for a nonviolent offense, regarding which he asserts his innocence. Richard also has a brother who has served prison time for a property offense.
>
> Abby Edwards, the community college instructor, has a son who a few years ago had accumulated traffic fines that he was unable to pay. He decided simply to serve the few days of jail time that would be required to eliminate the fines. While in jail, he was raped. We also heard in chapter 3 about the brother-in-law whose positive changes, despite a long history of crime and incarceration, had such an influence upon Abby's views.
>
> Burt Ruebel, the photographer, was once sentenced to probation plus a fine for drunk driving. Two of his siblings also have been arrested— one for drunk driving, another for shoplifting.
>
> Anne Girard, the aspiring writer, has a son who was arrested and held overnight after a fight in which he slugged an influential person.

Daniel Steinbach, the social worker, committed a variety of thefts as a juvenile and was incarcerated for a year.

Olivia Hassan, the bank teller, has a brother who has been charged, but never tried, for various offenses.

As a young man, Dexter Lane, the insurance agent, served a month's pretrial detention and then probation for a property crime, in an odd case of mistaken identity. At a later date, the charge was dismissed by a court and the offense expunged from his record. He has also been held overnight on several occasions for traffic offenses. Dexter has a brother who was incarcerated as a juvenile for armed robbery.

A few believers have had similar experiences:

Aram Isaac, the college-educated truck driver, has been the victim of false arrest and spent several days in jail before the mistake was cleared up.

Thelma Winters, the retired home health aide, has a grandson who as a juvenile has been incarcerated for offenses involving both burglary and drugs.

Violet Taylor, the retired waitress, has a niece—with whom she is very close—who has served time both in jail and in a halfway house.

Drew Snowden, the banker, has a son who has been arrested and charged with a serious traffic offense.

As a group, then, the dissenters I interviewed naturally may find it easier than the believers to imagine themselves in the shoes of criminal offenders. Most of the dissenters have had some firsthand experience either of being on the wrong side of the law—deservedly or undeservedly—or of relating to someone near and dear who was in that position. Few of the believers have had this experience. Perhaps, then, the dissenters are more easily able to look at criminal offenders and to say: this could be me, this could be my brother, this could be my son.

None of this is to say that experiences such as these directly lead persons to dissenting views. But it does suggest that they may be among a number of factors that, working together, create a fertile environment in which dissenting views may grow.[16]

Nonjudgmental Outlook

When this study was in its earliest stages, I spoke about it with a friend, explaining that I was seeking some understanding of why most people have harsh views about crime, and a few do not. Her response: "We are all just so judgmental." Here, then, is the germ of another hypothesis. What evidence can these interviews bring to this question? Is there any reason to believe that the dissenters are actually less judgmental about matters relevant to the crime issue than everybody else?

Let us turn first to the interviewees' views about the major causes of crime. When the believers hold forth on this issue, a substantial majority of them talk about a combination of causes—some of which imply nonjudgmental feelings on the participant's part, and others of which imply judgmental feelings. A believer may, for instance, mention unemployment, inadequate parenting, or poor schooling, but together with it he or she also mentions greed, the belief that one can get away with crime, or the evil inherent in human beings. Each and every dissenter, however, cites *only* causes of crime that imply nonjudgmental feelings—lack of self-esteem, the stresses of urban living, child abuse, mental illness, lack of housing, the demise of the family, and so on. In short, the dissenters mention only causes that suggest that some of the responsibility for the offense should be lifted from the shoulders of the individual offender.

Next we can turn to some questions that were asked near the end of the second interview, in a context purposefully divorced from the discussion of crime. Participants were asked for their feelings regarding four groups of people: the poor, the unemployed, dropouts, and people addicted to drugs and alcohol. Of course, most of the occupants of our prisons and jails are persons who are members of one or more of these groups.[17] So a consideration of whether there are notable differences between the dissenters and the believers in the degree to which they speak judgmentally of these groups should be highly relevant.

Almost never did a dissenter speak judgmentally of any one of these groups. Not one dissenter gave a judgmental description of the poor, dropouts, or addicts. Only in regard to the unemployed is there some small exception to this disinclination. This answer, from Olivia Hassan, the bank teller, is as judgmental as they come, for the dissenters:

> KTG: Now, what about unemployed people? Do you think most unemployed people really are willing and anxious to work, or do we have high unemployment because so many people are lazy or too picky about the kinds of jobs they're willing to take?
>
> OH: I don't feel real confident on giving an opinion on that because I'm not clear—I know they say that there are a lot of jobs out there, but I'm not clear of just how many jobs and what kind they are, out there. I do have a feeling, based on people I know, that people do have a tendency ... they have very high

expectations of jobs based on what they see on TV, based on
what jobs that they've had before, or something like that, to
not accept something beneath a certain level and try and work
their way back, or their way up, period. So I think that some
people are very unreal about how you get into the work world.

Three other dissenters do speak of the problem of people who choose
government assistance over minimum-wage jobs. But they emphasize the
socially created disincentives against their working and do not speak
judgmentally of the *individuals* who make these choices. Hear, for instance,
Dexter Lane, the insurance agent:

We have to take into account how one is conditioned. The welfare
system conditions persons, rewards persons, for not working, and to
that extent should be revised—eliminated, to some degree. Therefore,
with that caveat, most people would like to feel good about themselves
in terms of being able to produce . . . they would like to work. So most
people that are unemployed do not wish to be unemployed.

Thus, in all, there is a near complete lack of judgmental sentiments
expressed by the dissenters about the groups under discussion.

When we turn to the believers the picture changes noticeably. Asked
about drug addicts and alcoholics, only four of the thirteen believers
expressed completely nonjudgmental sentiments. Representative of the comments that the others made are these, from James Morton, the masonry
contractor:

They have completely given up on life. They know that they are not
going to be the big winner. They are not going to be a lawyer or a
doctor or a corporation president. And . . . although they wouldn't admit
it, they have probably proven that they are a loser, and this is a
manifestation of it.

Or these, from Barbara Damon, the transportation department official:

It's an easy out, I guess. It's a nice way to hide from reality. I don't
know if it's an easy way—it's expensive. I mean, if you could tunnel
some of that money—these people would be millionaires.

And these, from Violet Taylor, the retired waitress:

Because they get free money. All they do is wait for that check to come. A lot of them don't feed the kids. They start doping as soon as that check comes. If it comes eight o'clock, by twelve o'clock—oh, man—they partyin' back. But the rest of the month, they broke. Free money. Now if they would have to get out and work for that money, I don't think they would do it, but they lay around in their housecoats all day, and they wait for these checks to come and meet friends together, and they have a party. And that's every day of their life, till they get broke—and that goes on every month, for years.

The believers are more evenly balanced in their comments regarding the poor and the unemployed. About half of the believers express fairly nonjudgmental sentiments about each group. The rest have significant objections to the behavior of these groups. On poverty, for instance, hear Miriam Madamba, the secretary:

> *MM:* How did they come to be poor? I know that some single parents—like they are victims of divorce—they have not been trained to work, so they rely on welfare, and then they mostly have little kids, so they can't go out to work. And then I see some of these people in San Francisco who sit on the corners begging for money. Some of them—like the old people— probably don't want to be cooped up in a place where they keep these vagrants, so they prefer to stay out in the streets. *I don't know about those able-bodied people, how they can stand sitting on the corner, begging for alms....* (Emphasis added.)
>
> *KTG:* Do you think there are many able-bodied people doing that kind of thing?
>
> *MM:* It's like half. Some are old people, but the other half are able-bodied.

Or Clarence Peters, the glazing contractor:

> Part of it can be blamed on ... ignorance, because of poor schooling— poor attitude at school, perhaps when they had a chance for an education. And then when ... the chances were given them, they did not take advantage of the opportunities and preferred dole than work ... And there are circumstances where a person has tried to some extent and then has given up and prefers then a life of poverty than a regular life ... But also there is such things as ... abusing alcohol or

drugs, and there're certain habits that have been formed which have been bad, and principally the gambling that causes a good many people to be poor. Poor judgment in buying—spending the money that they have had . . . causes a good many people to be poor. Or allowing someone else to take advantage of them, and taking what money they might have had—and/or property.

On unemployment, there are comments like these from Violet Taylor, when I ask whether most unemployed people are "willing and anxious to work" or "lazy and too picky": "Too lazy . . . That's it—too lazy. They want somethin' for nothin'." Or these, from James Morton:

> I think that there is a very sizable portion of people who have grown up in some sort of a welfare environment that choose not to work because they find it not necessary, because the government gives them stamps for this and stamps for that. And illegitimate offspring become a way of life, and they are subsidized for their housing . . . They are not living in the lap of luxury . . . but by the same token, they are free to do whatever they want with what would have been their working day . . . And the guy might . . . elect to sell dope and maybe make more than everybody around him who are supporting government. And if it is a gal—God knows what she might be doing. . . .
>
> An awful lot of [unemployed people] make unemployment kind of like a way of life. Our unemployment insurance is another causative factor. It is too cushy. It doesn't make a person want to go out there and work, when they could be home in their own house, and getting paid for it—or whatever it is that they do with their time—maybe it's running out to the racetrack . . . .

Here, we find the same sort of argument that was expressed by some dissenters—that government is creating disincentives for certain people to work. But in this case, there are also judgmental remarks directed at the *individuals* who respond in this manner.

Then there is the topic of school dropouts. Here, the believers sound much more like the dissenters. Only three believers have judgmental comments to make about *kids* who drop out of school. When blame is assigned by the rest, it falls on parents, on the schools, and on poverty.

But in sum, when participants' sentiments about all four groups are considered, the differences between the dissenters and the believers are striking. The believers are a mixed group: some of them are much more judgmental than others; and individual believers generally are not uniformly judgmental across all of the questions. By contrast, the dissenters present a nearly uniform field of nonjudgmental feelings about the poor, the unemployed, dropouts, and the addicted.

Next, let us turn to two questions—also in the second interview, in a context removed from the issue of crime—that touched on the subject of failure: (1) In general, how difficult would you say it is for people to make their own lives better? (2) Some people's lives don't ever seem to get any better, or sometimes even get worse. Do you think that happens very much? Why do you think that happens? Criminal offenders certainly are experiencing some degree of failure in life—the criminal act perhaps being only the latest of many failures. So the extent to which dissenters and believers give judgmental answers to these questions—addressing failure in a more generic sense—should be relevant here.

A comparison between the responses of the dissenters and the believers reveals a picture very similar to that seen in their answers regarding the poor and the other groups discussed above. Among the dissenters, an answer that could be considered somewhat judgmental is given by only one individual—Olivia Hassan. Here, she speaks to the second question:

> I know people like that! ... They are just very comfortable. It's like, there's two somethings inside of them, and one area is very comfortable ... The other place that knows better is like—they'll try for a while to do better, but they just—for whatever was in that old way of being, they just go back to being that. It's just that they're more comfortable doing whatever they are doing.

In contrast, about half of the believers give answers that could be considered judgmental. Take, for instance, Miriam Madamba, the secretary, on the first question:

> *MM:* How difficult? It would depend upon their philosophy of life. Like I said, if they are content to be beggars, or they don't have incentive enough to look for a decent job, they stay there—for all they care.
> *KTG:* If you have the incentive or the will, does that make it easy to make your life better, or not?
> *MM:* Yes—if you have the will, and you study to raise your way of living. I think if there's a will, there's a way.

Or Barbara Damon, on the second question:

Why does it happen? Part of me wants to say because they want it to happen. The other part says, 'cause they are not willing to make the effort for it not to happen.

And Clarence Peters, on the second question:

I don't know that I can answer except to say too many dwell on self-pity and don't want to improve themselves—use excuses as to why they can't.

Thus, once again, the believers are a mixed bag, as we might expect any general assortment of people to be—some are very judgmental, some mildly so, and others not at all. But the dissenters stand out as quite different: judgmental attitudes about stagnation and failure are nearly absent from this group.

Finally, we might consider the area of "victimless crime." Participants were asked early on whether or not they felt that such acts should be considered criminal offenses and were given the examples of prostitution, gambling, and possession (as distinguished from sale) of illegal drugs. Seven of the nine dissenters either felt absolutely that these acts should not be considered crimes or felt that in some cases they should and in other cases they should not. But only four of the thirteen believers held either of these views.[18] Again, the views of the dissenters are strikingly less judgmental: the vast majority subscribe to the view that the criminal justice system has been assigned the task of responding to (judging) some behaviors that should either be accepted or be dealt with by social service agencies.

Considering all four areas that have been discussed—the causes of crime, explanations for poverty and other social problems, reasons for failure, and decriminalization of victimless acts—the dissenters, as a group, give a remarkably nonjudgmental collection of answers. This is not to say that they are wholly nonjudgmental persons. Kate Fontana rants about people with "Moral Majority" views; Burt Ruebel and Dexter Lane are quite judgmental toward the powers that be. It is more that the dissenters do not choose to be judgmental *in this arena*. And the believers are by no means their polar opposites: sometimes they are judgmental, sometimes not. But this is still a striking difference. These interviews definitely lend support to the proposition that a lack of relevant judgmental feelings is a significant factor in the formation of dissenting views regarding responses to crime.

Such a finding is consistent with the results of two other studies. Arthur

Stinchcombe et al. only speculated that "people who have a complex and merciful view of criminal responsibility are likely to be less punitive than those who believe that all offenders are criminals."[19] But a few years later Francis Cullen and his colleagues suggested a similar hypothesis and found it to be sustained in an analysis of written questionnaires completed by about 150 residents of Galesburg, Illinois:

> We hypothesize that those who hold a classical understanding of crime causation and hence believe that crime flourishes because it is a rational, utilitarian enterprise will be more punitive than those positivists in our sample who see crime as a manifestation of social constraint and social ills.[20]

And Dennis Cook, in an analysis of telephone interviews with 225 residents of Lincoln, Nebraska, found support for his hypothesis that "Belief about the Causes of Crime has an independent causal effect on Belief about the Best Treatment of Criminals."[21]

Liberal Attitudes

William Watts and Lloyd Free, in an analysis of a 1976 national poll, found that the category of respondents most receptive to prison reform and ghetto improvement was "self-designated liberals."[22] Vicki McNickle Rose obtained similar results in a Washington State poll taken a year earlier: "It appears that the more conservative respondents consider themselves, the less receptive they are to change and/or innovation in correctional systems."[23] And Stinchcombe and his colleagues, in their 1980 analysis of national poll data, found a small correlation between "general liberalism" (as measured by a civil liberties index) and lack of punitiveness.[24] However, they find that when they "examine this relationship in more detail, even the slight relationship of punitiveness and liberalism seems to be mostly due to a very few extreme liberals."[25] They elaborate further:

> In summary, there may be a small part of the total population, roughly 1 percent, whose members tend to answer all liberalism questions in a liberal direction *and* who also answer liberally those questions that have to do with punishments for crimes. The rest of the population sees a weaker connection between these questions of Enlightenment liberalism (civil liberties, sexual liberalism, feminism, and abortion liberalism) and the treatment of criminals by the courts.[26]

The earlier research has two implications for this study. First, it is clear that liberalness alone does not a dissenter make (indeed, the vast majority of Stinchcombe liberals are not dissenters), but it is probably one of those factors that, in combination with others, may coalesce to encourage the growth of dissenting views. Second, we should expect that the group of dissenters interviewed here will be comprised primarily of individuals holding quite liberal views.

This is indeed the case. Each respondent was asked this question: "Generally speaking, do you tend to think of yourself as a liberal, a conservative, or as something else?" All but one of the dissenters used the label "liberal" as at least part of their self-description.[27] (Only three believers called themselves liberals.)[28] Further, when respondents were scored on a twelve-point scale aimed at approximating just how liberal they would have been judged to be by Stinchcombe and his associates, seven of the nine dissenters scored 12, while the remaining two scored 11 and 11.5.[29] (Seven believers scored 10 and above; six scored below 10.)[30]

Finally, I used a broader definition of liberalism and conservatism than the one employed by Stinchcombe et al. to make my own evaluation of each participant.[31] Here, eight of the nine dissenters were categorized as liberals, while one was judged to be middle-of-the-road. (Among the believers, five were labeled liberals, four middle-of-the-road, and four conservatives.) Thus, by their own description, by a standard similar to that used by Stinchcombe et al., and by my definition, the dissenters are a group of liberal people. The believers, however, are like the public at large—persons of assorted persuasions.

Tolerance without Distress

Other analysts have suggested explanations for differences in harshness that hinge on attitudes somewhat related to the liberalism on which Stinchcombe et al. focused. In a 1984 study, Stuart Scheingold wrote:

> [The] data reveal that various forms of incivility or unusual behavior "may be interpreted as a sign of the social disorder and moral decay of which crime is a part and hence, be as threatening as more victim-oriented crime." Crime can become a convenient symbol for condensing a variety of stresses in our lives. Our frustrations are simply redirected into the issue of street crime for which punishment, we have learned, is a swift and effective remedy. According to this way of thinking, support for cracking down on criminals may be generated by

a convergence of cultural forces rather tenuously linked to a concern with the kinds of predatory street crime that threaten life, limb, or property.[32]

And in 1985 Francis Cullen, Gregory Clark, and John Wozniak offered this speculation about why harsh attitudes regarding crime have "reached high levels in recent times":

> Much of the answer, we suspect, lies in the general crisis in authority that confronted the nation and its people during the decade beginning in the late 1960's. As a number of commentators have argued, events ranging from Attica to Kent State, from urban riots to student protests, from women's liberation to humanistic secularism, and from failure in Vietnam to corruption in the Oval Office, all combined to rob people of their confidence in the prevailing order. Society seemed to be falling apart, and this prospect worried many Americans. In this context, rising crime rates became a source of special concern and fear because they signified, in Quinney's words, "the ultimate crack in the armor of the existing order." Similarly, the ostensible weakening of the social fabric led citizens to wonder if the discipline and traditional authority of previous days should not be forcefully invoked.[33]

We have seen that neither in terms of fear, nor in terms of the salience of the problem, does crime disturb the believers significantly more than the dissenters. But speculations like these just quoted should spur us to ask whether anything else of relevance is disturbing them differentially.

Here, the contrast between the believers and the dissenters is a stark one. In the realm of noncriminal, but not universally accepted, behaviors, all of the believers find certain things that are disturbing to them. And nearly all of the dissenters do not. Let us consider the views of five believers, chosen to display the continuum of their group's attitudes in this realm; the remaining believers are spread out more or less evenly between these five.

Clarence Peters, the glazing contractor, is clearly the most bothered of the believers. He believes that premarital sex is always wrong and opposes abortion except in cases of rape. He feels that homosexuality is "unbearable" and that gay persons, having abused the laws of nature, do not deserve equal rights. He agrees with the statement that "most men are better suited emotionally for politics than are most women" and advocates discrimination against women in job promotions because he considers them unstable employees: "So many of them are only filling in time until... [they] can get married and retire to a home life." Clarence disapproves of marriages between persons of different races and says of racism and discrimination:

"I don't think it exists as much as people think it does."[34] Particularly in Oakland, there is less discrimination than in other parts of the country, he asserts, and "the time that they would feel discriminated against would be circumstances that they have brought on by themselves." In a different context, he criticizes the behavior of recent immigrants to this country:

> [Something] that has bothered me is to find . . . groups such as the Orientals—Chinese—coming in from Hong Kong and forming gangs and taking things into their own hands . . . This has happened also with Vietnamese, or Laotians, I believe . . . The Mexican has taken a good many things into his own hands—he's demanded certain rights that haven't been given to him yet. . . .
>
> I'm inclined to think there are a good many immigrants coming into this country that aren't willing to work . . . I know the Cubans have created quite a problem in Florida. The Mexicans, . . . the Vietnamese, and especially the Chinese have created many problems in California.

Asked whether or not a book that supports communism should be allowed to remain in the public library, Clarence replies: "I'd favor removing it . . . Communism has no part in our democracy." Similarly, he objects to allowing someone who is against all churches and religion to make a speech in Oakland. And about the movements of the 1960s, he remarks: "I do still disagree with the hippie era. I think that too much energy was spent trying to destroy something that we had, instead of trying to improve it . . . They degraded themselves terribly to prove points, and they could have used that same amount of energy for self-improvement." Plainly, the world is brimful of people behaving in ways of which Clarence Peters disapproves. He marks the far end of the continuum of "botheredness" among the believers.

A step or two down the continuum is Sadie Monroe, the retired physical education teacher. She favors removing a book about communism from the library and opposes allowing an antireligious speech to be given in her city: "We need churches and religion. If they against it, there's no place for 'em in this society." She agrees with the statement that men generally are better suited for politics than women: "That's why we have so many more [men] than women." And she believes that people are less moral today than they were thirty or forty years ago:

> I think they're less moral. You look at the movies and the ones that live together, and they used to wouldn't dare think of livin' with someone unless they was married . . . And half of the movies are nude and all . . . Years ago they didn't show nude people on the movies.

Not far from Sadie is Gladys Jones, the hospital clerk, who also believes that men are generally better suited for politics than are women: "Most women have been in the home. They haven't been out in surroundings much as the men...And the women [are] more a motherly type figure." She advocates removing a book about communism from the public library: "I don't like communism." And she agrees with the statement that too many people in this country no longer have the proper respect for authority: "[It's] because of the top officials in the country, that are wrong, I guess. That's what they say, all the time. Too much corruption in government, local and national...That's one reason."

> Everything—the system has changed. Right now in government, in everything, it's a breakdown... Marriage, family, the whole structure. Authority to a lot of people don't mean anything anymore. I say in the last fifteen to twenty years, it changed quite a bit.

And at another point in our conversations:

> When I came out here [to California] in [the late 1960s] where they had this—well it was a movement going or something—the hippies and what not ... Before that, when I lived back in [the Midwest], people— they wouldn't never live together, anything like that. They'd always get married. But when I came back here I saw it was different—the moral standard.

However, Gladys expresses a principle of tolerance for certain of the behaviors that bother her. On homosexuality: "I don't like it, but still...they have their rights to do what they want...It's gotten out of proportion, and I don't think it's too much you can do about it now." On allowing a gay person to teach high school: "I think he should be able to teach 'cause I don't think he'd harm any of the students, or anything, as long as he teaches what they supposed to learn." Then, on abortion: "I don't like abortion. But I think a woman should have a right to do what she wants to."

Another step or two down the continuum would be Miriam Madamba, the secretary, who is bothered only by premarital sex and homosexuality. On the former: "I think it is wrong. But human nature such as it is, we find more and more couples having sexual relations before they are married." And on the latter: "I think it's sinful, but we have to be forgiving and accept them, because we're not perfect ourselves."

Finally, there is Adam Perlman, the speech therapist, who is the least bothered of the believers. He hems and haws and expresses some misgivings about abortion, but essentially concludes that he does not want to make a decision on that issue at the present time. And when asked what should be done about racial prejudice and discrimination, he objects to certain forms of affirmative action:

> I'm not sure that I agree with trying to compensate by going overboard and excluding—you have say a black and a white, and they're applying for the same job, and ... the white has more qualifications, but the black got the job because blacks have been excluded. I think it has to go on qualifications and on which person you think would fit in better at the job. And I think that should be regardless of what their race is or their religion is ... If you can find a case where a particular person ... had been discriminated against, maybe in that ... particular case you can impose sanctions on that individual or company to pay back for the losses ... and force them to ... hire a quota of minorities. But I don't think it should be an across-the-board thing in all ways of life.

But this is the extent of his disquiet.

On the whole, then, the believers are a pretty bothered group of Americans, considering that the remaining eight individuals are spread out fairly evenly amid these five. Most are not intolerant of everything that bothers them. In many instances they *choose* to honor the rights of others to engage in behaviors that they themselves find immoral or distasteful. But this cannot erase the underlying fact that on a gut level, they find various of the legal activities of their fellow citizens to be disturbing.

Turning to the dissenters, the picture is nearly the reverse image of the one just examined. Only one dissenter is much bothered by the sorts of things that disturbed the believers. Dexter Lane, the insurance agent, believes that abortion is "homicide" and that it should be outlawed except in cases in which the health of the mother or fetus is endangered. When asked whether or not he agrees with the statement that "Too many people in this country just don't have the proper respect for authority anymore," he replies:

> I would agree with that ... Basically I'm looking at the family and I'm thinking less of our political and legal institutions. It's healthy ... to challenge authority especially when it's presented to you from a nonbenevolent source ... But in the family situation, the lack of respect for authority—I use it in a sense of lack of respect for a system of rules and a system of values, and that lack of respect I think is the cause for much of the exercise of this bundle of what I call harmful free-

doms ... resulting in the demise of large groups of talented persons, who would otherwise live longer and contribute more to the well-being of humankind ... Say, for example, the freedom to engage in promiscuous sexual activity—one takes a chance ... of being killed from a disease ...

Dexter also believes that in "almost every way" people today are less moral than they were a decade or two ago:

There's less respect for family ... less respect for persons of differing cultural and ethnic backgrounds ... less respect for achieving on one's own effort, as opposed to achieving through some form of deceit— using an example of the widespread cheating that goes on in high schools and colleges now ... So the lack of moral fiber—moral fortitude—in this society is substantially less than it was fifteen to twenty years ago. And it's tapering off.

And he remarks at a later point:

In growing up, just looking at the behavior of not only my parents, but also my peers ... there was a great deal of tolerance of what I would consider to be now fairly aberrant, non-Christian, criminal behavior ....

Dexter, then, is very much the exception among the dissenters. Beyond him, about as close as any dissenter comes to expressing the sort of feelings that are under scrutiny here might be Abby Edwards's comment on my question about changes in morality over the past several decades:

I would have to say less ... I may be wrong about that ... I think people are less considerate of each other ... than they used to be. Maybe it's as we get bigger ... you're not so dependent on your neighbor—you're less considerate of him. I don't really know. I like to think of back in the olden days, when people depended on each other a lot more for what they have, that they respected each other more.

But this is pretty pale when compared to the remarks we have heard from the believers. Overall, we find a group of dissenters who are almost universally undisturbed by the types of behavior or presumptions that, in large or small measure, rattle all of the believers. These dissenters are not just liberal and tolerant, they are also unbothered. Here, it seems, is another of those factors that contribute to the creation of an environment in which dissenting views may grow.

Religious Questioning

In a 1975 article that reviewed the literature on public perceptions of crime, Graeme Newman and Carol Trilling wrote: "The one variable which has produced clear and consistent findings ... is that of strength of religious belief: the stronger the religious belief, the more punitive and indignant the response is likely to be."[35] Taking a somewhat different focus, Dennis Cook, in a 1979 survey in Lincoln, Nebraska, found that religious *orthodoxy* had no "significant, direct effect" upon respondents' "beliefs about the best treatment of criminals."[36] Finally, with yet another focus, national polling by the National Opinion Research Center has shown that respondents who subscribe to no religion are consistently less likely than Protestants, Catholics, or Jews to state that the courts are "not harsh enough" on criminals.[37] Certainly the evidence of the past two chapters indicates that this may be a profitable angle to consider: religious or spiritual beliefs appeared to be key influences in the lives of most of the complex believers and of those whose criminal justice views were not fully grounded in their political belief systems.

The existing analyses focus on different variables in different ways, yielding results that are at worst contradictory and at best difficult to cumulate. And two of the three studies fail to offer information about the criminological beliefs of respondents who subscribe to nontraditional religions. What more can we learn about the role of religion from intensive interviewing?

Near the end of the second interview, participants were asked a series of questions concerning religion: their religious affiliation, the degree to which religion was important to them in their daily living, the content of their religious beliefs, and so forth. In addition, there was the opportunity simply to be in the presence of each interviewee for a number of hours, noting the religious or spiritual references that peppered the conversations of some. I would assert that this allowed a much more reliable evaluation of religiosity than would a simple measure of church attendance (used in the first study referred to above).

Let us then consider first this issue of *strength* of religious or spiritual beliefs. Based on my overall evaluation of each participant's remarks, there are no striking differences between the strength of the beliefs exhibited by the dissenters as opposed to those of the believers. Seven of the nine dissenters seemed "highly religious or spiritual," as did half (seven out of thirteen) of the believers. Such a finding obviously stands in opposition to the results of the first study mentioned above.

Striking differences do emerge, however, in two other areas. First, there is a huge difference in the degree to which members of the two groups subscribe to religions that could be considered traditional in the United States.[38] All but two of the believers adhere (in varying degrees, of course) to such traditional religions—Judaism, Catholicism, and a variety of Protestant denominations. But only one dissenter has a traditional religious affiliation: Kate Fontana, the nurse-midwife, is a Catholic.

Second, there is a huge difference in the degree to which members of the two groups have questioned, and then changed, their religious beliefs. Not one dissenter was *raised* with the nontraditional beliefs (or lack of beliefs) that he or she now holds; thus, eight out of nine in this group at some point made a conscious decision to depart from the religious teachings of their youth. By contrast, only two of the believers have seriously questioned and then changed their beliefs. Consider, for example, these dissenters:

Abby Edwards, the community college instructor, was raised a Protestant. She still considers herself a Christian, but having been influenced by the study of yoga, she has adopted beliefs in karma and reincarnation that are "very, very important" to her.

> I believe in Christ, but I also believe that . . . people have the right to believe what they believe . . . I think sometimes that the Christians are a little prejudiced—some of the churches—because they think the only way to get to heaven or to God is through Jesus. And I don't believe that's true, although I believe that he was a supreme person.

Richard Niederhaus, the software designer, is the son of atheist parents, but as a child he attended a Protestant church with his grandmother. Today, he says he is a mystic, with leanings toward nondualistic yoga and Zen Buddhism.[39] "But I have a feeling for all the religious books and for people and their *striving* for religion—desire to be one."

Anne Girard, the aspiring writer, was raised a Catholic but no longer thinks of herself as a member of this faith. In recent years, she has followed a spiritual teacher. "My relationship to my creator . . . and being all that I can in this life is what is most important to me, and I think about it every day. And I live my life with that as the core of it, and toward that—being connected to the life force, and being in touch with the creation of my life." "There's an energy, a loving energy . . . that we are a part of and that we can know and we can enjoy. And we can learn what we're all about—what life is for."

Victor Rodriguez, the government administrator, was raised a Catholic but is no longer affiliated with any religion. Today, he says, "you can call me humanist type, with a little bit of maybe-something-is-happening-out-there. Still kind of a maybe. Because science has not proven it to me yet. I am open."

Dexter Lane, the insurance agent, was raised a Protestant but has investigated a number of faiths—Catholicism, Buddhism, Baha'i, and the ancient African religions. Now, however, he considers himself an Essene, asserting that Jesus was a member of the Hebrew sect that bore this name. He finds that many of the beliefs of the Christian, Jewish, and Coptic traditions coalesce in this faith.

Among the believers, however, only two individuals have changed their religious beliefs. Elizabeth Williams, the physical therapist, was raised a Catholic, but in her early twenties she entered into a "personal relationship with Christ" and could now be described as a Protestant evangelical. And Aram Isaac, for more than two decades a practicing Catholic, ultimately gave up all spiritual belief. He felt that he had the right to see some practical result from all his years of praying, attending church, contributing financially, and studying dogma and theology; and as this did not materialize, he reports, "I gave up."

This large difference between the dissenters and the believers in regard to religion may offer us considerable insight into the nature of the persons who hold these divergent criminological beliefs. The dissenters, it seems, are a group of questioners—a group composed almost exclusively of persons with a track record of challenging core beliefs. They have looked at traditional understandings about religious and spiritual issues, understandings that they and/or others have held dear, and have said, in effect: "This is not right," or "There must be something more." The personality that has challenged religious assumptions in this manner arguably is a personality that also will find it easier to make a challenge to other of the core assumptions with which most Americans have been raised—assumptions about crime and responses to crime most certainly being among them. In contrast, in the preceding chapters I have suggested that more traditional religious beliefs may have played a role in the formation of the criminal justice views of several of those believers who gave us the most reason to wonder why they were not dissenters: that is, the complex believers (who despite primary motivations in social critique or compassion were still believers); and the believers from chapter 4 (mostly the same individuals) whose harsh views were not consonant with their political belief systems.

Five areas in which the dissenters appear strikingly different from the believers have come under scrutiny here. What has been pieced together is a composite drawing of a prototypical dissenter: a person with a considerable empathy for offenders and a notable lack of judgmentalness in areas relevant to crime; a person who can be called a liberal and who also is undisturbed by various types of behavior that (though legal) are not universally accepted in our society; a person who is a questioner of traditional religious assumptions. A sixth factor—from the previous chapter—could join these: recall that each and every dissenter held a sophisticated political belief system in which his or her views on criminal justice appeared to be fully grounded.

This is by no means to say that an individual who fails to fit this profile in one or more of its elements will find it impossible to become a dissenter: indeed, the dissenters whose lives have been examined here do not all fit it in every regard.[40] Conceivably, an individual could become a dissenter without possessing any one of the attributes that have been discussed.[41] But we have striking evidence here that when a number of these key factors coalesce, they lay ground in which dissent can easily grow. I offer them as an explanation for differences that have been strangely resistant to reliable interpretation. These are explanations that have stood the test of in-depth interviewing; perhaps others will submit them to a quantitative review in a larger sample.

Personal Explanations for Dissent

Near the end of the first interview, participants were asked whether there had been any changes over time in their attitudes about criminal justice and, if so, why. Shortly thereafter, I pressed each dissenter to explain why he or she wound up with views on criminal justice that are so different from those held by most of the rest of the American public. Of course, this is the same question that I have been attempting to answer for myself throughout this chapter. So it is reasonable now to let these dissenters speak for themselves.

Although Kate Fontana, the nurse-midwife, developed most of her current views about crime and criminal justice only within the last decade, she feels that the foundation for her was the very strong sense of family, community, religion, and discipline that she received as a child. This helped her to develop a sense of right and wrong and gave her the self-esteem and security in her beliefs that allowed her to take the risk of moving thousands of miles from home to join a religious organization as a full-time volunteer working with the homeless. "What came out of that was this whole sense of awareness for me of social justice and the injustice of what exists today." Among the other members of this organization were persons who worked in the criminal justice system as "prisoner advocates who would go into prisons and . . . work for prison rights."

And so I learned all these things that I'd never heard of before ... and then you get into these circles ... You start thinking that everybody in the world are in these circles! And then you leave and you realize, no, you're wrong. You've become enlightened in your mind, but other people might think you've regressed.

Despite feeling that her early background was the ultimate foundation for her beliefs, Kate contrasts herself with the rest of her family in terms of the harsher views they still hold about criminal justice. "They look at it from a different angle," she says, "because they haven't read, maybe, or been given the education, or know that *people change*—people change with counseling, people change when they're ... helped to develop insight into their problems."

Abby Edwards, the community college instructor, reports that twenty years ago she was a supporter of capital punishment. "I really didn't know a lot who I was anyways, at that time. And other peoples' opinion meant a lot to me—that's what I based my thoughts on. And I don't do that anymore." For her, the major influence in a change of views was the study of yoga:

The ideals of yoga are more of a nonviolent nature. And if you look at everything nonviolently or nonjudgmentally, you just have to take a different look at the world, rather than saying this is the crime, and this is the punishment, and that sucker should be locked up.

Richard Niederhaus, the software designer, reports that he has always held the same views about criminal justice. Why did he turn out differently from the rest of the world: "Probably because I'm mixed races. I couldn't find anybody to relate to."[42]

Burt Ruebel, the photographer, describes his attitudes on criminal justice as having evolved over time but notes that he has held generally antiestablishment views since he was a child. On why he turned out to be a dissenter: "This is going to sound snotty, but I like to think ... I make a point of doing it. It is something of an obsession of mine." As a child, he notes, books were his best friends, and even today, the bottom line answer to my question seems to be, "I read books."

Daniel Steinbach, the social worker, notes that his views on criminal justice have changed several times during the course of his life. Early on, as has already been mentioned, he was himself a juvenile offender and served a period of incarceration. On the day he was released, he set out on foot to meet his mother at her workplace. He was tired and, spotting a car with the key in it, decided to steal it. Then, Daniel reports, "Something happened. I can't tell you what happened. Call it the hand of God, or whatever you want to call it, said, 'Hey, you don't wanna go back there,' and I didn't do it. That was my last crime." Some years later, in the late 1960s and the 1970s, Daniel "started to become a little bit more conservative as far as crime goes—in terms of leaning a little bit towards capital punishment, leaning a little bit towards throwing the keys away on some people ... not real conservative, but more conservative," especially as concerned violent crime. Finally, within the last decade, at a time of extreme crisis in his own life, he made a decision to get "in touch with other realities besides the scientific realities—ones you could measure and could verify ... And getting in touch with those other realities ... got me in touch with who I really am, and as a result of that my views changed on a lot of subjects."[43] In a nutshell, the source of his dissenting views: "going inside" himself.

As a young woman, Anne Girard, the aspiring writer, believed that murderers, kidnappers, and rapists should be given the death penalty immediately. Even in regard to lesser crimes, "I think maybe I felt more angry about it" and perhaps wanted to "punish them—get them—for what they did." She places the source of her changed views in "kind of an evolution within myself. Moving away from being judgmental with myself, and punitive, and critical." What kicked off the evolution? Besides the longer-term experiences of raising children and working with children, there was also a life crisis she endured: within the course of one year, she was divorced, lost a parent, and suffered a serious illness.

> It all just slowed me way down and opened me up to looking at things in a new way. And that included meditation, which I think has changed my life—has caused a real turning in a new direction—a transformation. And that's been gradual—to look inside myself ... daily, and in a quiet way. And to find there, something beneath all the emotions, and ... thoughts and ... ideas and ... judgments. To find there within myself something that's neutral ... It gives me strength, and that's where I feel that I get that positive, unconditional love right inside myself. And then see that that's the thing that I need—that other people need ... that that's the only thing that really nourishes and helps a person to be whole. ...

> And then I also did therapy for three and a half years and got in touch with my fears and my blamings and my judgments [of self] and saw how much of that goes on and how ineffective it all is ... So the meditation and the therapy both together have done all that transformation.

About his views on criminal justice, Victor Rodriguez, the government administrator, says, "It's a question of evolution," based on what he reads and on contacts with persons on both sides of the system.

I would say that the concept of rehabilitation—since I remember consciously thinking about this type of problem, I remember having that concept. The applicability of the concept to certain different people—that's what I have been, I think, changing, in a sense. I might have had a thought, years ago, that if you committed a crime—like snatching the purse of this poor lady, and beating her to pieces—you should go out—you know, the emotional reaction—you should go and be jailed ten years or something ... But after a while, you say, what good is that? What use is that?—putting into jail for doing that—when you go out and you're gonna do the same thing, only you are worse. I mean, what do we gain from that?

Why did he end up thinking differently than most of the rest of the public on this issue?

Maybe because I have never been a victim of crime. That might be a possibility. If I had been ... I might think differently, because I might react more emotionally....[44]

I think that basically I was brought up in a liberal household ... conservative politically and religiously, but also liberal in social thought ... We were brought up in a climate of no violence, a climate of help others ... I went to Catholic school, which—whatever you say about the Catholic school—they really strive to get into you some principles of life ... a lot of religious thought, moral thought. Of course, there is a lot more than that. But it does help.

Olivia Hassan, the bank teller, reports that she has gradually become more lenient than she used to be. When she was younger, she used to see things as being more "cut and dried." At that time, her views were very much shaped by those of her parents and of her grandmother, a strict fundamentalist Christian with whom she lived much of the time.

I had a very black-and-white view of right and wrong, which I don't have now. Now, I feel that I see more clearly reasons behind why people do things and that it's not black and white ... It's more difficult for me to make up my mind, just because I see more complications to what is right and wrong.

Olivia sees herself as having ideas on this subject that are quite different from those of most everybody she knows. I ask her why she thinks she ended up that way:

> I don't know ... That's hard ... I've just read a lot ... I think that I've always been interested in philosophies, in what people thought, how they thought that way, what it was like to think like a person—that type of thing, and how people come to decisions—that kind of thing. And plus, I work hard at being honest about what I'm thinking, what I'm feeling ... I think that I'm a lot more honest than a lot of people about things that they think—things that they do. . . .

Dexter Lane, the insurance agent, sees no major change in his attitudes on criminal justice over time. Here, he speaks to the question of why he, but so few others, adopted dissenting views:

> If we took each of those ideas, and we sat down with anyone, I think they would all agree that those are great ideas, but they would consider they are not attainable and too ideal. You take [even] the ... most conservative person ... would agree. . . .

> [The] only mitigating factor whereby these ideas would be different from ... the public at large is that it's a general human condition ... that human beings want vengeance if they ... feel that they've been done a wrong. They want their pound of flesh ... And this is why ... you ... find more people in favor of capital punishment than not ... because of the basic nature of humankind that says, vengeance is mine. And that's I guess basically where I would differ from the public at large on the capital punishment issue.

> On how to treat prisoners ... most people in the general public ... do not have the education or the understanding of human behavior to make that leap from saving money by not locking a person up and not throwing away the key. They see that as the only possible remedy. They haven't been educated as to the effectiveness of other remedies. So I don't consider that a real disagreement. I'd consider that a lack of enlightenment on the part of the general public ... as to what can be done with a human being. The public ... is generally pessimistic as to what kind of behavioral changes a human being can undergo. They figure a person ... who is engaged in criminal conduct is a permanent criminal, and that's it.

A dominant theme emerges from the explanations that these nine individuals offer, as we hear so many of them speak of thinking (especially independent thinking), reading, education, introspection, or broadening one's horizons. If there is a link between the explanations that these individuals give and those that I have myself presented, it lies in the proposition that these people have done some hard thinking and questioning. In the previous section, I showed that these are individuals who have been able to question the core assumptions of religious faith. In chapter 4, we saw that all of the dissenters hold sophisticated political belief systems in which their views on criminal justice appear to be fully grounded. And here they frequently invoke either the actual concept of free thought and questioning, or the types of experiences that conceivably may prepare persons to embark upon such questioning.

While the primary concern of this study is in explaining the development of a national consensus in which a significant portion of the American public has formed harsher views about criminal justice, it is interesting to note that two-thirds of these dissenters speak of developing *less harsh* views over time. Perhaps among the broader public, as well, there has been movement in each direction, that has been masked by the blunt instrument of national polling.

Although there are clear limits on the reliability of citizens' self-assessments of their political behavior, still these explanations are of interest for what they reveal about the participants' perceptions of themselves and others. Among the many contributions that intensive research can make, few are more basic than this: to let each individual tell his or her own story.

What makes the dissenters dissent? We have seen clearly that there is no one factor—no magic pill—that causes these unpopular views. Indeed, at least a half a dozen different factors are at work in the lives of the dissenters I have examined here. And as many other seemingly likely influences—fear, victimization, levels of information, and so on—appear to have no significant bearing on the formation of their dissenting views.

Here I have sought the etiology of a dissenter. But dissenters make up only a tiny fraction of the American public. I have placed this minority under the microscope less for its own sake than for what it can teach us about the formation of that enormous countervailing group: believers in the get-tough movement. We will need the lessons of this chapter, along with those of the two preceding, to form an answer to the question with which we began: why such consensus? It is to that question that we now turn.

CHAPTER 6

Explaining Consensus

We began with a mystery—a puzzle. Despite the enormous complexity and intractability of the problem of crime, the vast majority of Americans agree on what our nation's response should be: year after year, they tell pollsters that we need harsher criminal penalties. As we saw in chapter 1, this striking public consensus cannot be explained as a reaction to increased crime rates, as a subset of broader trends in social attitudes, or as a response to the great success of harsh policies. Each of these explanations plays loose with the facts.

In truth, the puzzle we are confronted with is this: in an era of falling crime rates and increased tolerance toward other forms of deviance and social change, still the vast majority of the American public supports harsh penal policies that they themselves acknowledge have been powerless thus far to reduce crime in our nation to an acceptable level. Why? How can we understand the formation and maintenance of this consensus?

Most of the pieces needed to make sense of this puzzle are now in place. But as with one of those large scenic mountain jigsaws, we have had to approach it in sections. These sections must be joined and the viewer removed by a few paces, before the finished product makes full sense to the eye. The sections that have been put together so far both have provided us with clues that can be used to construct the consensus puzzle and have offered a detailed look at how Americans form and structure their ideas about crime and criminal justice. Let us begin by summing up what has been learned:

Content. In chapter 2, we examined what the believers and the dissenters think about crime and criminal justice. Here we found that the essential distinction between the two groups lies not only in the fact that there generally is an obvious difference in the overall harshness or mildness of their views. More importantly, we saw that there is a fundamental difference in the way in which the believers and dissenters conceive of the basic aims of the criminal justice system. The believers maintain that harshness toward certain criminals is appropriate in order to serve the purposes of punishment, deterrence, or both. The dissenters see it differently. Although they may occasionally advocate measures that are inherently harsh, they never advocate them *because* they are harsh. For the dissenters, the only justification for a harsh sentence is incapacitation—the protection of society from further harm by the offender in question. Of course, most of the believers support the aim of incapacitation as well—alongside their convictions about punishment and/or deterrence. But for a dissenter, this is the *only* allowance made for harshness.

Motivation. In chapter 3, we looked at what respondents are trying to achieve with the policies they support. To what values or deep concerns are they responding when they express particular views? Four deep, underlying motivations sprang very clearly from the statements of the interviewees: *security*—the basic human desire for protection from loss or harm to self, family, or community; *desert*—a sense of what is right or proper, expressed especially in a striving for balance on the scales of life; *compassion*—a concern for the welfare of other human beings; and *social critique*—the conviction that a major change in our social, economic, political, or cultural arrangements is essential to the achievement of "the good society."

With both the dissenters and the believers, we saw two major patterns of motivation. While all of the dissenters draw the primary motivation for their harsh views from security alone, they are divided among those who find the primary motivation for their mild views in compassion and those who find it in social critique. The believers also are divided into two groups. Among the *traditional believers,* none reaches beyond security or desert to draw a primary motivation for their views, harsh or mild. Among the *complex believers* security and/or desert still provides the primary motivation for their harsh views, but values other than these play an important role in motivating their milder views.

Because security was found among the primary motivations of every one of these interviewees, it became clear that it is the *tension* between the other values—desert, on the one hand, and compassion or social critique, on the other—that has the greatest effect on the policy choices participants adhere to. Why do the believers believe? Either, it seems, because no strong motivation in compassion or social critique *prevents* them from accepting the traditional answers, or because even if they hold significant motivations from these two concerns, desert exerts an overpowering influence. As discussed in chapter 3, several questions naturally follow: Why do compassion and social critique have so little influence on these believers? Why does desert have so much? If the same interacting values that I found among my interviewees are at work among the broader public, why have the relative levels of these influences changed in recent decades, resulting in a consensus of public opinion? In this final chapter I suggest an answer to these questions.

Structure. In chapter 4, we examined the relationship of participants' views on criminal justice to their more general political beliefs. It was demonstrated that despite differences in levels of sophistication, a substantial majority hold criminal justice views that are well grounded in coherent political belief systems. A few participants—all believers—present an exception to this rule.[1] These individuals hold political belief systems that provide a plausible foundation for their mild views about criminal justice but seem to be lacking in the kinds of convictions that could fully undergird their harsh views. There was some indication that religious rather than political belief systems might hold the foundation for the harsh views of several of these participants, but my exploration of religious beliefs was not sufficiently detailed to substantiate this possibility.

A striking finding of this chapter was that all of the dissenters, but less than one-third of the believers, are among those whose criminal justice views appear to be *fully grounded* in *sophisticated* political belief systems.

Overall, part 1 of this book leaves the strong impression of a group of Americans whose views on crime and criminal justice are reasonably logical and, for the most part, internally consistent. In contrast to the widespread incoherence found by many scholars of public opinion when studying other issue areas, views on this doorstep issue, are remarkably well ordered. This finding only emphasizes the central role that issues of crime and criminal justice play in the American mind—for it is doubtful that results such as these would have been found on most other issues.

Dissent. Moving from examination into explanation, I began chapter 5 by asking what enables a dissenter to become and remain a dissenter, rather than a believer. Here I sought characteristics of background and outlook that coalesce in the lives of the dissenters, laying the ground in which their unpopular views can grow. I presented striking evidence to support this composite portrait of a prototypical dissenter: a person who has a substantial empathy for offenders; who is nonjudgmental in areas relevant to crime; who can be called a liberal; who is undisturbed by various types of behavior that (though legal) are not universally accepted in our society; and who is a questioner of traditional religious assumptions.

Why Consensus?

With this background, we can proceed to address the questions about consensus with which this book began. Three areas of the puzzle are in need of special examination: the public's curious devotion to incarceration, the surprising nonrelationship of criminal justice views and public views on certain other social issues, and the interesting case of forgiveness and crime.

Why Use More Prisons, If Prisons Do Not Work?

As noted in chapter 1, survey research has shown us that the vast majority of Americans support increasing our use of incarceration, despite the fact that they *also* feel that jails and prisons are not very effective at discouraging crime. Indeed, a substantial majority believes that our prisons are actually making criminals worse.[2] Why do Americans stand so firmly behind a policy that they themselves believe is not working? This is a critical question, because the more we understand about the reasons for this apparent contradiction, the more opportunity we should have to craft future policies that both acknowledge the public's concerns and inclinations and hold a greater chance of actual effectiveness.

Toward the end of the first interview, if it seemed appropriate, I asked participants this question: "What's the point in sending so many people to prisons, then—if they don't work very well?"[3] In addition, most of the believers offered spontaneous responses to this (unspoken) question at earlier points in the interview. From the answers of the believers, four themes emerge.[4]

First, there is the answer, expressed by eight of the believers at one point or another, that incarceration *would be* effective, if only it were more widely used, or the sentences were longer, or the conditions were harsher. Thelma Winters, the retired home health aide, makes this point:

> *KTG:*   What do you think would happen if tougher sentences were handed out to more criminals?
>
> *TW:*   I think they would be afraid to do a lot of things they do. It seems to me like they don't mind going to jail. [They] be in there a while and then get out. Then after they let them out, they go back and do the same things. I just think they didn't stay in there long enough to learn their lesson.

Second, two persons expressed the view that prisons could work if they made a sufficient effort at rehabilitation. Aram Isaac, the college-educated truck driver, makes this case:

> The reason why it doesn't work—the prison—[in] my point of view is just [that] the people [that] are responsible to keep the prisoners—they don't ... feel responsibility to teach them, to rehabilitate them ... The people working in the jail—what is their responsibility?—just to work days, months, and years? Or work [hard] in order to rehabilitate this criminal? ... Are they really working to rehabilitate the criminals or

not? It's very doubtful. Do they have the well-studied technique and specialities—psychologists, medical doctor, psychiatrists—to analyze and work day by day with this criminal or not? I doubt [it]. Just they stay there . . . counting days . . . That's why the jails do not work. . . .

Third, there is the view, expressed by four of the believers, that at least prisons and jails keep offenders off the streets. Clarence Peters, the glazing contractor, makes this point:

> *KTG:*   What's the point in sending so many people to prison, then—if they don't work very well?
>
>   *CP:*   To keep him out of society. To keep him from destroying lives of good civilians—destroying, upsetting the livelihood and happiness of citizens.

Finally, there is the response that says, in essence, what else is there to do? Five of the believers expressed this sentiment. Sadie Monroe, the retired physical education teacher: "They can't just let them walk around and commit more crime. Got to try to stop them some way. And that's the only way they have." Barbara Damon, the transportation department manager: "I don't have any other alternatives. What else can they do?" Interestingly, the believers who expressed this sentiment were not always so defeatist. Each one of them also expressed one of the other themes at some point in our conversations.

What should we make of this collection of opinions? The broadest message is that these believers are not walking around under a load of unresolved cognitive dissonance. Certainly there is the potential for contradiction and clash here. To simultaneously believe that a particular policy has not worked *and* to support our increasing use of that policy (even to advocate further increases)—these are not ideas that are automatically in harmony. But these believers manage to make them coexist peacefully.

Although several different themes were expressed, the key here lies in the first described above: there is a fundamental belief that, notwithstanding the ineffectiveness of our current institutions, sufficiently harsh prison sentences *would* work. A substantial majority of the believers hold this view (the eight who explained their support for an as yet ineffective policy in this way, plus two others).[5] Thus, if incarceration is not working in its present application, the answer is to apply it more widely, or for longer periods, or under harsher conditions. But the underlying premise that harshness works is not challenged by these believers. The only issue is the necessary level of harshness. Of course, this position might be debated by those who question the premise or argue that it cannot be made to succeed amid real-world constraints, but there is certainly nothing illogical or internally contradictory about it.

This conclusion also throws a monkey wrench at the notion that understanding this apparent contradiction in public opinion will assist us in developing alternative penal policies that are both acceptable to the public and practically effective. If in fact the public remains convinced that *this* penal policy will prove effective eventually, if only we use enough of it, then any quest for a politically feasible alternative will be restrained significantly before it even gets off the ground. Unless this widespread faith in the ultimate power of imprisonment fades in the face of further years of ineffectiveness or is confronted forcefully by some upper limit on the elasticity of government budgets, a change in the incarceration orientation of our justice system is unlikely.

A Puzzling Nonrelationship

A second area deserving closer scrutiny was suggested by the work of Arthur Stinchcombe and his colleagues, as described in chapter 1. The conventional wisdom is that less harsh views on criminal justice are a part of a general complex of liberal social attitudes. And statistical analysis also has found small but consistent correlations between less harsh views regarding penal sanctions and liberal views on certain other social issues. But the fact is that while public opinion regarding criminal justice has gotten more conservative in recent decades, attitudes about race and gender relations, abortion, civil liberties, and issues surrounding sex have liberalized. Stinchcombe et al. were able to show that the correlations that have been observed actually are due primarily to "a very few ideological liberals who view penal philosophy as a part of their liberalism." These individuals comprise about 1 percent of the American public. "The rest of the population," they write, "sees a weaker connection between these questions of Enlightenment liberalism ... and the treatment of criminals by the courts."[6]

The open question, then, is *why* so few Americans make a strong connection between these issues? Why this crisscross in the movement of public opinion? Why have we developed such a broad consensus about increasing our use of harsh sanctions for crime at the same time that we have become more tolerant on these other issues?[7] Of course, these are at least partially historical questions. And my research was designed neither to be a detailed study of the history of this era, nor to create a panel study measuring precise changes in the beliefs of specific individuals over time. But here we can rely on one of the key functions of intensive interviewing—the generation of new hypotheses—to provide a proposition that others may wish to test with different methods. Thus, there is sufficient evidence in these interviews, when viewed against the backdrop of the turbulent decades through which we have passed, to permit me to offer this assertion:

The public has not just become harsher on crime *and* more liberal on a collection of social issues, but has become harsher on crime at least in part *because* they have become more tolerant on these other issues. In suggesting this explanation I am relying heavily on the evidence presented in the section of the last chapter titled "Tolerance without Distress." There, following leads that came from the work of Stuart Scheingold and of Francis Cullen and his colleagues, I demonstrated that a significant factor that distinguished the believers from the dissenters was their attitude toward a variety of now legal, but not universally accepted, behaviors—abortion, homosexuality, equal opportunity for women and minorities, free speech for atheists and communists, cohabitation by the unmarried, and the like. In varying degrees, all of the believers were bothered by certain of these activities; in contrast, nearly all of the dissenters were not.

Importantly, there were many cases in which the believer was willing to tolerate the behavior in question but, deep down, was still bothered by it. Gladys Jones, for example, said, "I don't like abortion," but she still felt that a woman should have the right to make her own choice about the matter. Miriam Madamba referred to homosexuality as "sinful," but she still felt that we should be accepting and forgiving of gay persons. Elizabeth Williams said that she looked at sex as being a part of marriage, but as to those who engage in premarital sex, "I'm not here to condemn them." For these women and many other Americans, there exists what might be called a *botheration-toleration gap*. This is a phenomenon that we may presume has only multiplied in recent decades, as American society has come to tolerate so many previously proscribed behaviors. Like the believers we have just heard, no doubt a good many of these Americans are not as unbothered as they are tolerant. Indeed, for a fair number of these people, their tolerance may be born only of resignation. When the incidence and/or acceptance of a particular behavior in the population passes a certain level, someone who opposes it may simply reason that it is *impossible* to prohibit it. We can hear this kind of resignation in Gladys Jones's attitudes about homosexuality: "It's gotten out of proportion, and I don't think it's too much you can do about it now."

I should stress that when I talk about the American public becoming harsher over recent decades, I am not talking about everyone turning from dissenters into believers. Most of those people who changed their opinions probably never were dissenters to begin with. Note that the huge change that occurred in the public's response to the traditional poll question about whether the courts are harsh enough came from respondents moving out of the "about right" and "don't know" categories into "not harsh enough."[8] The percentage of respondents who have replied "too harsh" has remained roughly the same over the years. And only some of the former "about right" and "don't know" respondents would have ever been dissenters. What has most likely happened is that some dissenters have become believers, and *a lot* of people who were moderate believers have become much stronger, harsher believers.

A critical factor for explaining this change can be found in the botheration-toleration gap I have described. Many Americans have decided to tolerate behavior they nevertheless find bothersome. Thus they go about their lives, still carrying the burden of feeling that their fellow citizens are engaging in activities that are somehow distasteful, unnatural, sinful, dangerous, immoral, or uppity. But they choose not to release that psychological burden into advocacy of prohibitions on these activities.

What I am suggesting is that gradually over the years many Americans were developing a pool of insufficiently actualized negative feelings, and that they needed some place to put them. What better place than in strenuous opposition to the acts of criminal offenders? After all, they *had* stolen our property, assaulted our coworkers, raped our sisters, and killed our neighbors—year after year after year. If these Americans, wishing that life were different, had nevertheless chosen not to stand in the way of abortion, or open homosexuality, or blacks who wanted into the country club and women who wanted into the boardroom, then should we not expect that they would want, all the more, to *do something* about those acts to which we, as a society, had openly announced our intolerance—that is, crime?[9] Certainly this line of reasoning is compatible with the type of interpretation offered by Scheingold and by Cullen, Clark and Wozniak in the passages quoted in the last chapter, in which they emphasized the role that crime-related attitudes may play as a symbolic substitute for feelings about other forms of "incivility or unusual behavior."

These Americans, then, wanted to do something about crime. But what to do? A decision to act more diligently to solve a problem does not necessarily presuppose the use of one type of solution over another. But they chose to support the types of policies that had been traditional for our society: they chose to advocate the increased use of incarceration and the renewed use of capital punishment. Why this, instead of damning the failures of the past and pleading for new methods and experimental programs? Here, another of the lessons of chapter 5 may be relevant. There we saw that almost all of the dissenters had questioned and then changed their religious beliefs, while almost none of the believers had done so. I made the argument then that persons who were able to question the core assumptions of their religious upbringing might be persons who would more easily challenge other of the core assumptions of our society. Of course, to say that the dissenters tend more to be questioners than do the believers is not to say that the average American is a downright unquestioning person. Instead it may be the case that most Americans are simply all questioned out. In the past four decades Americans have been called to change their previous assumption that black persons were not the equals of whites. They have been asked to question whether their fundamental belief in freedom of speech applied to radicals in Berkeley and Nazis in Skokie. They have been asked to change their age-old assumption that a woman's place was in the home. They have been asked to question whether their political heritage of privacy rights called them to tolerate behaviors that their religious institutions had taught were morally repugnant: abortion and homosexuality. And for many Americans these questions and changes came at no small emotional cost. Would it be any wonder if Americans had little energy left to question traditional assumptions about crime and sanctions for crime?

This interpretation finds support also in the findings of chapter 3. There we saw that it was the tension between desert, on the one hand, and compassion or social critique, on the other, that made the critical difference in the motivations of the believers versus the dissenters. The traditional believers respond hardly at all to concerns of compassion or social critique, and there is little question about why they are believers. But for the complex believers there is a significant tension between desert and one of the other two concerns—the outcome of which makes them believers. Now look at the survey research: even before the vast growth in harsh attitudes among the American public, nearly 50 percent of the population already felt that the courts were not harsh enough. But for another 35 percent of the public there was a *change* that solidified by the late 1970s—and it is this change that requires an explanation. When concerns of compassion or social critique lose the power to stand up against an individual's additional motivations in desert, perhaps it is some of that exhaustion described above that is at work. One sometimes hears the term "compassion fatigue," in an era in which poverty confronts us so directly on the sidewalks of our cities; perhaps a sort of social critique fatigue also has come into play, limiting the degree to which Americans question inherited assumptions about criminal justice.

A focus on questioning may help to make sense of the findings of the previous section of this chapter, as well. There we saw that the key reason that most of the believers—despite their view that our prisons are ineffective—support the increasing use of incarceration is that they hold a fundamental belief that sufficient harshness will work. We have to wonder why they—and their fellow Americans—are not more mixed in their response to this acknowledgment of the inadequacies of our current efforts, with many more being led to seek alternatives to incarceration. Perhaps again the answer is that they are simply too weary of questioning to challenge the premise that lies beneath their choice of policy.[10]

The botheration-toleration gap described above, when combined with the understandable reluctance of most Americans to question traditional assumptions about criminal justice, goes a long way toward explaining how public attitudes about criminal justice and those about other social issues came to move in opposite directions. Based on this analysis, it is fair to say that the public has become more harsh on crime not *in spite of* but *because* of the contrary movement on these other issues.[11] Now let us turn to the final area of the consensus puzzle.

The Boundaries of Forgiveness

In chapter 5, we saw that the hypothesis that the believers and the dissenters might show significant differences in their attitudes toward forgiveness and vengeance was not supported by these interviews. Instead I found that most of the believers, just as the dissenters, considered forgiveness to be an important and worthy act between human beings. The comments of the dissenters were perhaps more intense, but on the whole not strikingly more so. In addition, nearly everyone in each group answered in the affirmative when asked whether it was possible to forgive persons who are not sorry, whether forgiveness could play any role in solving our social problems, and whether communal or societal acts of forgiveness were a possibility. As to vengeance, it was denounced by nearly everyone in each group.

Although I found little in their underlying attitudes on this subject that would distinguish between the believers and the dissenters, it is still a matter of considerable interest just to find that the believers have such strong feelings against vengeance and as much regard for the act of forgiveness as they do. If they have these beliefs, why is it that they are not exercising them much in their decisions about criminal justice? It seems that they feel that these standards of normal life do not much apply in this arena. Consider what Gladys Jones, the hospital clerk, has to say about vengeance:

> You got something against . . . [a] person. You want to get even. I don't like that. I don't believe in getting even with people . . . That's no good. I figure when you do that, you just as bad of a person . . . If they did something very wrong, the law should handle it, not you.

Gladys Jones is the only believer to put this sentiment into words, but based on the overall content of the interviews, I suspect that her perspective is shared by most of the others. When the dissenters reject the use of harsh sanctions for the purpose of punishment—that is, making criminals suffer because of their crimes—they conceive of this as a form of vengeance. But nearly all of the believers accept punishment as an aim of the criminal justice system, and it seems that they, like Gladys Jones, view these official actions of government as quite different from those, say, of angry neighbors who take turns putting dents in each other's cars. Government dispenses *justice,* not vengeance.

Likewise, the believers' regard for forgiveness is going largely unexpressed in the criminal justice sphere.[12] Certainly, it enters at some points, when the small magnitude of a crime, or the mitigating circumstances under which it was committed, are particularly compelling. But it is by no means an ever-present standard for action.

In puzzling out what it is that is happening here, it will be helpful to consider a concept suggested by Robert Lane in his study of the political ideologies of fifteen American "common men" in the late 1950s. There, he speaks of the "moral incorporation of the opponent," of "a willingness to grant a wrongdoer a moral character, however eroded this may be through misguided advice, or modified by misinformation." According to Lane, these men hold a broad view "that everyone is really basically the same and that everyone is basically 'like me.' " They apply this outlook "with respect to the Japanese and Pearl Harbor, the Negro and the Southern white in Little Rock, the corrupt politician, the chiseling businessman." But even they are willing to place a limited group of persons "beyond the pale"—most notably "those labeled Communist" and "moral delinquents."[13]

Here is the key to what is happening with my believers. To a significant degree, they have placed criminal offenders *beyond the pale.* They are not imputing to them good intentions; they are not looking upon them as really just like us. Forgiveness and the avoidance of vengeance may be important standards for the commerce of everyday life—with family, friends, schoolmates, and business associates—but the treatment of criminals is not a part of everyday life. Drew Snowden, the bank executive, hints at this perspective when he says of forgiveness: "That only works as long as I want to look at the positive for that person."

As we saw in the last chapter, one striking factor that distinguishes the dissenters from the believers is the difference in their level of empathy for offenders. But should we need further evidence that criminal offenders comprise an element of our society that is beyond the pale for most Americans, we may find it in the attitudes of the believers toward ex-offenders. Interestingly, when I asked the question, "How would you feel if a member of your family brought home to dinner a friend who was an ex-convict?" all but two of the believers expressed sentiments that could be considered accepting. And on the question, "How would you feel if an ex-convict was hired to work closely with you in your job?" nearly every one of them gave an accepting answer also. Some of their specific comments are instructive. From James Morton, the masonry contractor:

> ...Everyone needs an opportunity, and maybe the first one didn't go so great. So they're entitled to a chance. They shouldn't be judged entirely on what has happened in the past—unless it was an ax murder.

From Drew Snowden, the bank executive, who commented that he had attended a party at which a man who had previously been imprisoned for murder was present:

> He went to prison, and the book says that you go to prison and you come out a free man. That's the way it should work.

From Clarence Peters, the glazing contractor, who reports that he has knowingly hired an ex-convict and that it worked out:

> I have no qualms. Ex-convict, to me, does not mean he's a criminal any more.

And from Mary Bono, the receptionist, regarding how she would feel about having such a dinner guest:

> Treat him as a person—just like as a human being.

Here, I am quoting not from a group of dissenters, but from some of the harshest believers I interviewed. Throughout the preceding chapters, we have heard how they feel about criminals, and that sounds very different; now, however, they are talking about ex-criminals. Committing a crime, it seems, removes offenders from the normal human community, with its standards and expectations—among other things, expectations about forgiveness and vengeance. Adam Perlman expresses this state of affairs when he says, "If you violate somebody's rights, you forfeit some rights." But once offenders have paid the price for their crimes—these believers seem to be saying—they may be admitted back within the human community. They are taken back within the pale.

This phenomenon can help to explain further why American opinion on criminal justice has coalesced into the get-tough consensus that we want to understand. Lane argued that his 1950s men did not see the world "through moral glasses." "The criteria of 'right' and 'wrong,' 'good' and 'bad' are not usually the first to be applied to a man, a program, a party," he wrote of his interviewees.[14] But I would assert that our nation has changed since then. The furor over Vietnam and Watergate, the struggles over race and rights, the crusades of Jerry Falwell or even Ronald Reagan—intrinsic to these events were questions of morality, and they were debated in that language. Furthermore, if Lane perceived of his men as putting only communists and moral delinquents beyond the pale, might not this perception be hinged on a 1950s understanding of what that meant? If blacks had then been demanding to share not just schools, but also power, would it still have seemed that his men and others considered minority group members to be basically-like-me? What if the new boss on the assembly line had been black—or had the company president—or a candidate for mayor? Would they have drawn the inclusive circle that large? What if their wives had left their homes each day for education and then for employment—perhaps eventually to make a higher income than they? Or if a city councilman had announced before his reelection campaign that he was gay, what then?

Of course, in the decades that have intervened, we *have* drawn the circle larger. Grudgingly, we have stepped closer as a society to acknowledging that others really are like us—black, Hispanic, Asian, woman, gay, disabled. Kicking and screaming, we have, in varying degrees, taken them within the pale. Now who is left outside? Barely even communists, given the international changes of recent years. But certainly still criminals. Psychologically, there is a tremendous drive to leave somebody out. And if one group must now serve the purpose that was once served by many, surely our gut-level desires to treat them differently will only be intensified? Criminals have never much been within the circle of forgiveness. But as the world has changed around us, might we not desire to treat them even more harshly than before—with less forgiveness, with more vengeful punishments? This perspective both helps to explain the emergence of harsher views in recent decades, and recalls Durkheim's century-old assertion that punishment is addressed more to the upright citizen than to the criminal and that its "true function is to maintain social cohesion intact."[15]

In sum, it is the interaction of three major phenomena that I offer as an explanation for the broad get-tough consensus that has emerged and persisted among the American public in recent decades: first, the development of a *botheration-toleration gap* that left many Americans in need of an outlet for insufficiently actualized negative feelings about the behavior of their fellow citizens; second, a widespread exhaustion brought on by an era of forced questioning of prevailing social and moral beliefs, which only strengthened our underlying reluctance to question traditional assumptions about criminal justice—central among them the notion that imprisonment, like some patent medicine, will surely work if only we find the right dosage; and third, an exacerbation of our already strong tendency to place criminal offenders beyond the pale—this a natural reaction to our having moved to take so many others *in,* in recent years.

After Consensus

Whether or not my explanation of its origins is correct, the fact remains that Americans have reached an amazingly broad consensus in their attitudes toward criminal justice. A few final comments are in order about the view—held by well over three-quarters of our population—that the courts should be harsher still on criminal offenders. Not for naught has the public been sending this message to policymakers for over two decades. The message has been heard and heeded. As I described in chapter 1, the courts have gotten harsher. But there is considerable doubt as to whether this fact has registered in the minds of the public. No more than one or two of my believers indicated any recognition of this state of affairs. And other studies suggest that much of the public may share the feelings that Sadie Monroe, the retired physical education teacher, expressed when I asked her about the U.S. crime rate:

> It's going up—because the prisons are just—they keep saying they're overcrowded. And with these offenders—they being put in prison. So that the crime rate—*it would have to be increasing.* (Emphasis added.)

Have harsher policies actually backfired, in terms of satisfying the public? Sadie Monroe knows that the prisons are bursting at the seams, but rather than realizing that this is due to mandatory and stiffer sentencing, she simply assumes that it must mean that crime is up. Our changed penal policies have not assured her that crime is being dealt with more harshly, as she wishes: they may actually have made her world feel less safe. Not one of my believers realized that U.S. crime rates had actually gone down; four said they were about the same, and nine said they had gone up. Also instructive are the results of a 1985 national poll, in which respondents were asked, "The current overcrowding in prisons is largely due to which of the following?" and were not restricted to selecting one answer. Seventy-five percent chose the response, "increase in crime rate." But only 40 percent selected "increased commitment to incarcerate," only 36 percent selected "changing policy decisions regarding crime," and only 36 percent selected "increased use of longer sentences."[16] John Doble and the Public Agenda Foundation, in their 1986 interviews with focus groups in ten cities, came to a similar conclusion: "Americans believe that prison overcrowding is caused by an increase in crime. They simply do not believe that the crime rate has leveled off or that mandatory and stiffer sentencing are a cause of the problem."[17] Our burgeoning prison population probably is not the only factor that makes Americans feel that crime rates cannot possibly have fallen off, but if it is even one such factor, there is certainly some irony here.[18]

Of course, although the public wants harsh—and harsher—penalties, that is not all it wants. One of the clearest messages of these interviews involves the *complexity* of the participants' opinions and of their motivations for holding them. Certainly, national opinion polling had already suggested this phenomenon, but here we saw it in great and sometimes confusing detail. Importantly, the harsh views of the believers rarely are woven from a single thread. Almost always, two intertwined motivations are involved— security and desert—although one or the other may dominate. Further, the views of these believers are simply not all harsh. Most support alternatives to incarceration for certain nonviolent offenders. Most are willing—many anxious—to support further efforts at rehabilitation within prisons. Many include small expressions of compassion for offenders along with their sterner words invoking security and desert. And a few of these believers even have important motivations in social critique or compassion that lead them to heavily augment their otherwise harsh policy prescriptions with preventive and rehabilitative proposals.

There is an important message here for those who make, or attempt to influence, criminal justice policy. Left, right, and center, they have not always paid sufficient attention to the complexity of the public's views on this issue. Activists on the Left often have assumed that if they could only educate the public about the astronomical costs of our spiraling incarceration policies—if they could only convince them of the perpetual ineffectiveness of prisons in preventing recidivism and providing a general deterrence—if they could only demonstrate the effectiveness of alternative sanctions—then they could win public support. But they have not always given ample consideration to the public's desire for punishment. Most of the believers I interviewed feel that many criminals *deserve* to suffer because of their crimes, and they are joined by the vast majority of their fellow Americans. Unless and until some change can be made in that underlying conviction, efforts to move our nation away from its great devotion to incarceration are unlikely ever to meet with more than limited success.

On the other hand, more moderate to conservative policymakers also may find obstacles within the public's complex views. They might satisfy the widespread desire for punitiveness with longer sentences applied to more offenders and with frequent use of the death penalty (that is, they might satisfy it *if* they could ever get the message across that they had actually done so!). But desert is not Americans' only concern in advocating harsher penalties; they are motivated also by an enormous desire for security. So if these even harsher sentences do not work[19]—if the incidence of crime in our nation remains at unacceptable levels, and further, if an ever-increasing prison population leads some to *believe* that crime rates must be going up—then these policymakers too will meet with public dissatisfaction and disapproval. With constraints of budget placing some kind of upper limit on the degree to which harsh measures can be pursued in the search for an elusive effectiveness, where else will these policymakers have to turn for results, than to alternative sanctions and preventive social efforts? But given Americans' desire for *punishment,* would they support a sufficiently broad application of such programs, for them to become effective? This is a cycle, and a point of either exit or equilibrium is not clear. It seems that most Americans want it all—want to feel that criminals have been genuinely chastised; want to live in a safe society; want to be generous in their help to worthy others (while differing significantly in their definitions of worthiness); want not to bankrupt their government or its citizens with the burdens of seeking these ends. They cannot have it all.

My dissenters do not share the believers' sense of desert about harsh punishments. And they question the morality or effectiveness of harsh sanctions as deterrents. They want only the last three items on the list: safety, generosity, and solvency. This is still no easy bill to fill, but it is not as close to an impossible dream as the foursome above. Of course, the dissenters cannot seem to sell their position to much of anyone else. A few million Americans, perhaps, may espouse views that sound something like those we have heard from these nine. This is more than enough for a ball team, but paltry small for a social movement.

Examining the contrasts between the dissenters and the believers has provided us with important insights into the formation of a broad American consensus about criminal justice. But beyond this, why should we ponder the unpopular views of the dissenters any further? Why hearken to the call of such a small minority?

The constraints of the present age, as well as some important principles from the past, are prodding us to listen. *We want to be safe.* But we have found that the increasingly harsh penal policies that we have pursued in the past two decades have not proven to be the answer to our crime problem. Circumstances beg us to ask whether any level of harshness, short of one that would break our treasury and abrogate our standards of civilized behavior, would be sufficient to provide the deterrent effect we seek. And experience calls us to question whether harsh sanctions more often frighten offenders into a newfound righteousness or turn them into still more hardened and embittered persons—further inured to disrespect and violence. *We want criminal offenders to pay for their crimes*—to suffer as they have made others suffer, to get what they deserve. But have we given full consideration to the voices that urge us to call off our quest for a retributive justice? No doubt the most radical and controversial of these voices is that which two thousand years ago made the plea to "love your enemies" and "do good to those who hate you." But those who follow in the liberal tradition can look back even to that proponent of state terror, Thomas Hobbes, for the principle that any punishment inflicted without the intention or possibility of deterring wrongdoing is unacceptable: punishment unto itself is unjustified.[20]

We are a tired nation—tired from opening so often the boundaries of acceptance, of forgiveness, of understanding. If criminal offenders are the last frontier, then they are a tough frontier indeed. But to draw the circle of compassion large enough to include even these is not to condone their wrongdoing, not to sit passively as crime continues, not to unlock every prison door. Nor does accepting the ultimate failure of harsh methods to ensure our safety mean that we must throw up our hands in defeat and desperation. Rather, we might give preventive, rehabilitative, and restitutive solutions a genuine opportunity to show their effectiveness—and use confinement only where these measures have proven ineffective at preventing injury, or where the risks are too great to bear. To Kate Fontana, the nurse-midwife, I give the final word:

I think the way the decision [about appropriate penalties] should be made is, how can we, one, keep people safe in the community, but more importantly...how can we take this human being and the potential that they hold, and make the most of it?...I certainly think that [restitution] is important and that they realize that whatever they have done is not right...I mean, just as we want to treat them justly, they have to treat other people justly. But also...as opposed to just purely punishment, which is something I think that is really espoused today, we need to look at ways that it's not a waste of human potential and that we don't have hundreds of thousands of people locked up in prisons vegetating, when there's things that they can do and achieve....

Appendixes

APPENDIX A

Demographic Characteristics
of Participants, 1987

The Believers

Name	Age	Occupation	Education	Length of Oakland Residence	No. of Children
Mary Bono	34	Receptionist	High school; vocational courses	Since the mid-1970s	1
Barbara Damon	30	Manager, Calif. Dept. of Transportation	Some college	All but 4 years of her life	None
Aram Isaac	37	Delivery truck driver	BA	4-1/2 years	2
Gladys Jones	62	Hospital clerk	High school	19 years	1 (grown)
Miriam Madamba	56	Secretary	High school; secretarial courses	8 years	6 (grown)
Sadie Monroe	72	Retired PE teacher	BA; teaching credential	30 years	2 (grown)
James Morton	62	Masonry contractor	High school; trade school	All his life	3 (grown)
Adam Perlman	33	Director, speech therapy program	Master's degree	3 years	None
Clarence Peters	73	Owner, glazing company	1 year Jr. college	Since the Depression	3 (grown)
Drew Snowden	49	Bank executive	BA	Almost all life	1
Violet Taylor	63	Retired waitress	Tenth grade	30 years	2 (grown stepchildren)
Elizabeth Williams	34	Physical therapist	BS; BA	7 years	None
Thelma Winters	83	Retired home health aide	Eighth grade	42 years	5 (grown)

Note: See Appendix C for an explanation of changes made to protect the anonymity of the participants.

Race/ Ethnicity	Family Income	Religion	Spouse's Occupation	Spouse's Education
Filipino	$20-30,000	Catholic	(divorcing)	—
White	$50-70,000	Presbyterian	Plasterer	AA
Black (N. African)	$10-20,000	None (born Catholic)	Homemaker	Ninth grade
Black	$10-20,000	Baptist	(separated)	—
Filipino	$20-30,000	Protestant	(abandoned, then widowed)	—
Black	$10-20,000	Protestant	Retired optometrist	Dr. of Optometry
White	$50-70,000	No affiliation	Homemaker	High school
White	$30-40,000	Nonpracticing Jew	(single)	—
White	$30-40,000	Presbyterian	Retired elementary school principal	MA
White	Over $100,000	Protestant	Management consultant	BA
Black	$30-40,000	Christian	Retired gardener	Some high school
Anglo/Hispanic	$50-70,000	Christian	Architect	BA
Black	Under $5,000	Protestant	(widow)	—

The Dissenters

Name	Age	Occupation	Education	Length of Oakland Residence	No. of Children
Abigail Edwards	47	Community college instructor	High school; Red Cross certification	12 years	5 (grown children/ stepchildren)
Kate Fontana	33	Nurse-midwife	Master's degree	5 years	None
Anne Girard	45	Nursing student; dept. store clerk	Some college	5 years	2 (grown)
Olivia Hassan	36	Head bank teller	Some college	31 years	3
Dexter Lane	49	Insurance agent	Law degree	All his life	4 (minor and grown)
Richard Niederhaus	31	Software designer	Some college	10 years	1
Victor Rodriguez	37	Administrator, Dept. of the Interior	Master's degree	5 years	2
Burt Ruebel	34	Photographer	BA	5 years	None
Daniel Steinbach	48	Social worker	Master's degree	10 years	3 (grown)

Others

Name	Age	Occupation	Education	Length of Oakland Residence	No. of Children
Paul Bongolan	30	Makes floral deliveries	High school; attending community college	1 year	None
Evangeline Reed	68	Retired admin. asst., Dept. of Defense	High school; some nursing school	Almost all her life	3 (grown)

Race/ Ethnicity	Family Income	Religion	Spouse's Occupation	Spouse's Education
White	$50-60,000	Christian, plus reincarnation-karma	Plumber	High school
White	$40-50,000	Catholic	Self-employed cabinetmaker	BA
White	Less than $5,000	Follows a spiritual teacher	(divorced)	—
Black	$10-20,000	Multireligious	(divorced)	—
Black	$10-20,000	Essene	Not employed	High school
White/Asian	$40-50,000	Mystic	(single)	—
Hispanic	$50-70,000	Humanist, agnostic	Biologist	Master's degree
White	$10-20,000	Personal religion	(single)	—
White	$10-20,000	Nonpracticing Jew; spiritual	(divorced)	—

Race/ Ethnicity	Family Income	Religion	Spouse's Occupation	Spouse's Education
Filipino	$20-30,000	Catholic	(divorced)	—
Black	$10-20,000	Protestant	(divorced)	—

Interview Questions

Personal Information

1. How long have you lived in Oakland?
2. How do you feel about it as a place to live?
3. Where did you grow up?
4. What other places have you lived, and for how long?
5. How would you describe the neighborhood in which you live now?
6. Are there any people not of your race living in this neighborhood?
7. Do you plan to stay here?
8. What is your occupation? / (If appropriate) Are you currently employed?
9. What is your educational background?
10. May I know your age?
11. What is your marital status?
12. (If applicable) How about your spouse's education and occupation?
13. Do you have children?
14. (If yes) What are their ages?
15. (If grown) What are their occupations and education?

Definition of Crime

1. Would you tell me, first, what the meaning of the word crime is to you?
2. Could an act be considered a crime even if it did not actually break the laws of our country? Are there any other kinds of laws—moral or religious laws, for example—which you feel it would be a "crime" to break?
3. Could you give me any examples of actions that seem criminal to you, but are not against the laws of the United States? / What makes them seem criminal?
4. Looking at this now from the opposite angle, can you think of any acts that *are* illegal in this country, but *don't* seem like crimes to you?

5. One sometimes hears talk about "victimless crimes," actions which generally cause no *direct* harm to anyone besides the persons committing them. Prostitution, gambling, and possession of illegal drugs are examples of such acts. Should these be considered crimes, or not? How different or similar are they to "regular" crimes?
6. What does the phrase *white-collar crime* mean to you?
7. Are white-collar offenses really crimes, the same as, say, burglary or assault? How similar or different are they?
8. How serious of a problem is white-collar crime for our country?
9. Are governments or organizations ever guilty of crimes, or is crime a word we should use only to talk about the acts of individuals?
10. (If yes) Can you think of any examples of times when you felt that our government or some organization had committed a crime?

Causes of Crime

1. What do you think are the major causes of crime in our society today? / How? Why?
2. (If appropriate) You've mentioned several causes: could you rank them in order from the most to the least important?
3. Who do you think is generally more to blame for crime, individuals or society?
4. In your opinion, do the causes of white-collar crime differ from the causes of ordinary "street crime," or are they generally about the same?
5. (If different) What causes white-collar crime?

Government's Response to Crime

Opening Questions
1. In general, do you think the courts in this area deal too harshly, or not harshly enough, with criminals?
2. (If not harshly enough) Why should we be harsh on criminals?
3. (To those who answer no. 2, if appropriate) What would happen if tougher sentences were handed out to more criminals?
4. (To those who answer no. 1 "not harshly enough") Can you think of any earlier time in your life when the courts seemed to be harsher on criminals than they are now, or would you say the courts really haven't changed much in this regard? (If appropriate) / When? / How?
5. (To those who answer no. 4 in the affirmative) When you said that the courts should be harsher, did you mean that they should be as harsh as they were, say, in (time mentioned in no. 4), or did you have something more or less in mind?

6. (To those who answer no. 1 "too harshly") Why is that? / What problems does this cause?

Goals and Rationale
1. On this card I have listed several possible goals for our criminal justice system. Would you tell me which of these goals you think should be the most important, and so on, down to the least important, as well as pointing out any you don't think should be criminal justice goals at all: (Why?)

> punishment: making criminals suffer because of their crimes
> rehabilitation: teaching offenders how to become productive citizens
> deterrence: setting an example to discourage future crime

isolation: removing criminals from society
compensation: repaying victims for their losses
other_____

2. Criminal justice in this country is organized into separate systems for adult and for juvenile offenders. Would you rank the goals any differently when thinking just about the juvenile justice system?
3. Would you say that our current adult and juvenile criminal justice systems have the same priorities you've mentioned, or different ones?

Solutions
1. Suppose that you were in a powerful position in our government. What kinds of things would you propose that we do to solve the crime problem?
2. You've discussed several possible solutions. Now I'd like to show you a list including a few other ideas that are sometimes suggested. Would you tell me whether or not you think that each of these ideas would be effective in reducing crime, and whether you think pursuing it should be a high or low priority for our country:
   a. increasing educational and employment opportunities for all
   b. handing out stiffer sentences for convicted criminals
   c. hiring more police
   d. working harder to end racism and discrimination
   e. reforming our courts to make them fairer and speedier
   f. programs to reduce child abuse
   g. improving conditions in slum areas
   h. increasing scientific study of the causes of crime
   i. fighting drug and alcohol abuse
   j. making more use of alternatives to prisons

3. (If many are given high priority) You've indicated that a number of these ideas should be high priorities for our country. Which one or two do you think should have the *highest* priority?
4. Do you, or do you not, approve of capital punishment? Should some or all people who commit murder be executed? / Why (not?)
5. (If yes, and if appropriate) What kinds of murderers should be executed? Should all murderers be executed? / Why?
6. Should capital punishment be used for any other crimes?
7. Some people think that a ban on the possession of handguns would help to reduce the level of violence in this country. Others object that this would interfere with the rights of law-abiding citizens to keep guns for their own protection. What do you think—should handguns be banned or not?
8. It is sometimes suggested that the widespread use of violence in TV shows contributes to the high level of real-world violence in this country. But when proposals to regulate TV violence are made, objections are raised that this would involve an unacceptable level of government censorship. What do you think—should the showing of violence be limited in any way?

Prisons
1. What kinds of criminals belong in prison?
2. Many proposals have been made for changes in our prison system. Would you tell me whether you think each of these suggestions is a good or a bad idea:
   a. Work release programs that allow well-behaved prisoners to work in the outside world under supervision during the day, returning to prison at night and on weekends. Most of the prisoners' pay would go to compensate victims for their losses and to help the state pay for the cost of convicts' room and board.
   b. Expanded rehabilitation programs to teach prisoners literacy and job skills.
   c. Conjugal visits in special areas on the prison grounds, so that spouses and prisoners can spend a few full weekends a year together, thus helping to keep family ties intact.

Hardware and Money
1. In general, do you think our country is spending too much, too little, or about the right amount to address the crime problem?
2. During the past five years, the number of offenders in California's prisons has more than doubled. Weighing the costs against the benefits, do you think it is worthwhile for us to imprison so many people?

3. (If appropriate) Do you think the state of California needs more prisons, or not?
4. (If appropriate) Would you be willing to pay more taxes to build and operate them?
5. How much do you suppose it costs per cell to build a new maximum security prison these days—just a ballpark figure?
6. And about how much do you suppose it costs to *house* one prisoner for a period of a year in a maximum security prison—San Quentin or Folsom, for instance?

Hypothetical Crimes and Punishments
1. I'm going to give you a few examples of (hypothetical/imaginary) crimes. I'd like you to tell me what you feel should be done with the offender in each of these cases; and, if possible, please also tell me a little about what you were thinking about as you made your decision.
   a. A convenience store is robbed at midnight by a man carrying an unloaded gun. He grabs sixty dollars from the cash register and runs. The thief is nineteen years of age, a high school dropout, unemployed, and a drug addict. It is his first nondrug offense. What should the penalty be?
   b. The executive director of the local gas company is convicted of embezzling one million dollars from the public funds. What should the penalty be?
   c. A fifteen-year-old boy has been beaten and sexually abused by his legal guardian, an uncle, for the past ten years of his life. One night he takes the man's shotgun from a cupboard and kills him while he sleeps. What should the penalty be?
   d. A burglary of a home is committed while the occupants are sleeping. Five thousand dollars worth of goods are stolen. The burglars are a thirty-five-year-old female and a forty-one-year-old male. Both have served several prior prison sentences. This is their twentieth burglary this year. What should the penalty be for each?
   e. A twenty-eight-year-old woman meets a man of the same age at a night school music appreciation class. After class they adjourn to a nearby bar to share a few drinks. Later, he walks her home and, after refusing to leave her apartment, rapes her. When he is caught the next day, he confesses to two earlier rapes as well. What should the penalty be?
2. (If appropriate) Imagine for a moment that it were not possible to place any of the offenders we've just discussed in prison. Can you think of an appropriate alternative punishment for those you would otherwise have sent to prison?

Alternatives
1. Some communities have experimented with restitution programs in which offenders work to pay back their victims for what they stole, or in other cases do service work for the whole community, like cleaning up parks or highways. Do you approve or disapprove of this kind of program? Should it be used as an alternative to prison in some cases? /What kind of cases?
2. Studies have shown that the vast majority of offenders have problems with drug or alcohol abuse. Would you approve or disapprove of sending some of these people to outpatient programs or live-in halfway houses designed to help them conquer their addictions, rather than sending them to prison?
3. How would you feel if such a halfway house were built in your neighborhood?
4. (If appropriate) Where *should* halfway houses be built?

Punishment Styles
1. Do you think street crime and white-collar crime should receive different types of punishments, or the same types? / Why?
2. How about victimless crimes: prostitution, gambling, drugs, and so forth. Should they be punished any differently than crimes with direct victims? / Why?

Closing Question
Some people think that *government* will never be able to solve the crime problem. They insist that if change is ever to come it will have to start from some other source—moral or spiritual change in individuals, for example. Others are convinced that if government would finally enact the right policies, the crime problem could be brought under control. What do you think?

Crime and Voting

1. Have a candidate's views about crime and punishment ever made a special difference in whether or not you voted for him or her?
2. (If yes) Could you tell me a little about any of the cases in which this has happened?
3. Were you able to get to the polls to vote in the last presidential election?
4. How about the last election for governor of California?
5. And the last election for mayor of Oakland?
6. (For each, if did not) When was the last such election in which you voted?

7. Do you happen to know anything about the views on crime and punishment held by the politicians who won the elections I just mentioned, President Reagan, Governor Deukmejian, and Mayor Wilson?

Crime and Political Participation

1. Have you ever been involved in a community or political group which has attempted in any way, large or small, to do something about the crime problem?
2. (If yes) What does the group do?
3. (If appropriate) What effect has this had on the crime problem?
4. (If appropriate) Why did you join this group?
5. Can you think of any other public or political action you've taken to address the crime problem?
6. Besides voting, have you ever engaged in any other types of political activities, *not* addressed to the crime problem?

Concern over Crime as a Local and National Problem

1. How serious of a problem is crime for the city of Oakland, that is, when compared with other problems?
2. (If appropriate) What is there about crime that makes it so serious?
3. How about for your neighborhood—is there a significant crime problem in this neighborhood or not?
4. How about for the United States as a whole? How serious of a problem do you think crime is for our nation, again, compared to other problems?
5. I'd like to know what kind of emotional reaction you have when you read or hear about all the crime that goes on in this city. Would you read through the list of words on this card and tell me which two or three best describe your emotional reaction to crime:
   Anger
   Frustration
   Violation
   Helplessness
   Fear
   Sadness
   Outrage
   Confusion
   Pity
   Despair

6. Would any other words that are not on the list describe your emotional reaction better?

Fear of Crime

1. Is there any area within a mile of where you live where you would be afraid to walk alone at night?
2. (If yes) Would you describe it for me?
3. (If yes) Would you be afraid to walk there if you were accompanied by a friend?
4. How about during the daytime. Any area? (Describe.)
5. What about at home at night. Do you feel safe and secure, or not?
6. (If appropriate) And in the daytime, at home?
7. Thinking back over the years, would you say you feel any more or less uneasy at home and on the streets now than you used to? / When was this?
8. How likely do you think it is that you might someday become the victim of a violent crime?
9. And how likely is it that you might become the victim of a property crime, that is, theft or damage to something you own?
10. Are any members of your immediate family often in situations in which you fear for their safety more than you normally do for your own? (Describe.)

Perceptions of Crime Rates

1. Just your best guess—what percentage of the population of Oakland do you suppose were victims of a violent crime last year?
2. Would you say there was more or less crime in your neighborhood now than a year ago?
3. How about in our country as a whole, would you say the crime rate was going up, down, or staying about the same?
4. (To those who answer nos. 2 or 3 in the affirmative) What would you say was the cause of this increase?
5. Considering just your own neighborhood again, would you say it was more or less safe than most neighborhoods in Oakland?
6. And how about Oakland as a whole, would you say it was more or less safe than most large cities in this country?

Perceptions of Criminals

1. Thinking now about the United States as a whole, what percentage of our population would you guess have committed a crime sometime during their lives, for which they could have been sent to jail or prison?
2. In general, would you say that criminals today are more violent, or less violent, than they were five years ago, or about the same?
3. If you were forced to really generalize, how would you describe the average criminal, in terms of age bracket, education, income, and any other factors you might want to mention?
4. What do you think—does a person's race or class make him any more or less prone to commit crimes, or doesn't this make any difference? / Why (not)?
5. Why do you suppose women commit so many fewer crimes than men?
6. How do you think most prisoners react to being deprived of their freedom, their loved ones, and all the other privileges of the outside world? / (If prompting is needed) Do you think it causes them great pain, or is it just a normal and accepted part of the lifestyle for most criminals?
7. Now I'd like to ask you a few questions about how you personally would feel about having contact with persons who've committed crimes and have served time in prison:
   a. How would you feel if a member of your family brought home to dinner a friend who was an ex-convict?
   b. Has this ever happened to you?
   c. How would you feel if an ex-convict was hired to work closely with you in your job?
   d. Has this ever happened?

Perceptions of the Criminal Justice System

1. Thinking about the United States as a whole, in what percentage of all the crimes that are committed do you suppose the offender is caught and sent to jail or prison?
2. If a man snatches a purse containing forty dollars from an old woman on the street, what would you guess are the minimum and maximum penalties he can be given under the laws of the state of California?
3. How about for an armed robbery, say a robbery at knifepoint in which one hundred dollars is stolen and the victim spends two nights in the hospital. What do you suppose the minimum and maximum penalties would be?

4. How often do you think the courts *convict* innocent persons for crimes they didn't commit?

5. Do you think the criminal justice system in this country tends more to be fair, or to be biased, in regard to minorities and the poor?

6. How effective would you say our prisons are in discouraging convicts from committing new crimes when they are released?

7. Among those who have been to prison and are released, what percentage do you suppose go on to commit another crime?

8. How effective do you think the threat of prison sentences is in preventing people from ever starting a life of crime?

9. (If appropriate) What kinds of people are influenced by the threat of prison?

10. (To those who don't think prisons are very effective in nos. 6 and 8 above) What's the point in sending so many people to prison, then, if they don't work very well?

11. What do you know or have you heard about conditions in the jails and prisons of California? What do you suppose an average day in the life of a prisoner is like?

12. Now let's move on to consider the *victims* of crime for a few moments. Some people who have been crime victims feel that the police and courts have not treated them with the respect and care they deserve. Other victims have noted that many officers and officials went out of their way to be helpful and understanding. How do you feel about the way the criminal justice system treats the victims of crime? What should government do to help crime victims?

Personal Experiences with Crime

1. Have you ever been a victim of a crime? / (If yes) Could you describe what happened to you?

2. (If yes to no. 1) Was the crime reported to the police? / (If no) Why not?

3. (If never victimized) To what do you attribute this good fortune?

4. How about your family and close friends or neighbors: have any of them been victimized? / (Describe.)

Personal Experiences with the Criminal Justice System

1. (To those who were victimized and reported it) When X happened, did you have any involvement in a trial or other aspects of the case? / (If yes) Could you describe what took place?

2. (To those who reported a crime) How did you feel about the way you were treated by the (police/criminal justice system)?
3. Have you or any member of your family ever been arrested, indicted, convicted, or imprisoned for a crime? / (If yes) Would you tell me something about what happened? / (If imprisoned) When? / Where? / For how long?
4. How about any of your friends or acquaintances, neighbors or co-workers? / Who? / (Describe.)
5. Have you ever been to jail or prison as a visitor? / (If yes) Where?
6. (To those answer no to no. 3) Have you ever committed an act for which you could have been sent to jail or prison if caught?

Crime-Aware Behavior

1. Can you think of any ways in which you have changed your personal activities or lifestyle because of the crime problem?
2. What about (if not mentioned above):
   a. not going out at night alone
   b. putting extra locks on your doors
   c. installing a burglar alarm
   d. getting a dog
   e. not carrying much money with you
   f. putting bars on your doors or windows
   g. buying a gun for protection

Information Sources

1. Where do you generally get your information about crime?
2. Where do you generally get your information about the criminal justice system?
3. How accurate is the picture of crime we get from the news media? Would you say it was generally a pretty fair picture of crime in America, or does it tend to get sensationalized or blown out of proportion?

Attitude Change

1. Thinking back, have there been any major changes in your opinions about crime and punishment, compared to those you held, say five, ten, twenty or more years ago? / What? / Why?
2. Can you tie this change to any event in your personal life, the lives of friends or neighbors, or the news?

3. How *strong* would you say your opinions about crime and punishment are now, compared to the strength of your opinions on other topics, that is? How likely is it that your views on this topic could change somewhat in the next few years?

Concluding Crime Questions

1. When you think about the opinions of your relatives, friends, neighbors, and co-workers on crime and punishment, do they seem pretty similar or rather different from your own?
2. (If different) Can you give me any examples of differences in the way you think about this issue?
3. (If different) Why do you think you ended up with different ideas?
4. Do you spend much time talking with your friends and family about topics like we've discussed here today? And have you thought about these issues much before, or aren't these the kinds of things you tend to think and talk about?

Financial Information

1. On this card I have listed a number of different income brackets. Would you be willing to tell me into which one of these brackets your (family) income falls?
   a. Less than $5,000
   b. $5,000–$10,000
   c. $10,000–$20,000
   d. $20,000–$30,000
   e. $30,000–$40,000
   f. $40,000–$50,000
   g. $50,000–$70,000
   h. $70,000–$100,000
   i. More than $100,000
2. When you were growing up, was your family's financial situation very different from what yours is now?

Final Question

That's all the questions I have for today. Is there anything else you'd like to add?

Second Interview

Opening Question

Do you have anything on your mind from the last interview? Anything you'd like to discuss again or clarify?

Punishment in the Home

To those with children:
  1. Would you describe the *kinds* of things you punish(ed) your children for?
  2. What types of punishment do / (did) you use in different circumstances?
  3. Would you say you tend(ed) to be a strict parent, a lenient parent, or somewhere in between?
  4. How about your own experiences as a child? What sorts of punishment did you receive then? Were your parents more or less strict with you than you are / (were) with your children?

To those without children:
  1. Would you describe the *kinds* of things you were punished for?
  2. What *types* of punishment were used in different circumstances?
  3. Would you say your parents tended generally to be strict, to be lenient, or somewhere in between?

General Question

If you were in a powerful position in our government, what sorts of changes might you recommend in order to make life in the United States better for its citizens?

Justice

  1. What does the word justice mean to you?
  2. Are there any groups or types of people you think are treated unjustly in America today? Who?
  3. What kinds of rights do you think all people should have from birth?
  4. (If only constitutional rights are mentioned) You've mentioned several of our constitutional rights. Do you think people should have any other basic rights which are not included in the Constitution?

5. (Unless covered in no. 3 or no. 4) What about food, shelter, health care, and education? Should any of these be rights from birth, or would you say not?

6. Thinking about your own life, have you ever been treated unjustly, or had any important rights denied to you? / (Describe.)

Criminal Justice

1. Is the type of justice we've been discussing any different from the justice referred to in the phrase *criminal justice.* How would you define justice in this sense?

2. People sometimes talk about "the rights of the accused," that is, the rights of persons suspected of having committed crimes. How important are these rights? Should these constitutional principles be strictly adhered to at all times, or would you say that they could be waived on occasion in order to catch and convict particularly dangerous criminals? / (If waive) When? / Why?

3. Under our constitution, it is the responsibility of the state to prove in a trial that a criminal suspect is guilty, rather than for the suspect to prove that he is innocent. Do you think this is the way it should be, or not?

4. Once a person has been proven guilty, what types of things should the court consider when deciding how to punish him? How should the judge decide whether or not to send him to prison?

Racial Justice

1. To what degree and in what ways do you think blacks and other minorities are still subject to discrimination in America and, particularly, here in Oakland?

2. (If appropriate) What do you think should be done about this remaining prejudice and discrimination?

3. What is the best advice you could give to minority group members who want better jobs and more respect in the community?

4. In general, do you favor or oppose the busing of children for the purposes of integrating our public schools?

5. Do you personally approve or disapprove of marriages between people of different races? (Why not?)

Freedom and Authority

1. What does the term freedom mean to you?
2. What limits do you think there should be on people's freedom? Are there any dangers involved in having too much freedom?
3. How about too little freedom? What kinds of problems are there when there is too little freedom?
4. Do you ever feel that listening to all the different points of view on a subject is too confusing and time-consuming, and that you would like to hear just one point of view from somebody who knows? / (If yes) For example?
5. Are there ever times when laws and government authorities are wrong and should be disobeyed, or would you say that citizens should obey their government under all circumstances? / (If disobey) When? / Why?
6. I wonder if you agree or disagree with this statement: "Too many people in this country just don't have the proper respect for authority anymore." / Why?

Equality

1. The Declaration of Independence states that "all men are created equal." In what ways would you say that all people are created equal? In what ways are they unequal?
2. Should we be working toward greater equality between people in this country, or are we equal enough already? / (If the former) What kind of equality between people should we work toward?
3. Are there any ways in which freedom and equality conflict with each other?
4. Which do you think is the more important value, freedom or equality?
5. How would you feel if everyone received the same income, whatever his or her job was? Would people act any differently than they do now?

Human (Political) Nature

1. Next I'd like to know whether or not you think there is any such thing as human nature—any characteristics which are widely shared by human beings in different places and times?
2. (If yes) What does this human nature look like? What kinds of attitudes and behavior does it include?

3. (If appropriate) Would you say that human nature is pretty much an unchangeable fact of life, or do you think that human beings can improve upon their basic nature? / (If can change) How does change come about?

4. Do you think there will always be crime in the world, or not? / Why?

5. How about poverty? / Why?

6. Racial problems? / Why?

7. In general, how difficult would you say it is for people to make their own lives better? / Why?

8. Some people's lives don't ever seem to get any better, or sometimes even get worse. Do you think that happens very much? Why do you think that happens?

9. Do you think people now are more or less moral compared with people thirty or forty years ago? / Why?

Forgiveness

1. Now I'd like to hear your thoughts on the concept of forgiveness. Think for a moment about the last time you forgave a relative or friend for something important, or the last time you remember being forgiven by one of them. You needn't go into the personal details of the incident unless you wish to, but can you describe for me the *process* of forgiveness? What happens when someone forgives someone else?

2. Is it possible for someone to forgive another person if that person is not sorry for what he or she has done?

3. Could forgiveness play any role in solving our social problems? / (If yes) How?

4. Would you say that forgiveness is a concept that can only be put into effect between individuals, or could a whole community or society use it? Is it possible, for instance, for a nation to forgive another nation or for a city to forgive the kids who cover its subways with graffiti?

Vengeance

1. How about vengeance—what does this term mean to you?

2. In what kinds of circumstances, if any, do you think that vengeance is the best way to respond?

3. (If appropriate) Thinking about vengeance and then about forgiveness— which would you say we need more of in our society?

Democracy

1. How would you define *democracy*?
2. What are the advantages of democracy compared to other systems?
3. Can you think of any ways in which the United States is undemocratic?
4. If the majority rules in a democracy, what rights should the minority have?
5. It is sometimes pointed out that democracy means that everyone, no matter how ignorant or careless, has an equal vote. Do you think this is the way it should be?
6. Think for a minute about what an ideal "good citizen" in a democracy would be like. Regardless of whether there really is such a person or not, what kinds of things would he or she do? What kinds of attitudes toward politics would he or she have?
7. How close do most people come to this ideal? How close do you come?
8. Some people say that democracy creates confusion and prevents important things from getting done? What do you think about this?
9. Who really knows what is best for a person in the long run, the individual, or some of our leaders, or who? Do government officials know better than others what is good for people in this country?
10. Are there any groups or individuals in our country that you think have too much power? / (If yes) Who?

Governmental Force

1. Sometimes it seems necessary for the government to force people to do things against their will. Is this acceptable or right? / (If yes) Under what kinds of circumstances? / Why?
2. When, if ever, is a government justified in using *physical* force to control the behavior of its citizens?

Lifestyles

1. Why do you think some young people became hippies or protesters back in the sixties?
2. Do you see any of our young people doing comparable things today?
3. Is this behavior harmful?
4. These days, many people regard homosexuality as a reasonable and acceptable alternative lifestyle. Others argue that it is harmful or sinful. What do you think?

The Unfortunate

1. Think for a moment about very poor people: How do you think they came to be that poor? What causes poverty? Do poor people deserve to be poor? / Why?
2. How about people who never finish school? What do you think are the biggest reasons kids drop out of school?
3. Now, what about unemployed people? Do you think most unemployed people really are willing and anxious to work, or do we have high unemployment because so many people are lazy or too picky about the kinds of jobs they're willing to take?
4. Finally, what about people with serious addictions? Why do you think we have so many drug addicts and alcoholics?

Women's Rights

1. Would you tell me if you agree or disagree with this statement: "Most men are better suited emotionally for politics than are most women." /Why?
2. Can you think of any circumstances in which a woman doing the same job as a man should not be paid the same wage as he, provided that she has comparable education and experience?

Abortion

1. How do you feel about abortion? Should a woman have the right to terminate a pregnancy if she so chooses, or not? / (If yes) Why?
2. (If no) Are there *any* circumstances under which you would condone abortion, for instance, if the woman has been raped, or if her health is seriously endangered by the pregnancy? / (If no) Why not?

Sexual Liberalism

1. There's been a lot of discussion about the way morals and attitudes about sex are changing in this country. If a man and a woman have sexual relations before marriage, do you think it is always wrong, wrong only sometimes, or not wrong at all? / Why?
2. Are you for or against sex education in the public schools? / Why?

Civil Liberties

1. What if someone who is teaching at one of the Oakland high schools admits to being a homosexual. Do you think that such a person should be allowed to continue teaching or not?
2. Suppose that a man who admits he is a communist has written a book in support of communism. This book is in the public library. Would you favor removing the book from the library or should it be allowed to remain?
3. What if somebody who is against all churches and religion wanted to make a speech here in Oakland. Should he or she be allowed to speak or not?

Utopia

1. If you could design a utopia, a society where everything was just as you'd like it to be, what would it look like? / How would people behave there?
2. What kinds of things that you, personally, do now, would you not have to do in an ideal society?
3. Suppose that a few people didn't like this utopia, however perfect it seemed to everybody else. What should be done with them?
4. Would there be any crime in a utopian society? / (If no) Why not? / (If yes) What would be done about it?
5. In creating a perfect society, which would you say was more important, a new type of people, or new ideas and ways of doing things?
6. Are we getting any closer to this perfect world? Could such a society come about, or is it just an unattainable ideal?

Commitment to the Present Sociopolitical Order

1. Generally speaking, do you tend to think of yourself as a liberal, a conservative, or as something else?
2. (If liberal or conservative) How strong of a liberal/conservative would you say you were? / (If other) How would you describe your political views?
3. How would you say the liberals differ from the conservatives? Are there any ways in which they are the same?
4. Sometimes people talk about "capitalist society" or "capitalism." What do these terms mean to you?

5. How about the phrase socialism—what does that mean to you?
6. Which do you think is the better way to organize a society, capitalism or socialism? What problems do you see in each system?
7. In general, do you think that our government should try out more new ideas or is it better off sticking to existing ways of doing things? / Why?
8. Some people think that the *type* of government we have here in the United States is about the best government that it is realistically possible for human beings to achieve. Others believe that it could still be improved upon. What do you think? Could we *realistically* create a better government?
9. Can you imagine a situation in your life in which you would want to move out of the United States to another country?
10. (If no) Suppose that circumstances forced you to do so, how would you feel about this?

Religion

1. Would you describe your religious affiliation, if any?
2. What does your religion mean to you? / Is it important to you in your *daily* living? Do you think about it much?
3. Do you go to (church/synagogue/other) regularly?
4. (If yes) Generally speaking, would you say it is or isn't possible to have a (religious/Christian) approach to life without going to (church/synagogue/other)?
5. What would you say are your most important religious beliefs?
6. Does your religion have any special teachings about crime and punishment?

Personal Assessment and Philosophy

1. If you had to describe yourself to someone who didn't know you, what would you say? What are your best and worst qualities?
2. What was the most important event in your life, the best thing that ever happened to you?
3. What would you say was the biggest disappointment in your life? / Why did this happen?
4. What would you say the most important *lessons* of life have been for you?
5. What really matters in life? What are the things you believe most in, or think most important?
6. What is the point of living? Why are we here?

Concluding Questions

1. Do you spend much time talking with your friends and family about topics like we've discussed here today? And have you thought about these issues much before, or aren't these the kinds of things you tend to think and talk about much? / (If mixed) Which?
2. Is there anything else you want to add to today's discussion?
3. Are there any questions you want to ask me?

APPENDIX C
Methodological Commentary

This commentary addresses the history and capacities of the methodology that I have employed, and the process of selecting, soliciting, and interviewing the participants in this study.

Intensive Interviewing

The use of intensive interviewing techniques to study political attitudes goes back at least as far as the 1956 work *Opinions and Personality* by the psychologists Brewster Smith, Jerome Bruner, and Robert White. Their exhaustive study of ten Boston men was outwardly focused on attitudes toward Russia, but ultimately sought to understand "the psychological processes involved in forming an opinion."[1] In political science, Robert Lane is credited with pioneering the use of intensive interviewing in his late 1950s study of the political ideologies of fifteen "common men."[2]

Several strong claims can be made for the value of depth interviews. First, even for the researcher who is wary of placing too much credence in the results of small sample studies, these can be an important source of new ideas—ideas which ultimately may be developed into more refined hypotheses and subjected to quantitative analysis. Smith, Bruner, and White described this function, in their early work:

> In the development of a science, there is a strategy of discovery as well as a strategy of proof. In envy of the precision of method and theory attained by the physical scientists, psychologists and social scientists have in recent years focussed their efforts perhaps too exclusively in the direction of proof. Our purpose in this book, and in the research that underlies it, is of the other sort: *not to establish beyond reasonable doubt insights already in our repertory, but to gain new insights* into the relations of opinions and personality. We also seek to develop a coherent framework for conceptualizing these relations, and to illustrate this framework sufficiently to encourage more systematic investigation of the research problems to which it gives rise. (Emphasis added.)[3]

Second, intensive interviews can, in Jennifer Hochschild's words, "flesh out the skeletal findings of the pollster."

> They can fill in gaps left by opinion research through providing data that surveys are unable to produce. In opinion polling, the *researcher infers* the links between variables; in intensive interviewing, the researcher induces the *respondent* to *create* the links between variables as he or she sees them ... The conclusions from both types of research may be equally valid, even identical, but they emerge from different types of data, which are collected in different ways to yield different types of explanations for the same phenomenon.[4]

A look at one of the issues addressed in this book will illustrate this function. Surveys have told us that the vast majority of the American public both feel that jails and prisons are not very effective at discouraging crime and want an increased use of incarceration. Given this knowledge, survey researchers may be able—on their own—to suggest several reasonable explanations as to why Americans hold these potentially contradictory views. But the intensive interviewer can ask respondents to explain it for themselves—as indeed I have done in these interviews.

Third, although depth interviewing is typically conducted with small numbers of respondents, still, for each of those individuals it yields a result which is as close as social science is likely to come to "the whole picture." We can ask about nearly every topic we feel could conceivably have relevance to the issues under consideration, and interviewees—given free rein to speak their minds—will tell us about matters we could not think to ask about. Then, not only are we possessed of a larger quantity of information about each individual than is the typical survey researcher, but also, we are able to conduct what Lane has called "contextual analysis:"

> An opinion, belief, or attitude is best understood in the context of other opinions, beliefs, and attitudes, for they illuminate its meaning, mark its boundaries, modify and qualify its force. Even more important, by grouping opinions the observer often can discover latent ideological themes; he can see the structure of thought: premise, inference, application. There is no other satisfactory way to map a political ideology.[5]

Given the superior depth and breadth of information about each individual that the intensive interviewer has to work with, he or she may, as Hochschild asserts, "find results where surveys find only noise." Thus, at times, the findings of intensive interviewing "may even justify rejection of some interpretations of survey results."[6]

Of course, I make no claim that intensive interviewing will offer information about *proportions* of Americans who hold particular views. Even when interviewees are carefully chosen in stratified random samples that seek reasonable demographic balance, we cannot say that they are fully representative. The numbers are simply too small. At times—predominantly in chapter five—I have mentioned numbers when referring to my interviewees. But this is in no way to suggest that an equal percentage of *all* American dissenters or believers hold that opinion: I note specific proportions only to make the point that differences or similarities between the groups are striking.

Thus, when we generalize from intensive interviewing, we must do so cautiously. There is less to offer in the way of statistical representativeness, but so much more in depth of understanding. It is in exploring and explaining varying patterns of opinion or belief that this tool can prove its value. In sum, this is a methodology that serves not to supplant the large sample survey, but to complement it.

Selecting and Soliciting Participants

All of the participants were chosen from among United States citizens who were residents of the city of Oakland, California. Believers, of course, are easily found; dissenters are rare and must be sought after. Thus, the first step in the selection process was to identify Oakland residents who might reasonably be considered to be dissenters. For this purpose, I made use of a screening questionnaire (see fig. 1). This one-page form, along with a cover letter, was mailed to 370 Oakland residents chosen randomly from a street directory of the city. Two follow-up mailings were sent to those who failed to return the questionnaire: first, a reminder postcard, and later, a different letter with a fresh copy of the questionnaire. The final response rate was 64 percent. A small number of persons who were not U.S. citizens, or who had moved out of the city of Oakland, were among those who completed the questionnaire; these persons were not considered eligible to become interview participants.

Respondents to the questionnaire were classified as probable believers or dissenters. In order to qualify as a dissenter, a respondent should *not* have given any of the following answers:

- that the courts are "not harsh enough"
- that a goal other than rehabilitation should be the most important purpose of the criminal justice system
- that "overly lenient courts" are a key cause of crime
- that prison conditions are "too soft" or "about right"

In general, do you think the courts in this area deal too harshly or not harshly enough with criminals?

_____Too harshly
_____About right
_____Not harshly enough

What do you think should be the most important purpose of our criminal justice system?   (check one)

_____punishment: making criminals suffer because of their crimes
_____rehabilitation: teaching offenders how to become productive citizens
_____deterrence: setting an example to discourage future crime
_____isolation: removing criminals from society
_____other _____
                                (Please indicate)

Which of the following would you say were the three most important causes of our country's high crime rate?
    (Please indicate by the numbers, "1," "2," and "3")

_____Widespread abuse of drugs and alcohol
_____Overly lenient courts
_____Poor parental influence
_____Poverty and unemployment
_____Inadequate police
_____Child abuse
_____Breakdown of moral standards
_____Violence on TV and in the movies
_____Other _____
                                (Please indicate)

Some people think that prisons today have gotten pretty soft, and that they often end up coddling criminals. Others feel that a life lived in prison is still a hard, brutal life. What do you think?

_____Prison conditions are generally too soft
_____Prison conditions are generally about right
_____Prison conditions are generally too hard

Do you think that the state of California should build more prisons to deal with overcrowding and to allow for longer sentences; or would you say that California already has enough prisons to house all those who really belong behind bars?

_____We need to build more prisons
_____We already have enough prisons

Some people feel that many non-violent offenders should be placed in alternative programs, such as community work-service or victim re-payment projects, instead of being sent to prison. Others are concerned that such programs do not adequately punish offenders or protect the safety of the community. Generally speaking, how do you feel?

_____I support alternatives to prison for non-violent offenders
_____I oppose alternatives to prison for non-violent offenders

Are you a citizen of the United States?   _____Yes _____No

Fig. 1. Prescreening questionnaire

- that we need to build more prisons
- that alternative sentencing should not be used even for nonviolent offenders

However, I allowed some leeway for the occasional aberrant answer if, for instance, comments the respondent wrote in the margins indicated that he or she was probably a dissenter.

Then, among those classified as believers, a further distinction was made between those who supported the use of alternatives to incarceration for nonviolent offenders, and those who did not. As only one in seven persons who returned usable questionnaires took the latter, very harsh position, I decided that I should set out purposefully to include a few of these "alternative opposers" in my sample. Their presence among my interviewees would help to ensure that a diversity of views, even among believers, was represented.[7]

In addition to those in the categories just described, I also sought to interview a few persons who had failed to return the questionnaire. Viewed from the perspective of a simple mail survey, the response rate had been quite good. But my only use for this questionnaire was as a screening device. Thus, I wanted to avoid screening *out* of the pool of potential interviewees anyone who was unwilling or unable to complete it. Functional illiteracy, for instance, is an enormous problem in Oakland, where an estimated 24 percent of the adult population cannot read well enough to understand a newspaper.[8]

Table 2 provides further details of the selection process. In the believer and nonrespondent categories, a stratified random sample of potential interviewees was drawn, using criteria designed to maintain a reasonable balance between males and females, and between persons living in better vs. worse off areas of the city.[9] In the dissenter category, the selection was not purely random. Instead, it was designed to maximize the likelihood that those interviewed would indeed prove to be *bona fide* dissenters, and at the same time to maintain the standards for gender and economic balance described above.[10] Thus, before these latter criteria were applied, the sixteen eligible questionnaire respondents were ranked according to my (admittedly somewhat subjective) appraisal of the degree of certainty that they actually were dissenters.

Once the names of the desired interviewees were determined, these persons were gradually contacted over the course of several weeks, with some substitution of names being made to maintain gender and economic balance when the pattern of rejections and acceptances had disturbed it. Each potential interviewee was contacted first by letter, and then by telephone.

Remarkably, two of the four questionnaire nonrespondents who were interviewed turned out to be dissenters. Given statistical realities, I had assumed that all four would be believers. To be able to have non-respondents represented in both categories was a much appreciated stroke of luck.

A chart listing the twenty-four persons who were interviewed, and their "vital statistics," can be found in appendix A.

The Interviews

The twenty-four participants were interviewed between April and early July of 1987. Typically, two sessions, each lasting two to two-and-a-half hours, were held with each interviewee. But there were exceptions: one woman polished off both interviews in slightly more than two hours total. And the longest-winded individual required three sessions totaling over ten hours to answer all my questions.

Nearly all of the interviews were held either in the homes of the participants, or in a conference room made available to me in the administrative building of a downtown church. Here there were exceptions as well: one participant preferred to be interviewed on his boat moored in the Oakland harbor. Another, extremely pressed for time before a trip abroad,

TABLE 2.   The Selection Process

	No. of Persons Eligible	No. of Interviewees Sought	Final No. Interviewed	Total No. of Contacts Made in Order to Get Final No. to Agree[a]	No. Who Agreed Only Reluctantly to Participate
Dissenters	16	8	8	8	1
Believers Alternative Opposers Remainder	26 143	4 6-8	4 8	8 10	2 2
Non-respondents	117	4-6	4	10	2
Total	302[b]	24	24	36	7

[a]In addition to those persons who, when contacted, refused to be interviewed, there were also seven potential interviewees with whom I was never able to make contact.

[b]Three hundred seventy questionnaires were sent out. Later, sixty-eight names had to be removed from the list of persons eligible for selection, because of one of the following reasons: the questionnaire was returned undelivered; it had been addressed to someone who turned out to be dead or otherwise incapable of completing it; it was completed by someone who was a noncitizen; or it was completed by someone who had moved out of Oakland.

asked if he could be interviewed at the laundromat! We settled on a quieter location where both aims could still be accomplished.

Each interview session was tape recorded and later transcribed verbatim. The interviewees were offered anonymity and an honorarium of $50.00 in exchange for their participation. All twenty-four accepted the remuneration. The promise of confidentiality has been kept here through the use of pseudonyms for the participants and by altering many of the details of their lives. I have tried to make these changes subtle, in order that the true character of these twenty-four individuals will not be unduly masked. Five critical descriptors—gender, race, sexual orientation (where it was acknowledged), religion, and income bracket—have been reported without any changes. Everything else—occupation, age, description of spouse, number of children, etc.—was subject to change if I deemed it either (1) too revealing of the individual or (2) easily amenable to slight change without significant distortion of the participant's essential nature.

Interviewees were asked a series of open-ended questions.[11] These are listed in appendix B. Questions in the first interview dealt exclusively with the participants' views and experiences regarding crime and criminal justice. The second interview contained a handful of crime-related questions, but was predominantly devoted to discerning the interviewees' political, religious, and personal philosophies. The prepared questions were designed with the dual purpose of maximizing opportunities for individuality of response, while providing, as well, a consistent foundation that would allow comparison among the participants. In addition to the prepared questions, many ad hoc and probe questions also were posed.

Analysis of the Transcripts

After the tapes had been transcribed, I read each participants' interview with a long list of questions in hand. Some were simply duplicates of individual interview questions: Does this person approve of work release programs? Has she ever been a victim of crime? Other questions called for broader assessments based on an entire interview: How empathetic is this person toward offenders? Toward victims? How complex of a problem does he consider crime to be? Thus, as I read each interviewee's transcript I was compiling a very detailed set of notes. Although these notes by no means replaced consultation with the original transcripts, they became my primary analytical tool. I have been through them time and again, in a dozen different configurations: reading about individuals unto themselves, and comparing between participants on points from the minute to the very broad.

Postinterview Classification

Although all but four interviewees were prescreened by means of the mail questionnaire, the advance designation of each as a believer or a dissenter was only tentative. Naturally, not everybody said exactly the same things in person as in the mail, and the interviews also provided a vastly greater level of detail. Once the interviewing was completed, a final determination had to be made regarding the category into which each participant should be placed. I decided at that time to remove two of the prescreened participants from the believer and dissenter categories altogether. These individuals expressed views which were sufficiently incoherent as to defy meaningful interpretation. Their views were discussed in some detail in chapter four, but have been excluded from consideration in the remaining chapters.

Ultimately, I decided that each of the other prescreened participants had received the correct designation from the start, but this was not a simple or obvious conclusion. As discussed in the body of this work, a great many believers hold mixed views—part harsh, part mild. It is the same with the dissenters; their views are not perfectly pure in mildness. Thus, it was at times a difficult call, whether the balance of a participant's views should tip him or her over the line in one direction or the other. The final determination was made on the basis of the realization that there is a critical difference in the way in which the believers and the dissenters conceive of the basic aims of the criminal justice system. Whatever their other differences, each of the (coherent) prescreened believers (plus two of the mail questionnaire nonrespondents) was alike in this critical foundation. So too for the dissenters. The details of the criteria by which the interviewees were classified were discussed in chapter two.

This commentary has described the justifications for and the mechanics of the methodology used in this study. Clearly, this was not a representative sample, in the sense of figures and proportions. But I sought to offer nothing new to our quantitative knowledge of public opinion about criminal justice. Just as clearly, it was not a quick and easy sample. I used a stratified random sample of the city's residents, avoiding the pitfalls associated with studies relying on college students, members of certain organizations, or volunteers solicited through newspaper advertisements. Represented among my twenty-four interviewees was a considerable diversity of age, education, income, race, and religion. Nearly one third of the participants were persons who were initially quite reluctant to become involved in this study. Most importantly, these interviewees form a group of Americans whose views about criminal justice span the spectrum of belief from one extreme to the other. This has allowed me to understand more deeply, and then to compare, the beliefs both of those who stand with the get-tough consensus and of those who dissent from this view.

Notes

Chapter 1

1. Maguire, Pastore, and Flanagan, *Sourcebook 1992*, 196–97. An average of 3 percent said "too harsh" and 5 percent said "don't know." An average of 9 percent volunteered the response that the courts were "about right," an answer that, depending on the respondent's perceptions of the criminal justice system, could mean either support or rejection for a policy of tough sentencing. During these ten years, the proportion answering "not harsh enough" ranged from 79 to 86 percent.

2. President's Commission, *Challenge of Crime.*

3. Hindelang, *Public Opinion,* 12; Maguire, Pastore, and Flanagan, *Sourcebook 1992*, 196–97. In 1965, 2 percent said "too harshly," 34 percent said "about right," and 16 percent said "don't know."

4. Ekland-Olson, Kelly, and Eisenberg, "Crime and Incarceration," 397.

5. Gilliard, "Prisoners in 1992," 1; Beck, Bonczar, and Gilliard, "Jail Inmates 1992," 1.

6. Caringella-MacDonald, "State Crises," 102; "Prisoners in 1988," 5. I have taken average figures from the ranges in percent of capacity given in this report, which listed both proportions of highest rated capacity and proportions of lowest rated capacity.

7. "Prisoners in 1990," 6.

8. Caringella-MacDonald, "State Crises," 102. On these changes, see also Friedman, *Crime and Punishment,* 305–9.

9. Breed, "State of Corrections Today," 5.

10. Greenfield, "Capital Punishment 1991," 1. See also Friedman, *Crime and Punishment,* 316–23.

11. Austin and McVey, "NCCD Prison Population Forecast," 1.

12. "Prisoners in 1990," 7. The crimes under consideration were murder, nonnegligent manslaughter, rape, robbery, aggravated assault, and burglary.

13. Foote, *Prison Population Explosion,* 1, 5, 7.

14. Quoted in Scheingold, *Politics of Law and Order,* 77.

15. President's Commission, *Challenge of Crime.*

16. Hindelang, *Public Opinion,* 12.

17. Quoted in Scheingold, *Politics of Law and Order,* 78.

18. McGarrell and Flanagan, *Sourcebook 1984,* 226–27.

19. Department of Justice, *National Update,* 1.

20. Foote, *Prison Population Explosion,* 9.

21. Scheingold, *Politics of Street Crime,* 178. Scheingold apparently draws on Wilson and Herrnstein, *Crime and Human Nature* (New York: Simon and Schuster, 1985) for the notion that crime can act as a valence issue. For a more detailed discussion of valence issues, see Stokes, "Valence Politics," esp. 147 and 150.

22. Scheingold, *Politics of Law and Order,* 54–55.

23. Komarnicki and Doble, *Crime and Corrections,* 120. Several different polls have covered this question, which seems to be particularly sensitive to wording effects. For instance, in the same year (1982), a national poll done for *Time* magazine found that 41 percent selected the response, "to get violent criminals off the streets," 19 percent chose "to punish offenders, teach them a lesson," 15 percent selected "to rehabilitate the morals and skills of criminals," and 20 percent chose "to act as a deterrent to crime" (Komarnicki and Doble, *Crime and Corrections,* 119). My point is not about how many took which position, but that there were a variety of positions.

24. "One Household in Four Victim of Crime," 24–25.

25. Maguire and Flanagan, *Sourcebook 1990,* 200–201; Komarnicki and Doble, *Crime and Corrections,* 117. In a more specific question on this topic, 82 percent of a 1989 Gallup sample favored "making it more difficult for those convicted of violent crimes like murder and rape to be paroled" (Maguire and Flanagan, *Sourcebook 1990,* 188).

26. McGarrell and Flanagan, *Sourcebook 1984,* 190, 196. Sixty-seven percent agreed strongly; 22 percent agreed somewhat.

27. Flanagan and Caulfield, "Public Opinion and Prison Policy," 39. On the other hand, a different study found that 81 percent of a national sample selected incarceration as the most suitable penalty for household burglary with losses of one thousand dollars or more. (Department of Justice, *Bureau of Justice Statistics Data Report, 1987,* 35.)

28. In 1986, the year before I spoke with my interviewees, over $53 billion was spent nationwide on justice system expenditures, over $15 billion of which went to corrections. By 1990, over $64 billion was being spent nationwide, with almost $25 billion going to corrections (Jamieson and Flanagan, *Sourcebook 1988,* 2; Flanagan and Maguire, *Sourcebook 1991,* 2). In his report for the Center on Juvenile and Criminal Justice, Caleb Foote writes: "A few years ago the United States gained the dubious distinction of having the highest imprisonment rate in the world, passing South Africa and the Soviet Union . . . By 1990, 455 adult Americans per 100,000 population were behind prison and jail bars, compared to South Africa's rate of 311. Among black males our lead is overwhelming; the American black male imprisonment rate at 3,370 per 100,000 is almost five times greater than South Africa's 681 per 100,000 black males. Our total rate of 455 is more than four times that of Britain, five times that of Germany or France, and in most developed western countries the rates range between 50 and 90" (Foote, *Prison Population Explosion,* 1).

29. A 1982 ABC News poll found that 86 percent of a national sample disagreed with this statement: "If a person spends time in jail, chances are good he won't commit any more crimes after he gets out of jail." Eleven percent agreed and 4

percent gave no answer (McGarrell and Flanagan, *Sourcebook 1984,* 199). The Figgie study (1980) found that 80 percent of a national sample replied "not particularly effective" or "totally ineffective" to this question: "How effective are most prisons in rehabilitating criminals and helping their return to society as law-abiding citizens?" Twenty percent replied "effective" or "very effective" (*Figgie Report Part I,* 126 and 143). And a 1981 Harris poll found that 78 percent of a national sample answered "doesn't discourage crime" to this question: "From what you know or have heard, do you feel that our system of law enforcement works to really discourage people from committing crimes, or don't you feel it discourages them much?" Another 2 percent volunteered the answer that it "encourages crime." Sixteen percent said that it "really discourages crime" and 3 percent were "not sure." These figures are my readings from a line graph (Brown, Flanagan, and McLeod, *Sourcebook 1983,* 245).

30. A 1984 Roper poll found that 84 percent of a national sample "on balance" favored "harsher prison sentences for those convicted of crimes." Seven percent opposed it, and 10 percent volunteered that they had mixed feelings or didn't know (Public Opinion Location Library (on-line), Roper Center for Public Opinion Research, University of Connecticut).

31. Flanagan and Maguire, *Sourcebook 1991,* 204–5. Four percent responded that the courts were too harsh, and 5 percent responded "don't know."

32. See *Criminal Victimization: 1973–90 Trends* for data from the National Crime Victimization Survey (NCVS) of the Bureau of Justice Statistics, U.S. Department of Justice. For the years prior to 1973, the only data available are the FBI's Uniform Crime Reports (UCR), which are highly vulnerable to variations over time and locale in the degree to which crimes are reported to local police departments and reliably recorded there. To wit, compare the years 1973–90, when both UCR and NCVS data were available: although the rates move up and down slightly from year to year, the UCR shows a significant increase in the crime rate over the full period, while the NCVS shows an overall decrease in crime rates (Maguire, Pastore, and Flanagan, *Sourcebook 1992,* 357).

33. Stinchcombe et al., *Crime and Punishment,* x; *General Social Surveys, 1972–87,* 114–15, 117, 118–19, 163–64, 167, 226–27, 229–31, 236–39. See also McClosky and Brill, *Dimensions of Tolerance,* 435–38.

34. To wit: consider the efforts of then vice president George Bush to brand Governor Michael Dukakis as a *liberal* who was soft on crime, in the 1988 presidential election.

35. Stinchcombe et al., *Crime and Punishment,* x, 74, 88–92. The correlations calculated by these researchers are for pre-1980 data. More recent NORC data confirm that attitudes on each of these social issues have either held steady or continued to liberalize through 1987—the year of my interviews. The data also show that harsh views on sentencing by the courts and on the use of capital punishment have hovered around the same figures during the 1980s.

36. Ibid., 85, 87–92.

37. I continue the use of the terms liberal and conservative, initiated by Stinchcombe et al., to state the issues about these contrary directions of opinion movement.

However, I make absolutely no implication that the average American—or my interviewees—uses these concepts as organizing devices in the development of their various opinions and beliefs (See Converse, "Nature of Belief Systems"). The fact that aggregate public opinion has moved in directions that can be given these labels does not presuppose anything about the thought processes of the millions of individuals who make up that public.

38. See for instance, Blumstein, "Planning for Future Prison Needs," 209–10.

39. Friedman, *Crime and Punishment*, 452.

40. Scheingold, *Politics of Law and Order*, 55.

41. See, for instance, Sacco, "Effects of Mass Media"; and Skogan and Maxfield, *Coping with Crime*.

42. See, for instance, Barrie, *Television and Fear;* Liska and Baccaglini, "Feeling Safe by Comparison"; and Sheley and Ashkins, "Crime, Crime News."

43. Barrie, *Television and Fear*, 93.

44. See Barrie, *Television and Fear*, 91–97; and Scheingold, *Politics of Law and Order*, 62–64.

45. See the bibliography for a selection of references, including studies of public views on the causes of crime, appropriate responses, and the justifications that are employed for those responses; research on levels of victimization, fear, and the salience of the crime problem; and research on perceptions of crime, crime rates, and the criminal justice system. Also included are studies of public beliefs about the relative severity of crime, sources of information upon which people base their perceptions and opinions, and similarities or differences in the attitudes of the public and policymakers.

46. See Cullen et al., "Attitudes toward Sanctioning"; Cullen, Clark, and Wozniak, "Explaining the Get Tough Movement;" *Figgie Report Part V;* Rosch, "Crime in American Politics," in Fairchild and Webb, *Politics of Crime;* Scheingold, *Politics of Law and Order;* Stinchcombe et al., *Crime and Punishment; Figgie Report Part I;* Carter, "Hispanic Attitudes toward Crime"; Cook, "Ideology's Effects"; Taylor, Scheppele, and Stinchcombe, "Salience of Crime"; Duffee and Ritti, "Correctional Policy and Public Values"; Rose, "Public Opinion Concerning Correctional Policies"; Thomas and Cage, "Correlates of Public Attitudes"; Watts and Free, *State of the Nation III;* Newman and Trilling, "Public Perceptions of Criminal Behavior"; Boydell and Grindstaff, "Public Opinion toward Sanctions"; and Dow, "Role of Identification."

47. There was an exception in 1986, when the Public Agenda Foundation conducted a qualitative study (Doble, *Crime and Punishment*) utilizing "focus groups" of a dozen individuals in each of ten U.S. cities. Although this study can be praised for its national scope and demographic balance, it has quite serious flaws. Only one two-hour interview was held with each group, allowing any individual on average only ten minutes to speak, no doubt even less for the reticent. Further, the questioning of participants in a group presents a serious problem with acquiescence and bias.

48. See Hall et al., *Policing the Crisis,* for an examination of similar questions regarding British views on crime (from a different methodological base).

49. See appendix C for a more detailed discussion of the capacities of this methodology.

50. The remaining two interviewees expressed incoherent views; they will be discussed in detail in chapter 4.

51. Scheingold, *Politics of Law and Order,* 59–77.

52. The term believer, and this notion of a dominant social ethos also recalls Antonio Gramsci's concept of hegemony. "Hegemony consists . . . in 'an order in which a certain way of life and thought is dominant, in which one concept of reality is diffused throughout society, in all its institutional and private manifestations, informing with its spirit all tastes, morality, customs, religions and political principles, and all social relations, particularly in their intellectual and moral connotations'" (Gwyn Williams, *"Egemonia* in the Thought of Antonio Gramsci," *Journal of the History of Ideas* 21, no. 4, (Oct–Dec. 1960): 587, quoted in Femia, "Hegemony and Consciousness," 30–31).

53. Oakland's 1987 population was 356,200 (*California Statistical Abstract, 1987,* 16). By 1993, it had grown to slightly over 375,000. The 1987 population was approximately 47 percent black, 38 percent white, 10 percent Hispanic, and 8 percent Asian and Pacific Islander (Zimmerman, "Oakland," A-5).

54. Oakland Chamber of Commerce brochure, 5.

55. Walters, *The New California,* 69–72; Viviano, "The Powerlessness of Black Power." In this December 1986 article, Viviano wrote: "Today, the president and chief proprietor of the [Oakland] *Tribune* is [Robert] Maynard, the first black editor of a major American daily. Just up Broadway is the office of Lionel Wilson, Oakland's first black mayor. The city manager is black. The director of the museum is black. One black woman chairs the Board of Education. Another is port commissioner. On a per capita basis, Oakland has the largest number of black-owned businesses of any city in the United States. Black doctors and lawyers are among the potentates of Pill Hill and the Alameda County bar" (10).

56. Zimmerman, "Oakland"; Evenson, "City's Chinatown Bustling with Growth"; Bagwell, *Oakland,* 263.

57. Dorgan, "Under Siege."

58. Still, to place this in perspective, relatively placid-sounding cities like Portland and Seattle reported higher crime rates (Department of Justice, Federal Bureau of Investigation, *Crime in the United States,* 63–110). The full list of cities reporting higher crime rates: Portland, Miami, Ft. Worth, Detroit, Atlanta, Dallas, Seattle, Newark, and Boston.

59. A letter and supporting materials from the office of Henry L. Gardner, then the Oakland city manager, indicate that the best estimate of the poverty rate for 1988 would be 25 to 30 percent.

60. Evenson and Zimmerman, "Residents Question Priorities," A-6.

61. In addition, a city council election was held in Oakland in April 1987, two weeks after I began my interviews. Judging by the published statements of the candidates, the issue of crime received no extraordinary attention at this time.

62. *San Francisco Chronicle Index,* April–June 1987, 265 and July–September 1987, 301. Eleven of the articles appeared on the front page.

63. "Three Nude Women Freed from Chains," *Oakland Tribune,* March 26, 1987; "Bizarre Torture Case Detailed," *Oakland Tribune,* March 27, 1987.

64. See for instance, Converse, "Nature of Belief Systems" and "Public Opinion and Voting Behavior"; or Zaller, *Nature and Origins.*

65. Converse, "Public Opinion and Voting Behavior," 85.

66. A 1984 California poll showed that "crime and law enforcement" ranked first among a list of sixteen issues regarding which Californians were asked about their degree of concern. Seventy-three percent were "extremely concerned" about it, and 23 percent were "somewhat concerned" (Field, "High Degree of Public Concern").

Chapter 2

1. Recall that in order to keep my promise of confidentiality for the participants, pseudonyms have been used throughout, and many of the details of participants' lives have been altered. Five critical descriptors—gender, race, sexual orientation (where it was acknowledged), religion, and income bracket—have been reported without any changes. Everything else—occupation, age, description of spouse, number of children, and so on—was subject to change if I deemed it either too revealing of the individual, or easily amenable to *slight* change without significant distortion of the participants' essential nature.

2. Interviewee quotes are reported verbatim with two exceptions: Space fillers like "um" or "you know" and unnecessarily repeated words have been deleted except where they impart some significant meaning. Words that might indirectly identify an interviewee have been changed or omitted.

3. For details, see the section entitled "Hypothetical Crimes and Punishments" in the list of my interview questions given in appendix B.

4. An accurate recidivism rate is difficult to measure. To begin with, there are the uncountable recidivists who are never apprehended for new crimes that they commit. Then, there is some confusion caused by the fact that researchers have used a variety of different measures for this phenomenon. One Bureau of Justice Statistics study that followed some four thousand young parolees (ages seventeen to twenty-two at time of release in 1978) from twenty-two states found that 69 percent were rearrested for a serious crime within six years of release. Fifty-three percent were convicted for a new offense. The report points out that the conviction rate actually understates the true recidivism rate because not all of these individuals are prose-cuted (parolees often have their parole revoked and are reincarcerated to complete their original sentences, rather than being prosecuted for a new offense) and because data on new convictions were sometimes incomplete (Beck and Shipley, "Recidivism of Young Parolees"). Another BJS study, using a different methodology, estimated that a "first-timer" in state prison had a 29–38 percent "lifetime chance of returning to prison to serve a second sentence." A second-timer was estimated to have a 40–46 percent chance of return, and a third-timer a 42–53 percent chance (Langan, "Prevalence of Imprisonment," 6). The California Department of Corrections reports that 34.5 percent of prisoners (of all ages) released in 1985 were returned to custody within one year by the Board of Prison Terms; 12.9 percent returned within the year

because of a new felony commitment. Thus a total of 47 percent were reincarcerated within one year (California Department of Corrections, *Challenges in Corrections,* 25). Finally, an article in the *San Jose Mercury News* reports that "nearly 70 percent [of state parolees] are arrested before finishing their second year" (Wright, "Prison's Revolving Door").

5. Just as with the terms believer and dissenter, discussed in the first chapter, I struggled long and hard over the choice of these terms, harsh and mild. They oversimplify the matter, of course. Probably any two single words chosen to distinguish between complex areas such as these would oversimplify; if there are those that would not, I failed to find them. I chose these two words because they are basically factual, descriptive terms and avoid the even greater pitfalls of value-laden terms such as liberal, conservative, progressive, punitive, and so on.

6. All nine dissenters oppose capital punishment.

7. Here I mean, in addition to the actual words "punish" and "deter" and their variations, phrases such as "making criminals think twice," "setting an example" with a harsh sanction, or comments that a certain offender "deserves" such and such a penalty.

8. Of interest are some of the results of a 1987 national survey in which respondents were asked how important certain purposes were in choosing penalties for various offenses. The aggregate data show that 91 percent felt that "special deterrence" ("to scare the offender so he/she will not do it again") was important; and 87 percent felt that "general deterrence" ("to scare off other people who might do the same thing") was important. Eighty-nine percent felt that "desert" ("to give the offender what he/she deserves") was important; and 46 percent felt that "retribution" ("to get even with the offender by making him/her suffer for what he/she has done") was important. Seventy-two percent felt that "incapacitation" ("to lock up the offender so while he/she is in prison he/she won't be able to commit more crimes") was important (Flanagan and Jamieson, *Sourcebook 1987,* 157).

9. See appendix B.

10. I am referring to the first quote given in this section about Mrs. Jones.

11. The exception is Richard Niederhaus, whose enormous reluctance to overgeneralize complicates the analysis of his views. Richard rejects deterrence outright and, judging from the collectivity of his views, can be considered an opponent of punishment. He allows for the possibility that incarceration may occasionally be appropriate but never actively supports this on grounds of public safety. It is only by process of elimination that at least tacit support for a limited policy of isolation can be imputed to him.

12. The 1986 Survey of Inmates of State Correctional Facilities conducted by the Bureau of Justice Statistics showed that 55 percent of inmates in state prisons had been incarcerated for violent offenses (Innes, "Profile of State Prison Inmates, 1986," 1–3). The 1989 Survey of Inmates in Local Jails conducted for the Bureau of Justice Statistics by the U.S. Bureau of the Census showed that only 23 percent of inmates in local jails had been charged or convicted for violent offenses (Beck, "Profile of Jail Inmates, 1989," 4).

Chapter 3

1. When I say that the dissenters *by definition* take this position, I do not refer to a definition that I pulled out of a hat—or even out of some scholarly tome. What I speak of is rather something of a "push-me-pull-you": part empirical finding, part definitional stipulation. In using a mailed screening questionnaire, I began with a provisional definition of who would be eligible to be interviewed as a dissenter. But once the interviews were completed, I turned to the content of the conversations for guidance in better defining the difference between the groups, especially in the difficult marginal cases. From the *empirical* finding that the dissenters I had prescreened (as well as two of the mail questionnaire nonrespondents I interviewed) shared a perspective on the basic aims of the criminal justice system that differed significantly from that of the believers, I went on to form a finalized definition of the two groups.

2. I cannot state with certainty the primary motivation behind the *mild* views of three of the believers: Thelma Winters, Miriam Madamba, and Mary Bono. Only a small minority of the mild statements from these interviewees give the listener any indication of what value or concern may have led them to that conclusion. In my research design, the believers were asked specific preplanned questions about their reasons for holding harsh views, but no such predetermined questions were asked about why they hold their mild views. Nonetheless, most believers made the motivations for their mild views clear, either because these views were very important to them, or because they were comfortable with detailed talk about political and social issues and took seriously my broad encouragement to think aloud about the answers they would give. Unfortunately, neither of these factors much applied in the case of these three women.

Still, some speculation is in order. Motivations in compassion or social critique that are strong enough to be the *primary* motivations for an interviewee's mild views will, I believe, generally be motivations that that interviewee will defend or at least elaborate upon. For many dissenters, the task is to defend these values against the countervailing weight of public opinion. They cannot make simple statements of their views and assume that the sense of them will be obvious to any listener. But even a believer who responds strongly to compassion or social critique may feel compelled to defend, or at least to fully describe, this influence, because of its obvious contrast to his or her *own* harsh views and motivations. We have good examples of this from among the complex believers in this chapter.

What I am suggesting is that when compassion or social critique is held as the primary motivation for the mildness of an individual who also holds quite harsh views, it is highly likely to be an *active* motivation. Security and desert, on the other hand, are better suited to function adequately as fairly passive motivations in believers whose feelings about the mild views that they express are not particularly strong. They make no stark contrast to the motivations that influence these believers' harsher views: indeed, they are the very same values that operated there—now differently applied.

Following this logic, it seems most likely that these three women are primarily motivated in their mild views by security and/or desert. These women have very little to say about why they hold the mild views they do, but in this context, these motivations demand no huge defense. They may feel simply that rehabilitative or preventive programs are worth trying (provided they do not overly threaten our present safety), because they may possibly reduce future criminality: security. Just as likely, they may feel that some crimes simply are not bad enough to deserve a very harsh punishment: desert. Perhaps both.

Let me stress that it is *not* the case that these women hold inconsistent or incomprehensible views, but simply that they have failed to reveal the values motivating them to hold a minor portion of their views. This is omission, not incoherence. While the mild views each woman expressed were not a major part of her opinions about crime, I have little doubt that each could have given a rudimentary explanation of her motivations for holding them—had I asked her.

3. By comparison, the dissenters also believe that the mild policies they advocate will be the most effective means of reducing crime. But they do not hold up effectiveness (security) as a value to as great a degree as Elizabeth does.

4. See for instance, Rosenau, *Post-modernism and the Social Sciences,* 44–45, 53, 88; Edelman, *Constructing the Political Spectacle,* 3, 9; Edelman, *Symbolic Uses of Politics,* 172–87; Edelman, *Politics as Symbolic Action,* 3–5; Tversky and Kahneman, "The Framing of Decisions," in Hogarth, *Question Framing and Response Consistency;* Converse, "Nature of Belief Systems" and "Public Opinion and Voting Behavior"; and Zaller, *Nature and Origins.*

5. As noted in chapter 1, only two interviewees out of the twenty-four were distinguished by their incoherence. These two individuals will be discussed in detail in chapter 4.

6. Saudi Arabia is *not* Aram's homeland.

7. The language of the interview question was: "Some communities have experimented with restitution programs in which offenders work to pay back their victims for what they stole, or in other cases do service work for the whole community, like cleaning up parks or highways. Do you approve or disapprove of this kind of program? Should it be used as an alternative to prison in some cases?" Earlier in the interview I showed the interviewees a list of possible solutions to the crime problem. Included was "making more use of alternatives to prisons." About that, Mrs. Monroe remarked: "Make more use of alternates to prisons, and that would eliminate the whole requirement of prison."

Chapter 4

1. Here I follow in the tradition of Robert Lane. See his *Political Ideology.*

2. It should be stressed that my evaluation of coherence was both subjective and holistic. I had no simple litmus test. It is always possible that an individual may have possessed a personal coherence that I could not see or a type of sophistication that I did not comprehend. I present this as only my best effort to understand and would note that because of its limitations, I have tried to be generous in my assessments. In the few cases where I have labeled individuals incoherent or virtually

lacking in any political belief system, it seemed to me clear that these persons were not just slightly, but *significantly* more deficient in coherence or content than *any* other of the interviewees. And when I divide the political belief systems of the remaining interviewees into sophisticated and not so sophisticated, this is, of course, to draw a line on a continuum, rather than to make an all-or-nothing categorization.

3. In fact, about one-third of the interviewees with coherent political belief systems could not even give a reasonable definition of the terms liberal and conservative. On the broader issue of how to measure a political belief system, there has been a long-standing debate between Robert Lane and Philip Converse, as well as others who have taken their lead. See especially, Lane, *Political Ideology,* and "Patterns of Political Belief"; Hochschild, *What's Fair,* 229–37; Converse, "Nature of Belief Systems," and "Public Opinion and Voting Behavior"; Kinder, "Diversity and Complexity"; Niemi and Weisberg, *Controversies in Voting Behavior,* 319–28; Zaller and Feldman, "Answering-Questions," and "Political Culture of Ambivalence"; and Zaller, *Nature and Origins.*

4. See for instance, Prothro and Grigg, "Fundamental Principles of Democracy."

5. Converse, "Public Opinion and Voting Behavior," 85.

6. Zaller, *Nature and Origins,* 42–51.

7. Interestingly, these participants also have *stable* views on criminal justice—at least as measured by consistency between the mail questionnaire and the interviews. (The mail questionnaires were completed during February and March of 1987, the interviews during April to early July of the same year.) Of these thirteen interviewees, eleven completed a mail questionnaire. Of these, only one person expressed completely different or contradictory views about any of the six topics covered in both settings. (This individual—Elizabeth Williams, the physical therapist—did so on four of the topics. She explained to me after her interviews that when she received the questionnaire, it was shortly after her home was burglarized and that she was undergoing a largely temporary shift of opinion about criminal justice, in reaction to this violation.) By and large, the rest of the participants have fairly stable criminal justice views also, but not quite as stable as those in the first group. Of the eight remaining interviewees with coherent political belief systems, six completed a mail questionnaire. Of these, one gave completely different or contradictory answers on three of the topics covered; one did so on two topics; three did so on one topic; and one did so on no topics.

8. A word should be said about differences in educational levels between the two groups of interviewees. Eight of the nine dissenters I interviewed had completed at least some college coursework, whereas only seven of the thirteen believers had done so. (See appendix A for details.) Based on NORC's survey question about the harshness of the courts, however, there is some reason to question whether such a high proportion of all American dissenters would hold this level of education. In 1987 (the year in which my interviews were conducted), 3 percent of those with a college education said the courts were too harsh, as did 3 percent of those with a high school education, and 5 percent of those with a grade school education. (For the volunteered answer "about right," the percentages were: college, 14; high school, 9; grade school, 18 [Flanagan and Jamieson, *Sourcebook 1987,* 142–43].) Of course,

the standard I used to screen potential dissenters via a mail questionnaire was more stringent than simply avoiding an answer of "not harsh enough" to the NORC question. I required respondents to qualify on five additional questions and then prioritized the eligible by perceived certainty that they would truly turn out to be dissenters. Thus, there may be some degree to which having *consistent* dissenting views is associated with a higher level of education, although it is also possible that some of what we are observing here is sampling error. If it is the latter, however, this took place under conditions that should have discouraged it. The first eight eligible dissenters I contacted all agreed to be interviewed, and I was even fortunate enough to discover that two of the four mail questionnaire nonrespondents who agreed to be interviewed actually were dissenters. Furthermore, I made it a stipulation that at least 40 percent of each subgroup should live on the poorer side of the city of Oakland. (See appendix C for further details.)

9. This seeming inconguity is one of which Adam does not appear to be aware. The same could be said about each of the other participants whose criminal justice views do not appear consistent with their broader political ideologies.

10. The fact that one desires the law to be respected absolutely should not predetermine the choice of any particular method of obtaining respect. It matters only that one believe that the chosen method will work.

11. In chapter 5, I will discuss scores that I gave my interviewees, based on a twelve-point scale aimed at approximating just how liberal they would have been judged to be by Arthur Stinchcombe and the other authors of *Crime and Punishment—Changing Attitudes in America.* For all their incoherence, it is astonishing that Paul scored a 12, and Mrs. Reed received an 11.5 on this scale. The questions upon which this scale was based involved certain social issues—women's rights, abortion, sexual liberalism, homosexuality, interracial marriage, racist sentiments—and applications of civil liberties. Generally speaking, these questions were more closed-ended and were asked in a more cut-and-dried manner, with less probing for any underlying rationale, than were the typical questions of the second interview. Somehow, Paul Bongolan and Evangeline Reed were able to give consistently liberal answers to these questions. This does not mean that they are consistent liberals. First, there is arguably more to being a liberal than is included in these Stinchcombe-inspired questions. And further, when these two individuals leave the relatively safe shoals of guided-reply questions and begin to speak in depth about broader political concepts, they soon develop problems of incoherence. Perhaps it is a case of their having picked up surface elements of the liberal party-line, virtually by rote, without retaining as well an understanding of the rationale beneath this perspective.

12. Taylor, Scheppele, and Stinchcombe, "Salience of Crime." The authors make this point in connection with their finding that people living in high crime areas exhibit increased cognitive consistency about the crime problem. But the idea applies as well to the comparison between crime and policy issues that have less overall salience for the general public.

13. It may be important, as noted earlier, that Sadie Monroe came to our conversations with a mind preoccupied with personal problems. Her interviews were

quite brief, and she may not have described her beliefs as fully as she would have at a more propitious time.

14. Gladys Jones, for instance, gives us a clue when I ask about her most important religious beliefs: "When you die you go to heaven, *if you do right*" (emphasis added).

Chapter 5

1. Figgie Report Part I, 127. These researchers looked at two types of fear. "Concrete fear" was based on an index that measured how often a person worries about being the victim of six crimes: murder, sexual assault, mugging, knifing, beating, and armed robbery. Their "formless fear" index measured "how often people worry about being alone during the day and at night, in their homes, in their neighborhoods, and in their central business district or shopping center" (18–19).

2. Stinchcombe et al., *Crime and Punishment,* x. The authors used poll data from Gallup and the National Opinion Research Center. Since this book was published in 1980, the situation has remained the same for blacks but has changed somewhat for women. Stinchcombe et al. used two measures for punitiveness: level of support for the use of capital punishment for murder and level of support for the proposition that the courts are not harsh enough on crime. While women continue to support capital punishment in lesser numbers than men, they have since 1982 favored harsher sentencing by the courts in slightly higher numbers than have men (Maguire, Pastore, and Flanagan, *Sourcebook 1992,* 196–97 and 206–7).

3. Stinchcombe et al., *Crime and Punishment,* 125–26.

4. Ibid., 70–72. Salience was measured by whether or not a respondent mentioned a social control problem as the nation's most important problem.

5. See Cullen et al., "Attitudes toward Sanctioning," 318; *Figgie Report Part V,* 97–98; and Taylor, Scheppele, and Stinchcombe, "Salience of Crime," 415.

6. Only one member of each group—Anne Girard, the aspiring writer (a dissenter), and Thelma Winters, the retired home health aide (a believer)—could be described as highly fearful.

7. Participants were asked how likely they thought it was that they might someday become the victim of a property crime, or of a violent crime. In their estimates for property crime, there was no difference between the dissenters and the believers: virtually everyone thought that it was conceivable—most thought it likely. The estimates from the two groups about violent crime were also quite similar to one another, although more mixed within each group: only a few thought this to be a likely eventuality; some thought it "possible," and as many, unlikely.

8. By "close" I mean family and friends, as opposed to acquaintances.

9. To discuss the salience of the crime problem for individuals who are spending several hours conversing on that very subject with an interviewer is in some ways problematic. The process itself is bound to increase the level of salience for these individuals. But it can probably be assumed that the participants' perceptions are more or less equally altered. And because what is of interest here is not the absolute

magnitude of salience, but any relative differences between the dissenters and the believers, their opinions on this question should still be of value.

10. Only three believers, and none of the dissenters, made this an important focus of their comments.

11. Several prior studies have touched on aspects of the public's lack of accurate information about crime and criminal justice. See for instance, Henshel and Silverman, *Perception in Criminology;* Warr, Gibbs, and Erickson, "Contending Theories"; and Sheley and Ashkins, "Crime, Crime News." There are also the frequent Gallup polls on perceptions of local crime increases or decreases (Maguire, Pastore, and Flanagan, *Sourcebook 1992,* 187); as well as a 1982 ABC News poll in which 83 percent of the respondents said that the crime rate was going up (McGarrell and Flanagan, *Sourcebook 1984,* 168). For some countervailing evidence, see Warr, "Accuracy of Public Beliefs" and "Accuracy of Public Beliefs: Further Evidence."

12. California Department of Corrections, *Challenges in Corrections,* 5 and 7. I arrived at this figure by averaging the per cell cost for the two new maximum security prisons for which prices were given in this report.

13. Department of Justice, *Criminal Victimization: 1973–90 Trends.*

14. Stinchcombe et al., *Crime and Punishment,* 80, 77.

15. Dow, "Role of Identification."

16. This finding is interesting, given research that has shown that citizens' personal problems do not have a significant effect upon their voting choices. An important difference, however, is that here I am speaking of a likely effect of experience only upon attitudes—and very specifically related attitudes. See Kinder and Kiewiet, "Sociotropic Politics"; and Brody and Sniderman, "Life Space to Polling Place."

17. The 1989 Survey of Inmates of Local Jails showed that 54 percent of jail inmates had not completed high school. Thirty-six percent were unemployed when arrested. Seventy-eight percent of those who had been free for at least one year prior to arrest had prearrest incomes of less than fifteen thousand dollars annually, and 62 percent made less than ten thousand dollars annually. Fifty-five percent had used a "major drug" at some point prior to arrest (Beck, "Profile of Jail Inmates, 1989," 3, 8). The 1986 Survey of Inmates in State Correctional Facilities showed that 31 percent of state prison inmates were unemployed when arrested. Sixty percent of those who had been free for one year prior to arrest had had an annual income of ten thousand dollars or less. Sixty-two percent of inmates had at some point used illegal drugs on a regular basis (Innes, "Profile of State Prison Inmates, 1986," 1–6).

18. Five dissenters felt absolutely that these acts should not be criminalized; two believers agreed.

19. Stinchcombe et al., *Crime and Punishment,* 77.

20. Cullen et al., "Attitudes toward Sanctioning," 310. These researchers (using Likert-style questions) developed scales to measure classical versus positivist views of crime causation, punitiveness, attitudes toward rehabilitation, attitudes toward the death penalty, and views about the treatment of white-collar criminals. They write, "Attribution—the positivist-classical scale—has a statistically significant effect on three of the dependent variables. The only exception was with the punishment of

white-collar crime . . . The three significant relationships are in the expected direction in that a positivist orientation is positively associated with support for rehabilitation and negatively related to support for a general punishment philosophy as well as for capital punishment."

21. Cook, "Ideology's Effects," 29, 63–75, 101–2, 111, 113. Cook measured the two areas of belief with sets of statements to which respondents were asked how strongly they agreed or disagreed. He found roughly a .5 correlation between scales he created for the two beliefs.

22. Watts and Free, *State of the Nation III*, 185–86. Respondents were asked: "Which two or three of the [six] approaches listed on this card do you think would be the best way to reduce crime?" Fifty-nine percent of self-designated liberals chose "Cleaning up social and economic conditions in our slums and ghettos that may breed drug addicts and criminals," while only 46 percent of the entire sample did so. Thirty-six percent of self-designated liberals chose "Improving conditions in our jails and prisons so that more people convicted of crimes will be rehabilitated and not go back to a life of crime," while only 28 percent of the entire sample did so. And only 36 percent of self-designated liberals chose "Really cracking down on criminals by giving them longer prison terms to be served under the toughest possible conditions," while 43 percent of the entire sample did so.

23. Rose, "Public Opinion Concerning Correctional Policies," 65, 71–72. Self-ascribed political ideology was the variable that explained the greatest percentage of the variance in respondents' receptivity to correctional reform. Still, this was only 9 percent; and all ten of her independent variables explained only 19 percent of the variance.

24. Stinchcombe et al., *Crime and Punishment,* 81–85. See also Cook, "Ideology's Effects," 108–17.

25. Ibid., 85.

26. Ibid., 87–88. Indeed, 94 percent of the respondents who answered all their liberalism questions in a liberal direction still did *not* give liberal/lenient answers to both of their punitiveness questions (no to capital punishment; "too harsh" on the questions about the sentencing practices of the courts).

27. Further, the remaining portions of their descriptions never included the word *conservative*. The one dissenter who did not refer to himself as a liberal—Dexter Lane, the insurance agent—called himself a "responsible libertarian."

28. Three more believers referred to themselves as a mix of liberal and conservative.

29. This scale was composed of one point for a liberal answer to each of the nine questions listed in appendix B (second interview) under the headings Women's Rights, Abortion, Sexual Liberalism, and Civil Liberties; one point for a liberal answer to the question about homosexuality under the heading Lifestyles; one point for a liberal answer to the question about interracial marriage under the heading Racial Justice; and one point for my subjective estimation that the participant was not a racist nor a person who made "illiberal" comments about race relations. See Stinchcombe et al., *Crime and Punishment,* 149–61, for the wordings of the poll questions that these researchers used in their analysis.

30. The mean score for the believers was 9. The range was from 2 to 12.

31. My definition involved an index of six factors (each essentially a continuum) on which each participant's overall attitudes were subjectively rated: (1) Reform versus Tradition/Order; (2) Optimism versus Pessimism regarding Human Nature; (3) People are Equal versus People are Naturally Unequal; (4) Strong versus Limited Government Role in Social Change; (5) Social versus Individual Responsibility for Failure; and (6) Tolerance for Dissent versus the belief that we need Strong Leaders and Strict Morals to control Human Appetites. (To create this index, I distilled the definitions given in several sources. See Rossiter, "Conservatism," and Smith, "Liberalism," in Sills, *International Encyclopedia of the Social Sciences,* 276–82 and 290–94; Minogue, "Conservatism," and Cranston, "Liberalism," in Edwards, *Encyclopedia of Philosophy,* 195–98 and 458–61; McClosky, "Conservatism and Personality"; and McClosky and Zaller, *American Ethos,* 189–90.) To be judged liberal or conservative overall, a participant was required to receive that designation on at least five of the items; or on four of the items with two middle-of-the-road designations.

32. Scheingold, *Politics of Law and Order,* 75. Scheingold quotes DuBow, McCabe, and Kaplan, *Reactions to Crime,* 8.

33. Cullen, Clark, and Wozniak, "Explaining the Get Tough Movement," 21. On this point, see also, Rosch, "Crime in American Politics."

34. Interestingly, in answer to a later question, he says that he feels that the criminal justice system is biased against minorities and the poor.

35. Newman and Trilling, "Public Perceptions of Criminal Behavior," 230. This conclusion apparently was based upon a 1970 study conducted in the Canadian city of London, Ontario, which sought public opinion regarding the appropriate sanctions for various crimes of violence (Boydell and Grindstaff, "Public Opinion toward Sanctions"). Church attendance was the measure of religiosity.

36. Cook, "Ideology's Effects," 101–2, 114. Cook measured orthodoxy by means of three questions concerning life after death, the Devil, and the divinity of Jesus. Excluded from this portion of his analysis were those respondents who were not Christians (77).

37. Maguire, Pastore, and Flanagan, *Sourcebook 1992,* 196–97. For the ten polls conducted between 1980 and 1990, the average differential between those with no religion and the next highest religious group is 9 percent. Not reported, unfortunately, are the answers of respondents who subscribe to religious views other than Christianity or Judaism. A quantitative researcher interested in this question could go further with the NORC data. The General Social Survey has included questions regarding church attendance, self-assessed strength of religiosity, and changes in religious affiliation over time, as well as some about specific religious beliefs. Regressions could be run on these and the GSS's criminological questions regarding capital punishment and harsher courts. See *General Social Surveys, 1972–1986: Cumulative Codebook.*

38. There is no difference, however, when it comes to rejecting religion altogether. One dissenter and two believers fall into this category.

39. Richard describes dualism as the concept of "the God above and the man below."

40. Five of the dissenters *do* fit the profile in every regard. They are Abby Edwards, Richard Niederhaus, Burt Ruebel, Daniel Steinbach, and Anne Girard.

41. No one of these nine is missing every attribute.

42. Richard's father is white, his mother Asian.

43. Among the problems that Daniel resolved at this time was a serious addiction to drugs. For the record, Richard Niederhaus, the software designer, is also a former drug addict.

44. Victor's remarks a few moments later are also of interest. I ask, "Do you think you would feel any differently if tomorrow you were suddenly the victim of a violent crime or something?" He replies: "I might. I cannot deny that . . . But so far that is the way I see it. And even when my wife was ripped off of her purse . . . I said, this guy obviously needs the money, because otherwise who is going to be risking, sometimes his . . . life . . . Because you never know when somebody is going to shoot you if you try to steal money . . . Probably [he] was desperate, I thought, and it's done. No harm done, except that my wife had to go through the trauma and had to go to all these calls and all that. But in the end, I said, listen, it could have been worse . . . Why dwell in the problem? Just, let's get on with our lives."

Chapter 6

1. In addition, as was fully discussed in chapter 4, two interviewees had criminal justice views and general political beliefs that were incoherent, and one very elderly and poorly educated interviewee appeared to have no *political* belief system.

2. A 1982 national poll conducted for *Time* asked this question: "Do you feel that conditions today in most prisons result in rehabilitating those who are committed there or are conditions turning them into more hardened criminals than before?" Thirteen percent said "rehabilitating"; 72 percent said "making them more hardened criminals"; and 15 percent volunteered the answer that they were "not sure" (Komarnicki and Doble, *Crime and Corrections,* 127).

3. For obvious reasons, this question was not asked of most of the dissenters. There were two exceptions. As noted in chapter 2, Olivia Hassan, the bank teller, had said "yes" when I asked whether or not it was worthwhile to imprison as many people as we now do—perhaps because of a misperception as to what types of offenders we are currently incarcerating. Dexter Lane, the insurance agent, who tended to distinguish between least-of-evils policies he would sanction in the present political climate and his ideas for a very different sort of criminal justice system (which he felt there was little chance of selling to the public or policymakers at the present time), gave the same answer to that question. Later, when asked what was the point in making heavy use of incarceration, both invoked the principle of incapacitation. Olivia: "The only point is that it isolates them. It's better than having them all killing other people or destroying other people's lives and stuff." Dexter: "[Given current political realities] prisons are going to remain the same for the foreseeable future. And I'm interested in doing business without threat of . . . my

place [being] broken into, my car stolen, and so forth. So I'd just as soon have these . . . people off the street too."

4. Two believers are not included here. Miriam Madamba, the secretary, had said that she felt that prisons were effective. And Elizabeth Williams, the physical therapist, had favored reducing our use of jails and prisons. Neither was quizzed on this point, nor did they speak to it spontaneously.

5. Not included in this majority are three believers. Adam Perlman, the speech therapist, has mixed feelings about whether or not a deterrence policy can work. James Morton, the masonry contractor, holds that capital punishment is a deterrent, but as to the threat of incarceration: "It doesn't seem to be effective at all today. When I was a young fellow, I think it was almost 100 percent effective. And we have had a turnabout in moral standards and . . . so many other influences in our lives that it has lost all of its power. It just doesn't seem to be a viable thing." Elizabeth Williams, the physical therapist, shares Mr. Morton's view about capital punishment, but, as mentioned earlier, she favors a reduction in our use of jails and prisons.

6. Stinchcombe et al., *Crime and Punishment,"* x, 74, 85–92.

7. There has been some controversy among political scientists regarding the issue of increases in tolerance. Sullivan, Piereson, and Marcus have argued that "claims that the public is now more tolerant than in the 1950s are either untrue or greatly exaggerated." Their study asked respondents to select two groups that they liked the least, and then to answer questions measuring tolerance toward those groups (Sullivan, Piereson, and Marcus, *Political Tolerance and American Democracy,* 60–63, 250). I place more credence in the position of McClosky and Brill, who write that "there are . . . reasons, both empirical and intuitive, to believe that support for civil liberties has been on the rise in recent decades and that the drift of opinion since . . . the early 1950s has been toward greater acceptance of diversity, nonconformity, and dissent." They offer several criticisms of the Sullivan et al. study, among them "that the Sullivan group, in essence, takes the respondent's attitudes toward a single group (or at most two groups) as the proper indicators of the respondent's general level of tolerance—this despite the obvious fact, demonstrated repeatedly in our studies, that a respondent may be highly tolerant toward a large number of unpopular groups or groups he or she strongly dislikes, but yet feel that a *particular* group . . . is so dangerous that it should not be permitted to engage in such activities as teaching or holding public rallies in the city. In addition, an individual might, over the years, grow increasingly more tolerant of many different groups and activities, but might continue to be as repelled by (and as intolerant of) a *particular* group as he or she was at the start. Sullivan and his colleagues would be compelled in this case to classify this individual as no more tolerant at the end of the measuring period than he or she was at the beginning—obviously an incorrect inference" (McClosky and Brill, *Dimensions of Tolerance,* 435–36).

8. For some reason, throughout the years that Gallup and NORC have asked the traditional question about the courts, they have given respondents only the options of replying that they were "too harsh" or "not harsh enough." "About right" was not an invited answer, although it was volunteered by some respondents—in early years, by a significant percentage of them. Perhaps this question wording has been

continued through the years in order to maintain comparability within the time series. But in some future year, it would be well worth trying out an *additional* version that would make "about right" an explicit option.

9. Of course, there is little need to explain why persons who are conservative enough to have *intolerant* feelings about very many of these social issues also would have harsh and conservative feelings about criminal justice. But if any of these conservative Americans have become even harsher on crime over the years, some explanation might be found in circumstances similar to those involving their more tolerant but still bothered fellow citizens. Consider that in some cases social outlets for the intolerant feelings of the former group have become severely restricted over the years. James Morton, for instance, clearly realizes that his views on the relations between the races would not be welcomed in most social or business settings; indeed, he feels the need to apologize for them even when speaking to an interviewer he will never see again, under guarantee of anonymity. Thus, even Americans like Morton may have a need to displace some negative feelings onto a different issue.

10. This reluctance to question traditional assumptions—both about the ultimate effectiveness of prisons and about the necessity of offenders getting their "just deserts"—probably explains some apparently contradictory poll results. I refer to the contrast between the repeated polls that find that over 80 percent of the public will say that the courts are not harsh enough on crime, and at least two other polls that found that 61–81 percent of the public chose the approach of attacking social problems over that of more prisons and police, when asked about efforts to lower the crime rate (see Flanagan and Maguire, *Sourcebook 1991,* 202 for a 1989 Gallup poll question; a similar 1988 Harris poll question is available on-line through the Public Opinion Location Library of the Roper Center for Public Opinion Research, University of Connecticut). When poll question wording links the causes of crime, by definition, with these socioeconomic problems and rules out issues of just punishment by limiting the frame of reference to effectiveness issues only, respondents' assumptions can be stretched a good deal. But in the setting of intensive interviews using open-ended questions, we can see how critical a role these generally unquestioned assumptions play.

11. The reader may be interested in a later book by Stuart Scheingold, published after my study had been completed, which reaches conclusions compatible with these, from the perspective of political culture (see Scheingold, *Politics of Street Crime,* esp. 18–22 and 172–79).

12. Elizabeth Williams, the physical therapist, is a partial exception. But then, she sounds almost like a dissenter until she reaches the point of dealing with the most serious offenses.

13. Lane, *Political Ideology,* 321–45, 367–68, 473.

14. Ibid., 323.

15. Durkheim, *Division of Labor,* 108.

16. Figgie Report Part V, 126.

17. Doble, *Crime and Punishment,* 33.

18. In polls taken between 1981 and 1989 an average of only 16 percent felt that

there was less crime in their area than a year before (Flanagan and Maguire, *Sourcebook 1991,* 185).

19. Recall, as was discussed in chapter 1, that the lowered crime rates of recent years should *not* be taken as evidence that harsher sentences are already working. Population research has shown that the decrease in crime is largely due to demographic changes that have reduced the percentage of our population who are in the crime-prone age bracket. See, for instance, Blumstein, "Planning for Future Prison Needs," 209–10.

20. Hobbes, *Leviathan,* part 2, chap. 28.

Appendix C

1. Smith, Bruner, and White, *Opinions and Personality,* 5.

2. Lane, *Political Ideology.* Other uses of this methodology by political scientists include Karl Lamb's *As Orange Goes,* a study of the political beliefs of suburban families in Orange County, California; Jennifer Hochschild's *What's Fair,* in which interviewing focused on beliefs about distributive justice; and Robert Botsch's *We Shall Not Overcome,* a study of the attitudes of Southern blue-collar workers.

3. Smith, Bruner, and White, *Opinions and Personality,* v. On this point, see also, Eckstein, "Case Study and Theory."

4. Hochschild, *What's Fair?* 25, 24.

5. Lane, *Political Ideology,* 9–10.

6. Hochschild, *What's Fair?* 25.

7. This category of "alternative opposer" did not turn out to be a very good predictor of extreme harshness. During the interviews, only one of these persons even maintained his stern opposition to virtually all alternatives. Except for this one man, it was from among those who *supported* alternatives on the mail questionnaire, that my harshest interviewees came. For these reasons, no further use of the category "alternative opposer" has been made here.

8. Second Start Adult Literacy Program, *Project Description;* Bureau of the Census, *1980 Census of Population,* vol. 1, chap. A, part 6, 1, 14.

9. My concern here, given the small sample size, was that I not end up accidentally interviewing a group of people who, for example, all made over twenty-five thousand dollars per year. Since only a very rough measure was needed, and because Oakland is a city that can roughly be said to have its better and worse off halves, I simply drew an imaginary dividing line on the map and took care not to select a disproportionate number of my interviewees from one side or the other.

10. Unlike gender and level of affluence, race most often could not be deduced from an individual's name and address. My hope was that with a city such as Oakland—and with attention given to economic balance—a racially diverse sample could be achieved without special effort. Fortunately, this turned out to be the case. (See appendix A.)

11. While most of the questions were developed specifically for this study, some were "borrowed" from others. Professor Robert Lane of Yale University and Professor Jennifer Hochschild of Princeton University graciously gave permission

to use certain questions that they had posed in their studies of political ideology and distributive justice, respectively (Lane, *Political Ideology,* 481–93; Hochschild, *What's Fair?* 292–308). Various other questions were drawn from among those that have been asked repeatedly in national opinion polls conducted by the National Opinion Research Center (General Social Survey) and the Gallup poll.

Bibliography

Abelson, Robert P., et al., eds. *Theories of Cognitive Consistency: A Sourcebook.* Chicago: Rand-McNally, 1968.

"Americans Evaluate the Court System." *Public Opinion* 5, no. 4 (August–September 1982): 24–26.

"Americans Express Domestic Rather than International Concerns." *Current Opinion* 3, no. 10 (October 1975): 94–95.

"Americans See Surge of Crime and Take Preventive Measures; Crime Wave Laid to Variety of Economic and Social Problems." *Gallup Report* 187 (April 1981): 4–19.

Arkoff, Abe, and Gerald M. Meredith. "Consistency in Attitudes toward Civil Liberties." *Journal of Social Psychology* 70 (December 1966): 265–74.

Austin, James, and Aaron David McVey. "The NCCD Prison Population Forecast: The Growing Imprisonment of America." *NCCD Focus* (April 1988).

Austin, Thomas L., and Eve S. Buzawa. "Citizen Perceptions on Mass Transit Crime and Its Deterrence: A Case Study." *Transportation Quarterly* 38, no. 1 (January 1984): 103–20.

Bagwell, Beth. *Oakland: The Story of a City.* Novato, Calif.: Presidio Press, 1982.

Balkin, Steven. "Victimization Rates, Safety, and Fear of Crime." *Social Problems* 26, no. 3 (February 1979): 343–58.

Barrie, Gunter. *Television and the Fear of Crime.* London: John Libbey, 1987.

Baumer, Terry L. "Research on Fear of Crime in the United States." *Victimology* 3, nos. 3–4 (1978): 254–64.

Beck, Allen J. "Profile of Jail Inmates, 1989." *Bureau of Justice Statistics Special Report.* Washington, D.C.: U.S. Government Printing Office, 1991.

Beck, Allen J., Thomas P. Bonczar, and Darrell K. Gilliard. "Jail Inmates 1992." *Bureau of Justice Statistics Bulletin.* Washington, D.C.: U.S. Government Printing Office, 1993.

Beck, Allen J., and Bernard E. Shipley. "Recidivism of Young Parolees." *Bureau of Justice Statistics Special Report.* Washington, D.C.: U.S. Government Printing Office, 1987.

Bellah, Robert N., et al. *Habits of the Heart: Individualism and Commitment in American Life.* New York: Harper and Row, 1985.

Bennett, W. Lance. *The Political Mind and the Political Environment: An Investigation of Public Opinion and Political Consciousness.* Lexington, Mass.: D. C. Heath, 1975.

Biderman, Albert D., et al. *An Inventory of Surveys of the Public on Crime, Justice, and Related Topics*. Washington, D.C.: U.S. Government Printing Office, 1972.

"Bizarre Torture Case Detailed." *Oakland Tribune*, March 27, 1987, sec. A.

Blumstein, Alfred. "Planning for Future Prison Needs." *University of Illinois Law Review* 1984, no. 2: 207–30.

Blumstein, Alfred, and Jacqueline Cohen. "Sentencing of Convicted Offenders: An Analysis of the Public's View." *Law and Society Review* 14, no. 2 (winter 1980): 223–61.

Botsch, Robert Emil. *We Shall Not Overcome: Populism and Southern Blue-Collar Workers*. Chapel Hill: University of North Carolina Press, 1980.

Boydell, Craig L., and Carl F. Grindstaff. "Public Opinion toward Legal Sanctions for Crimes of Violence." *Journal of Criminal Law and Criminology* 65, no. 1 (1974): 113–16.

Breed, Allen. "The State of Corrections Today: A Triumph of Pluralistic Ignorance." Speech delivered in February 1986. Printed by the Edna McConnell Clark Foundation, New York.

Brody, Richard A., and Paul M. Sniderman. "From Life Space to Polling Place: The Relevance of Personal Concerns for Voting Behavior." *British Journal of Political Science* 7, part 3 (July 1977): 337–60.

Brown, Edward J., Timothy J. Flanagan, and Maureen McLeod, eds. *Sourcebook of Criminal Justice Statistics - 1983*. U.S Department of Justice, Bureau of Justice Statistics. Washington, D.C.: U.S. Government Printing Office, 1984.

Brown, Steven R. "Intensive Analysis in Political Research," *Political Methodology* 1, no. 1 (winter 1974): 1-25.

Bureau of the Census. *1980 Census of Population*. Washington, D.C., 1982.

California Department of Corrections. Challenges in Corrections. 1986–87 Annual Report.

California Statistical Abstract, 1987. Sacramento: Economic Development Agency, State of California.

Campbell, Angus, et al. *The American Voter*. New York: John Wiley and Sons, 1960.

Campbell, J. B. "Cognitive Dissonance." In *Encyclopedia of Psychology*, vol. 1, edited by Raymond J. Corsini, 235–36. New York: John Wiley and Sons, 1984.

Caringella-MacDonald, Susan. "States Crises and the Crackdown on Crime under Reagan." *Contemporary Crises* 14 (1990): 91–118.

Carter, David L. "Hispanic Attitudes toward Crime and Justice in Texas: A Study of Perceptions and Experiences." Ph.D. diss., Sam Houston State University, 1980.

Cicourel, Aaron V. *Method and Measurement in Sociology*. New York: Free Press, 1964.

"Citizens Say Crime on Increase." *Current Opinion* 3, no. 4 (April 1975): 32.

Clemente, Frank, and Michael B. Kleiman. "Fear of Crime in the United States: A Multivariate Analysis." *Social Forces* 56, no. 2 (December 1977): 519–31.

Conklin, John E. *The Impact of Crime*. New York: Macmillan, 1975.

Converse, Philip E. "The Nature of Belief Systems in Mass Publics." In *Ideology and Discontent,* edited by David E. Apter, 206–61. London: Free Press, 1964.

———. "Public Opinion and Voting Behavior." In *Handbook of Political Science,* vol. 4, edited by Fred. I Greenstein and Nelson W. Polsby, 75–169. Reading, Mass.: Addison-Wesley Publishing Co., 1975.

Cook, Dennis G. "Ideology's Effects on Beliefs about the Causes of Crime and the Best Treatment of Criminals." Ph.D. diss., University of Nebraska, 1980.

"Crime: The Public Gets Tough." *Public Opinion* 5, no. 5 (October–November 1982): 36.

"Crime Cited as Number One Community Problem in California." *Current Opinion* 1, no. 5 (May 1973): 43.

"Crime Cited as Top Community Problem." *Current Opinion* 3, no. 9 (September 1975): 86.

"Crime, Drugs, Environment, and Health are Highest Priorities for Spending." *Current Opinion* 2, no. 9 (September 1974): 106.

Cullen, Francis T., et al. "Attribution, Salience, and Attitudes toward Criminal Sanctioning." *Criminal Justice and Behavior* 12, no. 3 (September 1985): 305–31.

Cullen, Francis T., Gregory A. Clark, and John F. Wozniak. "Explaining the Get Tough Movement: Can the Public Be Blamed?" *Federal Probation* 49 (June 1985): 16–24.

Cullen, Francis T., and Karen E. Gilbert. *Reaffirming Rehabilitation.* Cincinnati: Anderson Publishing Co., 1982.

Cullen, Francis T., Bruce G. Link, and Craig W. Polanzi. "The Seriousness of Crime Revisited: Have Attitudes toward White-Collar Crime Changed?" *Criminology* 20, no. 1 (May 1982): 83–102.

Department of Justice. *BJS Data Report, 1987.* Washington, D.C.: U.S. Government Printing Office, 1988.

———. *Bureau of Justice Statistics National Update* 1, no. 4 (April 1992).

———. "Criminal Victimization 1986." *Bureau of Justice Statistics Bulletin.* Washington, D.C.: U.S. Government Printing Office, 1987.

———. "Criminal Victimization 1987." *Bureau of Justice Statistics Bulletin.* Washington, D.C.: U.S. Government Printing Office, 1988.

———. *Criminal Victimization in the United States: 1973–90 Trends.* Washington, D.C.: U.S. Government Printing Office, 1992.

———. *Criminal Victimization Surveys in Oakland: A National Crime Survey Report.* Washington, D.C.: U.S. Government Printing Office, 1977.

———. "Jail Inmates 1983." *Bureau of Justice Statistics Bulletin.* Washington, D.C.: U.S. Government Printing Office, 1985.

———. *Oakland: Public Attitudes about Crime—a National Crime Survey Report.* Washington, D.C.: U.S. Government Printing Office, 1978.

———. "Prisoners in 1987." *Bureau of Justice Statistics Bulletin.* Washington, D.C.: U.S. Government Printing Office, 1988.

———. "Prisoners in 1988." *Bureau of Justice Statistics Bulletin.* Washington, D.C.: U.S. Government Printing Office, 1989.

———. "Prisoners in 1990." *Bureau of Justice Statistics Bulletin.* Washington, D.C.: U.S. Government Printing Office, 1991.

———. Federal Bureau of Investigation. *Crime in the United States: Uniform Crime Reports—1985.* Washington, D.C.: U. S. Government Printing Office, 1986.

Dexter, Lewis Anthony. *Elite and Specialized Interviewing.* Evanston, Ill.: Northwestern University Press, 1970.

Dillman, Don A. *Mail and Telephone Surveys: The Total Design Method.* New York: John Wiley and Sons, 1978.

Doble, John. *Crime and Punishment: The Public's View.* New York: Public Agenda Foundation, 1987.

"Domestic Issues Top Concerns." *Current Opinion* 4, no. 9 (September 1976): 92.

Dorgan, Michael. "Under Siege: Oakland's Crack Crisis." *San Jose Mercury News,* February 28 and 29, and March 1, 1988.

Dow, Thomas E., Jr. "The Role of Identification in Conditioning Public Attitudes toward the Offender." *Journal of Criminal Law, Criminology, and Police Science* 58, no. 1 (1967): 75–79.

DuBow, Fred, Edward McCabe, and Gail Kaplan. *Reactions to Crime: A Critical Review of the Literature (Executive Summary).* Washington, D.C.: U.S. Government Printing Office, 1979.

Duffee, David, and R. Richard Ritti. "Correctional Policy and Public Values." *Criminology* 14 (February 1977): 449–59.

Durkheim, Emile. *The Division of Labor in Society.* Translated by George Simpson. Glencoe, Ill.: Free Press, 1933.

Eckstein, Harry. "Case Study and Theory in Political Science." In *Handbook of Political Science,* vol. 7, edited by Fred I. Greenstein and Nelson W. Polsby, 79–137. Reading, Mass.: Addison-Wesley Publishing Co., 1975.

"Economic Concerns Most Urgent." *Current Opinion* 4, no. 6 (June 1976): 61.

Edelman, Murray. *Constructing the Political Spectacle.* Chicago: University of Chicago Press, 1988.

———. *The Symbolic Uses of Politics.* 1967; reprint. Urbana: University of Illinois Press, 1985.

———. *Politics as Symbolic Action: Mass Arousal and Quiescence.* Chicago: Markham, 1971.

Edwards, Paul, ed. *The Encyclopedia of Philosophy,* vols. 2 and 4. New York: Macmillan and Free Press, 1967.

Ekland-Olson, Sheldon, William R. Kelly, and Michael Eisenberg. "Crime and Incarceration: Some Comparative Findings from the 1980s." *Crime and Delinquency* 38, no. 3 (July 1992): 392–416.

Endicott, William. "The Times Poll: Discontent over Crime Focused on Judiciary." *Los Angeles Times,* Feb. 2, 1981, sec. A.

"Energy Crisis One of Nation's Top Problems." *Current Opinion* 5, no. 11 (November 1977): 124.

Erskine, Hazel. "The Polls: Causes of Crime." *Public Opinion Quarterly* 38, no. 2 (summer 1974): 288–98.

————. "The Polls: Control of Violence and Crime." *Public Opinion Quarterly* 38, no. 3 (fall 1974): 490–502.

————. "The Polls: Politics and Law and Order." *Public Opinion Quarterly* 38, no. 4 (winter 1974-75): 623–34.

————. "The Polls: Fear of Violence and Crime." *Public Opinion Quarterly* 38, no. 1 (spring 1974): 131–45.

European Committee on Crime Problems. *Public Opinion on Crime and Criminal Justice.* Reports presented to the Thirteenth Criminological Research Conference. Strasbourg, France: Council of Europe, 1979.

Evenson, Laura. "City's Chinatown Bustling with Growth." *Oakland Tribune,* July 26, 1987, sec A.

Evenson, Laura, and Kathy Zimmerman. "Residents Question Priorities." *Oakland Tribune,* July 26, 1987, sec. A.

Ezorsky, Gertrude, ed. *Philosophical Perspectives on Punishment.* Albany: State University of New York Press, 1972.

Fairchild, Erika S., and Vincent J. Webb, eds. *The Politics of Crime and Criminal Justice.* Beverly Hills, Calif.: Sage Publications, 1985.

"Fear in the Neighborhood." *Public Opinion* 3, no. 4 (August–September 1980): 34.

"Fear of Crime Grows." *Current Opinion* 3, no. 9 (September 1975): 84–85.

Feldman, Stanley, and John Zaller. "The Political Culture of Ambivalence: Ideological Responses to the Welfare State." Paper presented at the annual meeting of the Midwest Political Science Association, Chicago, April 1988.

Femia, Joseph. "Hegemony and Consciousness in the Thought of Antonio Gramsci." *Political Studies* 23, no. 1 (March 1975): 29–48.

Field, Mervin D. "Voters Rate the Importance of Twenty-Five Campaign Issues." *California Poll,* October 20, 1982.

————. "High Degree of Public Concern about Two State Issues: Crime and Law Enforcement, Schools and Education." *California Poll,* February 23, 1984.

Field Research Corporation. *Public Opinion of Criminal Justice in California.* Berkeley, Calif.: Institute of Governmental Studies, 1974.

The Figgie Report on Fear of Crime: America Afraid, Part I: The General Public. Willoughby, Ohio: A-T-O, 1980.

The Figgie Report Part V: Parole—a Search for Justice and Safety. Richmond, Va.: Figgie International, 1985.

Finckenauer, James O. "Crime as a National Political Issue: 1964–1976—from Law and Order to Domestic Tranquility." *Crime and Delinquency* 24, no. 1 (January 1978): 13–27.

Flanagan, Timothy, and Susan Caulfield. "Public Opinion and Prison Policy: A Review." *Prison Journal* 64, no. 2 (Fall–Winter 1984): 31–46.

Flanagan, Timothy J., and Katherine M. Jamieson. *Sourcebook of Criminal Justice Statistics—1987.* U. S. Department of Justice, Bureau of Justice Statistics. Washington, D.C.: U.S. Government Printing Office, 1988.

Flanagan, Timothy J., and Kathleen Maguire. *Sourcebook of Criminal Justice Statistics—1991.* U.S. Department of Justice, Bureau of Justice Statistics. Washington, D.C.: U.S. Government Printing Office, 1992.

Flanagan, Timothy J., and Edmund F. McGarrell, eds. *Sourcebook of Criminal Justice Statistics—1985*. U. S. Department of Justice, Bureau of Justice Statistics. Washington, D.C.: U.S. Government Printing Office, 1986.

Foote, Caleb. *The Prison Population Explosion: California's Rogue Elephant*. Center on Juvenile and Criminal Justice report. June 1993.

"Forty-five Percent Afraid to Walk Near Home at Night," *Current Opinion* 2, no. 9 (September 1974): 104.

Free, Lloyd A., and Hadley Cantril. *The Political Beliefs of Americans: A Study of Public Opinion*. New Brunswick, N.J.: Rutgers University Press, 1967.

Friedman, Lawrence. *Crime and Punishment in American History*. New York: Basic Books, 1993.

Furstenberg, Frank F., Jr. "Public Reaction to Crime in the Streets." *American Scholar* 40, no. 4 (Autumn 1971): 601–10.

Gandy, John Thomas. "Community Attitudes toward Creative Restitution and Punishment." Ph.D. diss., University of Denver, 1975.

Garofalo, James. *Public Opinion about Crime: The Attitudes of Victims and Non-Victims in Selected Cities*. Washington, D.C.: U.S. Government Printing Office, 1977.

General Social Surveys, 1972–1986: Cumulative Codebook. Chicago: National Opinion Research Center, 1986.

General Social Surveys, 1972–1987: Cumulative Codebook. Chicago: National Opinion Research Center, 1987.

Gibbons, Don C. "Crime and Punishment: A Study in Social Attitudes." *Social Forces* 47, no. 4 (June 1969): 391–97.

Gilliard, Darrell K. "Prisoners in 1992." *Bureau of Justice Statistics Bulletin*. Washington, D.C.: U.S. Government Printing Office, 1993.

Gottfredson, Stephen D, and Ralph B. Taylor. *The Correctional Crisis: Prison Populations and Public Policy*. Washington, D.C.: U.S. Government Printing Office, 1983.

Graber, Doris A. *Crime News and the Public*. New York: Praeger Publishers, 1980.

Greenfeld, Lawrence A. "Capital Punishment 1991." *Bureau of Justice Statistics Bulletin*. Washington, D.C.: U. S. Government Printing Office, 1992.

Hall, Stuart, et al. *Policing the Crisis: Mugging, the State, and Law and Order*. London: Macmillan, 1978.

Hamilton, V. Lee, and Steve Rytina. "Social Consensus on Norms of Justice: Should the Punishment Fit the Crime?" *American Journal of Sociology* 85, no. 5 (March 1980): 1117–44.

"A Harder Line on Crime." *Public Opinion* 3, no. 4 (August–September 1980): 37.

Harris, Louis, and Associates. *The Public Looks at Crime and Corrections*. Joint Commission on Correctional Manpower and Training. Washington, D.C.: U. S. Government Printing Office, 1968.

Hartjen, Clayton A., and Daniel Carratura. "Attitudes toward Crime and Punishment: A Comparative Analysis." *International Journal of Contemporary Sociology* 14, nos. 3–4 (July–October 1977): 185–96.

Henshel, Richard L., and Robert A. Silverman, eds. *Perception in Criminology.* New York: Columbia University Press, 1975.

"High Cost of Living Americans' Top Problem." *Current Opinion* 2, no. 11 (November 1974): 123.

"High Cost of Living Considered Nation's Top Problem." *Current Opinion* 3, no. 9 (September 1975): 84.

"High Cost of Living Considered Top Problem." *Current Opinion* 4, no. 2 (February 1976): 16-17.

"High Cost of Living Top Problem." *Current Opinion* 3, no. 4 (April 1975): 37.

Hindelang, Michael J. *Public Opinion Regarding Crime, Criminal Justice, and Related Topics.* Washington, D.C.: U.S. Government Printing Office, 1975.

Hobbes, Thomas. *Leviathan.* Edited by C. B. Macpherson. Harmondsworth, England: Penguin Books, 1968.

Hochschild, Jennifer L. *What's Fair? American Beliefs about Distributive Justice.* Cambridge, Mass.: Harvard University Press, 1981.

Hogarth, Robin, ed. *Question Framing and Response Consistency.* San Francisco: Jossey-Bass, 1982.

"How Fear Affects Attitudes." *Public Opinion* 3, no. 5 (October–November 1980): 31.

Inflation Considered Top Priority." *Current Opinion* 4, no. 5 (May 1976): 43.

Innes, Christopher A. "Profile of State Prison Inmates, 1986." *Bureau of Justice Statistics Special Report.* Washington, D.C.: U.S. Government Printing Office, 1988.

Jamieson, Katherine M., and Timothy J. Flanagan, eds. *Sourcebook of Criminal Justice Statistics—1986.* U. S. Department of Justice, Bureau of Justice Statistics. Washington, D.C.: U.S. Government Printing Office, 1987.

Jehl, Douglas. "Clinton Delivers Emotional Appeal on Stopping Crime." *New York Times,* November 14, 1993, sec. A.

Kahn, Robert L., and Charles F. Cannell. *The Dynamics of Interviewing: Theory, Technique, and Cases.* New York: John Wiley and Sons, 1957.

Katz, Daniel. "The Functional Approach to the Study of Attitudes." In *A Sourcebook for the Study of Personality and Politics,* edited by Fred I. Greenstein and Michael Lerner, 198–230. Chicago: Markham, 1971.

Keniston, Kenneth. *Young Radicals: Notes on Committed Youth.* New York: Harcourt, Brace, and World, 1968.

Kinder, Donald R. "Diversity and Complexity in American Public Opinion." In *Political Science: The State of the Discipline,* edited by W. Finifter, 389–425. Washington, D.C.: American Political Science Association, 1983.

Kinder, Donald R., and D. Roderick Kiewiet. "Sociotropic Politics: The American Case." *British Journal of Political Science* 11 (1981): 129–61.

Komarnicki, Mary, and John Doble, eds. *Crime and Corrections: A Review of Public Opinion Data since 1975.* New York: Public Agenda Foundation, 1986.

Lamb, Karl A. *As Orange Goes: Twelve California Families and the Future of American Politics.* New York: W. W. Norton and Co., 1974.

Lane, Robert E. "Patterns of Political Belief." In *Handbook of Political Psychology*, edited by Jeanne N. Knutson, 83–116. San Francisco: Jossey-Bass, 1973.

———. *Political Ideology: Why the American Common Man Believes What He Does*. New York: Free Press, 1962.

Langan, Patrick A. "The Prevalence of Imprisonment." *Bureau of Justice Statistics Special Report*. Washington, D.C.: U.S. Government Printing Office, 1985.

Langan, Patrick A., et al. *Historical Statistics on Prisoners in State and Federal Institutions, Year End, 1925–86*. Washington, D.C.: U.S. Government Printing Office, 1988.

Lewis, Dan A., ed. *Reactions to Crime*. Beverly Hills, Calif.: Sage Publications, 1981.

Liska, Allen E., and William Baccaglini. "Feeling Safe by Comparison: Crime in the Newspapers." *Social Problems* 37, no. 3 (August 1990): 360–74.

Luskin, Robert C. "Measuring Political Sophistication." *American Journal of Political Science* 31, no. 4 (November 1987): 856–99.

Luttbeg, Norman R. "The Structure of Beliefs among Leaders and the Public." *Public Opinion Quarterly* 32, no. 3 (fall 1968): 398–409.

Maguire, Kathleen and Timothy J. Flanagan, eds. *Sourcebook of Criminal Justice Statistics—1990*. U. S. Department of Justice, Bureau of Justice Statistics. Washington, D.C.: U.S. Government Printing Office, 1991.

Maguire, Kathleen, Ann L. Pastore, and Timothy J. Flanagan, eds. *Sourcebook of Criminal Justice Statistics—1992*. U. S. Department of Justice, Bureau of Justice Statistics. Washington, D.C.: U.S. Department of Justice, 1993.

Mathis, Frank O., and Martin B. Rayman. "The Ins and Outs of Crime and Corrections." *Criminology* 10 (November 1972): 366–73.

McClosky, Herbert. "Consensus and Ideology in American Politics," *American Political Science Review* 58, no. 2 (June 1964): 361–82.

———. "Conservatism and Personality." *American Political Science Review* 52, no. 1 (March 1958): 27–45.

McClosky, Herbert, and John Zaller. *The American Ethos: Public Attitudes toward Capitalism and Democracy*. Cambridge, Mass.: Harvard University Press, 1984.

McClosky, Herbert, and Alida Brill. *Dimensions of Tolerance: What Americans Believe about Civil Liberties*. New York: Russell Sage Foundation, 1983.

McGarrell, Edmund F., and Timothy J. Flanagan, eds. *Sourcebook of Criminal Justice Statistics—1984*. U. S. Department of Justice, Bureau of Justice Statistics. Washington, D.C.: U.S. Government Printing Office, 1985.

McGuire, William J. "The Nature of Attitudes and Attitude Change." In *The Handbook of Social Psychology*, vol. 3, edited by Gardner Lindzey and Elliot Aronson, 136–314. Reading, Mass.: Addison-Wesley Publishing Co., 1969.

McIntyre, Jennie. "Public Attitudes toward Crime and Law Enforcement." *Annals of the American Academy of Political and Social Science* 374 (November 1967): 34–46.

Menninger, Karl. *The Crime of Punishment*. New York: Viking Press, 1968.

"Most Support Life Sentence for Drug Pushers." *Current Opinion* 1, no. 4 (April 1973): 32.

"Most Think TV Violence and Crime Linked." *Gallup Report* 200 (May 1982): 35–38.

Mower White, C. J. *Consistency in Cognitive Social Behaviour: An Introduction to Social Psychology.* London: Routledge and Kegan Paul, 1982.

Muir, William Kerr, Jr. *Police: Streetcorner Politicians.* Chicago: University of Chicago Press, 1977.

National Research Council. Panel for the Evaluation of Crime Surveys. *Surveying Crime.* Washington, D.C.: National Academy of Sciences, 1976.

Newman, Graeme R., and Carol Trilling. "Public Perceptions of Criminal Behavior: A Review of the Literature." *Criminal Justice and Behavior* 2, no. 3 (September 1975): 217–36.

Nie, Norman H., Sidney Verba, and John R. Petrocik. *The Changing American Voter.* Cambridge, Mass.: Harvard University Press, 1976.

Niemi, Richard G., and Herbert F. Weisberg. *Controversies in Voting Behavior.* 2d ed. Washington, D.C.: Congressional Quarterly Press, 1984.

"1976 Election Issues." *Current Opinion* 4, no. 11 (November 1976): 119.

Oakland Chamber of Commerce brochure. Marcoa Publishing Co., 1988.

"One Household in Four Hit by Crime; Many Afraid to Walk Alone in Neighborhoods." *Gallup Report* 210 (March 1983): 3–9.

"One Household in Four Victim of Crime; Public Backs Local Crime-Watch Patrols." *Gallup Report* 200 (May 1982): 17–25.

"On Some Issues, Differences Are Still Insignificant." *Public Opinion* 5, no. 2 (April–May 1982): 28.

"Our Crowded Prisons." *Annals of the American Academy of Political and Social Science* 478 (March 1985).

Packer, Herbert L. *The Limits of the Criminal Sanction.* Stanford, Calif.: Stanford University Press, 1968.

Pearman, William A. "An Empirical Assessment of the Public's View of Retribution vs. Rehabilitation of Criminal Offenders." Paper presented at a meeting of the Pennsylvania Sociological Society, Villanova University, Villanova, Penn., November 1983.

"People Are Less Afraid They Will Be Victims." *USA Today,* October 12, 1983.

Pierce, John C., and Douglas D. Rose. "Nonattitudes and American Public Opinion: The Examination of a Thesis." *American Political Science Review* 68, no. 2 (June 1974): 626–49.

President's Commission on Law Enforcement and Administration of Justice. *The Challenge of Crime in a Free Society.* Washington, D.C.: U.S. Government Printing Office, 1967.

———. *Task Force Report: Crime and Its Impact—an Assessment.* Washington, D.C.: U.S. Government Printing Office, 1967.

Press, Aric, et al. "The Plague of Violent Crime." *Newsweek,* March 23, 1981, 46–54.

Prothro, James W., and Charles M. Grigg. "Fundamental Principles of Democracy: Bases of Agreement and Disagreement." *Journal of Politics* 22, no. 2 (May 1960): 276–94.

"Public Backs Wholesale Prison Reform." *Gallup Report* 200 (May 1982): 3–16.

"Public Blames Drugs and the Courts for High U.S. Crime Rate." *Current Opinion* 1, no. 4 (April 1973): 33–34.

Putnam, Robert D. "Studying Elite Political Culture: The Case of 'Ideology.'" *American Political Science Review* 65, no. 3 (September 1971): 651–81.

Rokeach, Milton. *Beliefs, Attitudes, and Values: A Theory of Organization and Change.* San Francisco: Jossey-Bass, 1968.

————. *The Open and Closed Mind: Investigations into the Nature of Belief Systems and Personality Systems.* New York: Basic Books, 1960.

Rose, Vicki McNickle. "A Survey of Public Opinion Concerning Correctional Policies and Prison Reform." Ph.D. diss., Washington State University, 1976.

Rosenau, Pauline Marie. *Post-modernism and the Social Sciences: Insights, Inroads, and Intrusions.* Princeton, N.J.: Princeton University Press, 1992.

Sacco, Vincent F. "The Effects of Mass Media on Perceptions of Crime: A Reanalysis of the Issues." *Pacific Sociological Review* 25, no. 4 (October 1982): 475–93.

San Francisco Chronicle Index, April–June 1987 and July–September 1987. Ann Arbor, Mich.: University Microfilms, 1987.

Scheingold, Stuart A. *The Politics of Law and Order: Street Crime and Public Policy.* New York: Longman, 1984.

————. *The Politics of Street Crime: Criminal Process and Cultural Obsession.* Philadelphia: Temple University Press, 1991.

Schuman, Howard, and Stanley Presser. *Questions and Answers in Attitude Surveys.* New York: Academic Press, 1981.

Scott, William A. "Attitude Measurement." In *The Handbook of Social Psychology,* vol. 2, edited by Gardner Lindzey and Elliot Aronson, 204–73. Reading, Mass.: Addison-Wesley Publishing Co., 1968.

Second Start Adult Literacy Program. *Second Start Project Description.* Oakland, Calif.: City of Oakland, 1985.

Sheley, Joseph F., and Cindy D. Ashkins. "Crime, Crime News, and Crime Views." *Public Opinion Quarterly* 45, no. 4 (1981): 492–506.

Sills, David L., ed. *International Encyclopedia of the Social Sciences,* vols. 3 and 9. New York: Macmillan and Free Press, 1968.

Skogan, Wesley G., and Michael G. Maxfield. *Coping with Crime: Individual and Neighborhood Reactions.* Beverly Hills, Calif.: Sage Publications, 1981.

Smith, David Lewis, and C. McCurdy Lipsey. "Public Opinion and Penal Policy." *Criminology* 14, no. 1 (May 1976): 113–24.

Smith, M. Brewster. "Personal Values as Determinants of a Political Attitude." *Journal of Psychology* 28 (October 1949): 477–86.

Smith, M. Brewster. "Political Attitudes." In *Handbook of Political Psychology,* ed. by Jeanne N. Knutson, 57–82. San Francisco: Jossey-Bass, 1973.

Smith, M. Brewster, Jerome S. Bruner, and Robert W. White. *Opinions and Personality.* New York: John Wiley and Sons, 1956.

Sniderman, Paul M. *Personality and Democratic Politics.* Berkeley and Los Angeles: University of California Press, 1975.

———. *A Question of Loyalty.* Berkeley and Los Angeles: University of California Press, 1981.

Sparks, Richard F., Hazel G. Genn, and David J. Dodd. *Surveying Victims: A Study of the Measurement of Criminal Victimization, Perceptions of Crime, and Attitudes to Criminal Justice.* Chichester, England: John Wiley and Sons, 1977.

"Spending Priorities: The Call for Arms." *Public Opinion* 3, no. 5 (October–November 1980): 22.

Stimson, James A. "Belief Systems: Constraint, Complexity, and the 1972 Election." *American Journal of Political Science* 19, no. 3 (August 1975): 393–417.

Stinchcombe, Arthur L., et al. *Crime and Punishment—Changing Attitudes in America.* San Francisco: Jossey-Bass Publishers, 1980.

Stokes, Donald. "Valence Politics." In *Electoral Politics,* edited by Dennis Kavanagh. Oxford: Clarendon Press, 1992.

Sullivan, John L., et al. "The More Things Change, the More They Stay the Same: The Stability of Mass Belief Systems." *American Journal of Political Science* 23, no. 1 (February 1979): 176–86.

Sullivan, John L., James Piereson, and George E. Marcus. *Political Tolerance and American Democracy.* Chicago: University of Chicago Press, 1982.

Taub, Richard P., D. Garth Taylor, and Jan D. Dunham. *Paths of Neighborhood Change: Race and Crime in Urban America.* Chicago: University of Chicago Press, 1984.

Taylor, D. Garth, Kim Lane Scheppele, and Arthur L. Stinchcombe. "Salience of Crime and Support for Harsher Criminal Sanctions." *Social Problems* 26, no. 4 (April 1979): 413–24.

Thomas, Charles W., and Robin J. Cage. "Correlates of Public Attitudes toward Legal Sanctions." *International Journal of Criminology and Penology* 4, no. 3 (August 1976): 239–55.

Thomas, Charles W., Robin J. Cage, and Samuel C. Foster. "Public Opinion on Criminal Law and Legal Sanctions: An Examination of Two Conceptual Models." *Journal of Criminal Law and Criminology* 67, no. 1 (March 1976): 110–16.

"Three Nude Women Freed From Chains." *Oakland Tribune,* March 26, 1987.

Toseland, Ronald W. "Fear of Crime: Who is Most Vulnerable?" *Journal of Criminal Justice* 10, no. 3 (1982): 199–209.

Tufte, Edward R. *The Visual Display of Quantitative Information.* Cheshire, Conn.: Graphics Press, 1983.

van den Haag, Ernest. *Punishing Criminals.* New York: Basic Books, 1975.

Viviano, Frank. "The Powerlessness of Black Power." *San Jose Mercury News—West Magazine,* December 14, 1986, 8–11, 22–25.

von Hirsch, Andrew. *Doing Justice: The Choice of Punishments.* New York: Hill and Wang, 1976.

Wallerstein, James S., and Clement J. Wyle. "Our Law-Abiding Lawbreakers." *Probation,* (April 1947): 107–12, 118.

Walters, Dan. *The New California: Facing the Twenty-first Century.* Sacramento: California Journal Press, 1986.

Warr, Mark. "The Accuracy of Public Beliefs about Crime." *Social Forces* 59, no. 2 (December 1980): 456–70.

———. "The Accuracy of Public Beliefs about Crime: Further Evidence." *Criminology* 20, no. 2 (August 1982): 185–204.

Warr, Mark, Jack P. Gibbs, and Maynard L. Erickson. "Contending Theories of Criminal Law: Statutory Penalties vs. Public Preferences." *Journal of Research in Crime and Delinquency* 19, no. 1 (January 1982): 25–46.

Warr, Mark, Robert F. Meier, and Maynard L. Erickson. "Norms, Theories of Punishment, and Publicly Preferred Penalties for Crimes." *Sociological Quarterly* 24, no. 1 (winter 1983): 75–91.

Watts, William, and Lloyd Free. *State of the Nation III.* Lexington, Mass.: D. C. Heath and Co., 1978.

West's California Codes—Penal Code. 1988 compact edition. St. Paul, Minn.: West Publishing Co., 1988.

White, Garland F. "Public Responses to Hypothetical Crimes: Effect of Offender and Victim Status and Seriousness of the Offense on Punitive Reactions." *Social Forces* 53, no. 3 (March 1975): 411–19.

Williams, Joyce E., and Karen A. Holmes. *The Second Assault: Rape and Public Attitudes.* Westport, Conn.: Greenwood Press, 1981.

Wilson, James Q. *Thinking about Crime.* New York: Vintage Books, 1975.

Wiltz, C. J. "Fear of Crime, Criminal Victimization, and Elderly Blacks." *Phylon* 43, no. 4 (winter 1982): 283–94.

Wolman, Benjamin B., ed. *International Encyclopedia of Psychiatry, Psychology, Psychoanalysis, and Neurology,* vol. 3. New York: Aesculapius Publishers, 1977.

Wright, Stephen E. "Prison's Revolving Door." *San Jose Mercury News,* June 21, 1987, 1.

Yin, Peter. "Fear of Crime as a Problem for the Elderly." *Social Problems* 30 (December 1982): 240–45.

Yoachum, Susan. "Clinton Wraps Up a Triumphant Week: He Concludes West Coast Tour in L.A. with Fervent Speech on Crime." *San Francisco Chronicle,* November 22, 1993, sec. A.

Zaller, John. *The Nature and Origins of Mass Opinion.* Cambridge: Cambridge University Press, 1992.

Zaller, John, and Stanley Feldman. "Answering-Questions vs. Revealing Preferences: A Simple Theory of the Survey Response." Paper prepared for delivery at the fifth annual meeting of the Political Methodology Society, 1988.

Zimmerman, Kathy. "Oakland: On Cusp of Revival, City Still Grapples with Legacy of Problems." *Oakland Tribune,* July 26, 1987, sec. A.

Index